The Vulnerability of Cities

For Ulli

The Vulnerability of Cities

Natural Disasters and Social Resilience

Mark Pelling

Earthscan Publications Ltd
London • Sterling, VA

First published in the UK and USA in 2003
by Earthscan Publications Ltd

ISBN: 1 85383 830 6 paperback
      1 85383 829 2 hardback

Typesetting by MapSet Ltd, Gateshead, UK
Printed and bound in the UK by Creative Print and Design Wales, Ebbw Vale
Cover design by Danny Gillespie

For a full list of publications please contact:

Earthscan Publications Ltd
120 Pentonville Road, London, N1 9JN, UK
Tel: +44 (0)20 7278 0433
Fax: +44 (0)20 7278 1142
Email: earthinfo@earthscan.co.uk
Web: **www.earthscan.co.uk**

22883 Quicksilver Drive, Sterling, VA 20166-2012, USA

Earthscan is an editorially independent subsidiary of Kogan Page Ltd and publishes in association with WWF-UK and the International Institute for Environment and Development

A catalogue record for this book is available from the British Library

Library of Congress Cataloging-in-Publication Data

Pelling, Mark, 1967-.
    The vulnerability of cities : natural disasters and social resilience / Mark Pelling.
        p. cm.
    Includes bibliographical references and index.
    ISBN 1-85383-830-6 (pbk.) — ISBN 1-85383-829-2 (hardback)
    1. Urban ecology—Developing countries. 2. Natural disasters—Developing
countries. 3. Disaster relief—Developing countries. 4. Urbanization—Developing
countries—Social aspects 5. Sustainable development—Developing countries. 6.
Urban policy—Developing countries. I. Title: Natural disasters and social resilience.
II. Title.

HT243.D44P45 2003
307.76'09172'4—dc21

                                                                              2003000697

Contents

List of Figures, Tables and Boxes   *vii*
List of Acronyms and Abbreviations   *ix*

SECTION I: CITIES AND ENVIRONMENTAL RISK

1 Tracing the Roots of Urban Risk and Vulnerability   **3**
Introduction   3
Sustainable Development, Disaster and the City   5
Environmental Hazard and the City   13
Outline of the Book   17

2 Cities as Sites for Disaster   **19**
Introduction   19
Urban Growth and Disaster Exposure   20
Disaster Impacts   38
Summary   44

3 Social Vulnerability in the City   **46**
Introduction   46
A History of Human Vulnerability and Environmental Hazard   47
Livelihoods and Vulnerability   55
Social Adaptation and Ameliorating Vulnerability   61
Case Studies of Livelihood and Vulnerability in Georgetown, Guyana   65
Summary   67

4 Urban Governance and Disaster   **68**
Introduction   68
Political Actors   70
Summary   90

SECTION II: THE CASE STUDIES

Case Study Selection   93

**5 Maintaining Civil Society in a Liberal Democracy: Bridgetown,
   Barbados**   **97**
Introduction   97

Democracy from Above: The Barbadian Path to Development   98
Social Vulnerability Amid Economic Development   101
Environmental Hazard   103
Disaster Mitigation and Response Capacity   104
The Pine Community   109
Summary   115

6   Post-socialism and Barriers to Building a Civil Society:
Georgetown, Guyana   **118**
Introduction   118
A Legacy of Mistrust: Guyana's Development History   119
Urban Poverty and Hazard   121
Urban Development and Governance   123
Disaster Mitigation and Response Capacity   129
Albouystown   131
Summary   137

7   Patrimonial Regimes and the Maintenance of a Constructive
Civil Society: Santo Domingo, The Dominican Republic   **139**
Introduction   139
Authoritarian Rule in the Dominican Republic   140
Environmental Hazard   141
Urban Governance and Adaptive Potential   142
Disaster Management Capacity   148
Los Manguitos   154
Summary   159

Section III: Towards Safer Cities

8   Action for Safer Cities   **163**
The Social Roots of Urban Vulnerability and Resilience   163
Urbanization, Environmental Change and Hazard   166
A Structural View: Institutional Frameworks and Adaptive Potential   168
Citizen Agency and Adaptive Potential   174
Opportunities and Barriers to Building Adaptive Potential   178
Urban Environmental Risk: A New Research Agenda for Policy
Reform   180

Appendix   *185*
References   *188*
Index   *205*

List of Figures, Tables and Boxes

FIGURES

1.1	Sustainable urbanization: main components and indicative issues	12
1.2	Everyday and catastrophic hazards in Georgetown, Guyana	16
2.1	Growth rates for urban populations by world region	23
2.2	World hazard zones and urban centres	25
2.3	Reported urban disasters 1998–2001	26
3.1	The components of environmental risk	48
4.1	Resource flows between partners	89
5.1	Urban settlement in Barbados	100
6.1	Flood risk, Georgetown	124
6.2	Economic status, Georgetown	125
7.1	Household poverty, Santo Domingo	143
7.2	Recorded household damages from Hurricane Georges, Santo Domingo	144

TABLES

2.1	Major cities at risk from natural disasters	27
2.2	Direct disaster impacts by hazard type	39
2.3	Disaster and socio-political change	43
3.1	Adaptive potential	63
4.1	Private sector involvement in disaster mitigation	75
II.1	The case studies	94
5.1	Assets for urban areas and for all Barbados	102
5.2	Vulnerability and risk	111
5.3	Social capital and adaptive potential	112
6.1	Squatting in Greater Georgetown	127
6.2	Vulnerability and risk	132
6.3	Health impacts of the most recent flood	133
6.4	Adaptive potential	133
6.5	Local group membership	134
7.1	INGO responses to Hurricane Georges	151
7.2	Community initiatives facilitated by the DDMC in Santo Domingo	153

7.3   Social organization, Los Manguitos   156
7.4   Summary of findings   157
8.1   City-wide adaptive potential   171
8.2   Social capital and social organization   175
A.1   The standard methodology   186

BOXES

1.1   Key terminology   5
1.2   Wildavsky's principles of resilient systems   8
2.1   The colonial roots of urban risk   24
2.2   Structural adjustment   31
2.3   Flood hazard and response in Rio de Janeiro   35
2.4   Building form and disaster resistance in the Himalayas   36
3.1   Community-based disaster management   57
4.1   The World Bank's Disaster Management Facility   72
4.2   Arup and earthquake mitigation in Turkey   76
4.3   The United Nations Risk Assessment Tools for Diagnosis of
      Urban Areas Against Seismic Disasters programme (RADIUS)   78
4.4   Networks, innovators and partners: three forms of INGO/NGO
      cooperation for disaster mitigation   79
4.5   Local government and community resilience in the Philippines   82
4.6   The Asian Urban Disaster Mitigation Program   84
4.7   The Citizens' Disaster Response Network, Manila   86
7.1   IDAC: integrating disaster response and social development   147
7.2   The Dominican Red Cross: state capture and release   149
7.3   The UNDP and grassroots rehabilitation   150

List of Acronyms and Abbreviations

ACHR	Asian Coalition for Housing Rights
ADN	Ayuntamiento Distrito Nacional (Dominican Republic)
AMDEM	Asociación de Mejoramiento y Desarrollo de Los Manguitos (Dominican Republic)
ANDA	Albouystown Neighbourhood Development Association (Guyana)
AUDP	Asian Urban Disaster Mitigation Program
B$	Barbadian dollars
BBC	British Broadcasting Corporation
BECT	British Earthquake Consortium for Turkey
BLP	Barbados Labour Party
CARE	Cooperative for Assistance and Relief Everywhere (*formerly the* Cooperative for American Remittances to Europe)
CBO	community-based organization
CDB	Caribbean Development Bank
CDC	Civil Defence Commission (Guyana)
CDERA	Caribbean Disaster Emergency Response Agency
CDRC	Citizens' Disaster Response Center
CERO	Central Emergency Relief Organization (Barbados)
CHPA	Central Housing and Planning Authority (Guyana)
CIDA	Canadian International Development Agency
CONDIC	Comité Nacional de Desarrollo Integral Comunitario (Dominican Republic)
CPRME	Comisión Presidencial para la Reforma y Modernización del Estado
DCC	Disaster Coordinating Council
DDMC	Dominican Disaster Mitigation Committee
DERO	District Emergency Relief Organization (Barbados)
DFID	Department for International Development (UK)
DR$	Dominican dollars
DRC	Dominican Red Cross
ECHO	Humanitarian Aid Office (European Commission)
ESRC	Economic and Social Research Council
FCT	Future Centre Trust (Barbados)
FUNDASAL	The Salvadorian Foundation for Development and Basic Housing

GCC	Georgetown City Council (Guyana)
GDP	gross domestic product
GGG	Good and Green Guyana
GNP	gross national product
GRC	Guyana Relief Council
GS&WC	Georgetown Sewerage and Water Commissioners
HIV/AIDS	human immunodeficiency virus/acquired immunodeficiency syndrome
IDAC	Instituto de Acción Comunitaria (Dominican Republic)
IDDI	Instituto Dominicano de Desarrollo Integral (Dominican Republic)
IFI	international financial institution
IFRC/RC	International Federation of the Red Cross and Red Crescent
IMF	International Monetary Fund
INGO	international non-governmental organization
IPCC	Intergovernmental Panel on Climate Change
LETS	local economic trading scheme
MOCUGRECA	Movimiento Cultural Gregorio Castillo
MP	Member of Parliament
NGO	non-governmental organization
ODA	Overseas Development Administration (UK)
ONAPLAN	Office of National Planning (Dominican Republic)
PAHO	Pan American Health Organization
PCW	Pinelands Creative Workshop (Barbados)
PDC	Pinelands Development Council (Barbados)
PLD	Dominican Liberation Party (Dominican Republic)
PNC	People's National Congress (Guyana)
PPP	People's Progressive Party (Guyana)
PRD	Dominican Revolutionary Party (Dominican Republic)
RADIUS	Risk Assessment Tools for Diagnosis of Urban Areas Against Seismic Disasters programme (United Nations)
SAP	structural adjustment programme
SIMAP	Social Impact Amelioration Programme (Guyana)
SDVC	Support Disaster Victims Campaign
SPARC	Society for Promotion of Area Resource Centre
SPSS	Statistical Package for Social Scientists
UCOREBAM	Unión Comunitaria para la Recogida de Basura del Barrio Los Manguitos (Dominican Republic)
UN	United Nations
UN-HABITAT	United Nations Human Settlements Programme (*formerly* UNCHS (Habitat))
UNCHS (Habitat)	United Nations Centre for Human Settlements (*now* UN-HABITAT)

UNCRD	United Nations Centre for Regional Development
UNDRCO	United Nations Disaster Relief Coordinator
UNDP	United Nations Development Programme
UNEP	United Nations Environment Programme
UNICEF	United Nations Children's Fund (*formerly* United Nations International Children's Emergency Fund)
UNPD	United Nations Population Division
UK	United Kingdom
USA	United States of America
USAID	United States Agency for International Development
WCED	World Commission on Environment and Development
WHO	World Health Organization
WRI	World Resources Institute (USA)
YMCA	Young Men's Christian Association

Cities and Environmental Risk

Tracing the Roots of Urban Risk and Vulnerability

INTRODUCTION

On 10 July 2000, 300 people were killed by a landslide in Manila, the Philippines. A shameful and avoidable loss, but just one from a growing list of urban disasters with a natural trigger. The event stands out because the landslide was not of soil, rocks or mud but of solid waste. This was truly an urban disaster. The disaster occurred in a squatter settlement, home to 300,000 people. The squatters lived on and around the Payatas rubbish dump, which takes garbage from Manila's 10 million inhabitants. The landslide and the response of survivors to it help in showing some of the fundamental characteristics of urban risk and vulnerability in Africa, Asia and Latin America and the Caribbean. First, it reminds us that urban areas are not immune to the forces of nature, which are more often associated with risk in rural communities. Second, it illustrates that it is communities of the poor and marginalized that face living with the greatest threats to health and livelihood from natural disaster, as well as having to cope with everyday risks from living and working in hazardous environments.

Responses to the Payatas landslide highlight the way in which the political–legal regime of a city can shape the capacity of different actors to cope with disaster impacts. The city government had in the past given up to US$200 to the families of victims of disaster – an appallingly low value to place on a human life, and hardly sufficient to replace the potential economic contributions to the household of an active household member. Knowing the city government's past record, relatives of victims pre-empted a statement from the city authorities by demonstrating outside the court in Quezon City, Manila. After some time, and with support from human rights lawyers, the survivors filed a US$20m legal claim against the city government for compensatory and moral damages based on the assertion that the city authorities were responsible for managing the Payatas dump. That the low-income victims of an urban disaster could launch such a well-orchestrated response relied upon specific kinds of social organization and legal rights in the city – basic conditions that are absent in some cities, and exceeded in others.

It is the objective of this book to explore the social attributes of at-risk communities and cities and examine the ways in which these assets shape human vulnerability to disaster. In Manila a long tradition of civil society organizing at the city and national levels provided a resource of human rights lawyers. Amongst community members experience of grassroots organizing and community-based self-help had fostered the skills necessary for leaders to organize community-level protest. More generally, it is a reflection of the relative power of civil society compared to the state, and of the attributes of the political–legal regime in place in Manila, that criticism of the state was allowed to be voiced by the survivors of the Payatas disaster, that open reporting of the event was possible in the press and that compensation could be discussed in a court of law.

In the course of the book we hope to go some way towards explaining why, at the beginning of the 21st century, urban areas in so-called developing countries appear to be increasingly affected by environmental risk. Environmental risk in the city is interpreted as an outcome of the political interests and struggles over power that shape the urban environment and society. As Harvey argues, 'all ecological projects (and arguments) are simultaneously political–economic projects (and arguments) and vice-versa. Ecological arguments are never socially neutral...' (Harvey, 1993, p25).

We will need to examine how power makes certain social groups within the city, and collectively, certain cities, more disaster-prone than others. Two expressions of power need to be considered: the material and the non-material (Braun and Castree, 1998). An example of a material expression of power is the contrasting ability of different actors to purchase land or secure housing in the city, with consequences for place of residence and access to basic services. Non-material expressions of power have been explored through discourse analysis, which argues that power resides in the control of ideas rather than things because it is ideas that shape the way in which things are used (Haraway, 1997). Examples of this form of ideological competition include contrasting perceptions of the role of and reason for participatory development approaches. Is participation a tool to facilitate grassroots empowerment and the transfer of skills to grassroots actors to challenge the status quo, or a mechanism to encourage grassroots actors to contribute labour in development projects and to undertake responsibility for maintaining new infrastructure to increase cost efficiency and project sustainability for funding agencies? To understand the geography of risk in the city we need to tackle both material and discursive forms of power. We need to identify the sources and uses of power that direct the distribution of resources in the city, and to understand this we need to be aware of the ideological positions of dominant actors in the city that justify decision-making for resource distribution.

SUSTAINABLE DEVELOPMENT, DISASTER AND THE CITY

Both disaster studies and urban studies are notoriously multi-disciplinary, and words often have multiple meanings. Box 1.1 provides definitions for some key terms.

Identifying disaster

The difficulty of disentangling natural hazards from other sources of threat to life and livelihood – especially from technological hazards and social hazards of violence and war – is frequently commented upon by disaster researchers (Burton, Kates and White, 1993; Blaikie et al, 1994; Tobin and Montz, 1997; Mitchell, 1999). The utility of an approach that singles out individual threats to humanity is greatest for research and policy that seeks to understand and mitigate a single type of physical process, but is reduced for work oriented towards understanding and intervening in human responses to hazard threats. As work on disasters over the last ten years has increasingly focussed on issues of human vulnerability and resilience, the more integrative approach has gained favour (White et al, 2002). Here, hazards are defined as 'human ecological interaction that can generate disaster' (Mitchell, 2001, p87). What constitutes a disaster is discussed in more length below, but clearly the term can operate at different scales. As the example from the Patayas landslide demonstrated, an event leading to a single casualty or death can become a disaster for any

---

Box 1.1 *Key terminology*

Risk: To be threatened by harm. To be at risk is to be under threat of harm.

Hazard: The potential to harm individuals or human systems. In this work, hazard is ascribed to natural, physical or environmental elements. It can be everyday (scarcity of clean drinking water) or episodic (volcanic eruption).

Vulnerability: Denotes exposure to risk and an inability to avoid or absorb potential harm.

Physical vulnerability: Vulnerability in the built environment.

Social vulnerability: Vulnerability experienced by people and their social, economic and political systems.

Human vulnerability: The combination of physical and social vulnerability.

Resilience: The capacity to adjust to threats and mitigate or avoid harm. Resilience can be found in hazard-resistant buildings or adaptive social systems.

Disaster: The outcome of hazard and vulnerability coinciding. Disaster is a state of disruption to systemic functions. Systems operate at a variety of scales, from individuals' biological and psychological constitutions or local socio-economies to urban infrastructure networks and the global political economy.

dependants of the person who has been injured or killed. At an urban scale, disasters are events of sufficient enormity to cause disruption to the urban system. This can be measured in a number of ways.

A common indicator of urban disaster is for the number of victims in proportion to the total population to be high, though there is no universally accepted ratio (Cross, 2001). Problems of data quality, particularly for historical events, limit the applicability of this approach (Pelling and Uitto, 2001). If 'impacted population' is used rigorously as a definition of disaster then the problem of proportionality will cause many small events in large populations to be hidden (Mossler, 1996). This is the case in large cities where events may directly impact on only a small proportion of the urban population compared to smaller urban centres, or where many small events may have a large cumulative impact but be overlooked by municipal or national authorities and international actors. An alternative measure of urban disaster may be to include only those events that have been felt to impact upon and cause dislocations within the 'urban system'. Within this we might include the economic functions of the city, its political regime and infrastructural integrity. Indicators for economic impact could include fluctuations in urban income, local rates of inflation and unemployment and the contribution of urban activities to national gross domestic product (GDP). Changes in political and social organization could be indicated by changing crime rates or periods of military control. Infrastructural integrity might be indicated by the number and proportion of, amongst other things, dwellings, industrial premises, hospitals, schools, sewers, roads and electricity cables etc destroyed or damaged by an event. For individual events much of this kind of data is available, but for the majority of cases it is not, again limiting the usefulness of this approach. A third source of definition might be to include only those events that have been recognized as disasters by a third party, be this a national government, municipality or international organization. This approach avoids the need for quantitative data but is open to political distortions where agencies might want to suppress or exaggerate the importance of an event (Albala-Bertrand, 1993). A deeper problem with these definitions of disaster is their failure to recognize the cumulative impact of small impact events. This is discussed below, but it should be noted here that cumulative disasters, including for example localized landslides or flooding, traffic accidents or the impacts of air pollution, cause more death and incapacitation in the city than larger scale events (Hardoy et al, 2001). To a great extent, therefore, fuzziness in the definition of disaster is less of a weakness than it may first appear.

The coevolution of urbanization and risk

Environmental risks, including chronic and catastrophic forms of 'natural disaster', occur as part of the development process (Hewitt, 1983; Castree and Braun, 2001). More than this, natural disasters are signifiers of the inequalities that underpin capitalist (and alternative) development, of unsound and manifestly unsustainable human–environment relations. With specific reference to mega-cities, Mitchell (1999) describes how urban disasters are not amenable to technological quick fixes alone, and rather that the nature of disaster risk is constantly being redefined as changes to urban landscapes and socio-economic characteristics unfold. Urbanization affects disasters just as profoundly as disasters can affect urbanization.

Norgaard (1994) describes the pattern of changing human and environmental processes acting in one place as coevolutionary. The metaphor of an evolving biological system is useful. Here, there is no simple one-way line of causality in the production of human or environmental conditions: 'nature' does not cause 'natural disasters'; rather risk in the city is an outcome of a myriad of feedback loops and thresholds and competing ideas, mechanisms and forms. In this way, the breaching of a critical threshold – perhaps by a relatively minor initial event – can initiate a cascading series of knock-on effects with wide repercussions throughout the urban system. The rate of change can be fast or slow, with catalysing events, such as catastrophic disaster or political reform, sometimes altering the context in which the combined human–environmental system operates. This creates space for rapid adaptation and hidden or new forms of human and/or environmental organization to evolve and rise to prominence – for a new equilibrium to establish itself before the next upheaval. There is of course no guarantee that successive periods of equilibrium will mark out a march towards progress, with backsliding and loss of human and environmental assets being as likely an outcome as the developmental progress that has been assumed in the post-Enlightenment era.

An example of a threshold-breaching event, which threatened to disrupt the stability of an urban system, comes from Metro Manila. Here, a small earthquake put one small section of the track of the city's 15km light rail system out of alignment. This minor failure caused the system to be closed for a number of days and reduced its overall capacity for several months, putting more traffic onto the road network and creating knock-on problems (Solway, 1994). In contrast, Webber (1990 in Cross, 2001) explains how the collapse of the Oakland expressway and the closure of the San Francisco Bay Bridge following the Loma Preta earthquake did not lead to disruption of the San Francisco Bay Area's transport system because of a high degree of redundancy in the metropolitan transport network. These examples highlight one way through which systems can be designed to have resiliency to unanticipated change such as natural disaster shocks.

The idea of resiliency suggests a proactive stance towards risk. It has been discussed within ecological theory, systems analysis and disaster studies (Tobin and Montz, 1997). Barnett (2001), in an analysis of policy responses to the uncertainty of climate change, draws on Wildavsky (1988) to identify six principles of resilient systems (see Box 1.2).

The local effects of global environmental change and economic, political and cultural globalization are adding greater uncertainty to development

---

Box 1.2 *Wildavsky's principles of resilient systems*

- *The homeostasis principle.* Systems are maintained by feedbacks between component parts which signal changes and can enable learning. Resilience is enhanced when feedbacks are transmitted effectively.

- *The omnivory principle.* External shocks are mitigated by diversifying resource requirements and their means of delivery. Failures to source or distribute a resource can then be compensated for by alternatives.

- *The high flux principle.* The faster the movement of resources through a system, the more resources will be available at any given time to help cope with perturbation.

- *The flatness principle.* Overly hierarchical systems are less flexible and hence less able to cope with surprise and adjust behaviour. Top-heavy systems will be less resilient.

- *The buffering principle.* A system which has a capacity in excess of its needs can draw on this capacity in times of need, and so is more resilient.

- *The redundancy principle.* A degree of overlapping function in a system permits the system to change by allowing vital functions to continue while formerly redundant elements take on new functions.

Source: Barnett (2001)

---

planning in general, and more specifically to the prediction and management of natural hazard and human vulnerability. Uncertainty amongst policy-makers comes from the increasing difficulty with which planning decisions can reliably be made based on extrapolating environmental hazard, human vulnerability and disaster experience from the past, when the physical and human conditions that contextualized past events are being re-shaped by local and global forces. Added to this, it is easy for local decision-makers working in agencies with limited financial and human resources to feel disempowered by the global scale of risk, that their ability to influence risk pressures is being undermined by their distance from, and the global scale of, sources of risk. When uncertainty and disempowerment are felt by decision-makers there is a danger that investment in disaster preparedness and mitigation will be left outside of urban development strategy, with disaster management reverting to a focus on post-disaster humanitarian relief and rehabilitation. Planners may well ask: 'How can we justify an investment in vulnerability reduction when we do not know beyond reasonable doubt the magnitude and frequency of future natural hazards nor the characteristics of populations at risk?', or question the effectiveness of local interventions into forces that are global in scale.

In such an atmosphere of growing uncertainty and reactive planning, dominant disaster mitigation tools based around physical engineering solutions to human exposure to hazard are becoming less attractive. The danger is that engineering-based solutions are not being replaced by alternative strategies, with urban societies being allowed to live under the shadow of increasing risk. One way around this impasse may be to emphasize the social as well as the physical dimensions of risk. This is where Wildavsky's principles of resilience can help us. They point a way towards identifying an array of basic principles out of which alternative policy options for building resiliency to a whole range of stimuli – economic, physical, social etc – can be built. Returning to the six principles developed by Wildavsky (1988), particular characteristics of urban systems can be identified, support for which would build resilience in general and an enhanced capacity to cope with natural disaster shock in particular:

- Communications systems in the city. Information should flow freely between experts, policy-makers and citizens. Local knowledge and development priorities need to be identified and risks must be clearly communicated.
- Risks are greatest when functions are dependent upon a single resource. At the individual level, multiple livelihoods provide some resilience. For big business, developing contacts with a range of suppliers will help limit production delays following disaster.
- Local participation in decision-making through formal democratic structures and also by involvement in local development projects will maximize the benefit gained by citizens from development programmes and projects.
- Social surplus invested in buildings insurance, life insurance, social services or emergency services will be available at times of need following disaster.

Most of these practical outcomes of Wildavsky's account of resilience are already being pursued in cities of the global South. But they continue to be seen as responding to individual sectoral risks, so that ameliorating social vulnerability to environmental risk is divorced from vulnerability to economic or socio-political risks. The aim of placing Wildavsky's principles within the context of coevolution is to emphasize the range of fundamental policy options available to urban decision-makers that bridge the gap between disaster mitigation and mainstream development policy.

Whilst coevolution is a useful device for framing urban development and environmental risk, it is a difficult concept to operationalize. Data requirements would make a complete coevolutionary study of a city exorbitantly expensive. Despite this, some attempts have been made. In a study of coastal cities, Timmerman and White (1997) found that policy-makers were ill-prepared to study or plan at the interface between the built and natural environmental components of the city. Policy and planning institutions were orientated towards disaster response rather than preparation or mitigation. Citizens and firms who were in a position to respond to risk tended to react to perceived risk individualistically: the rich distanced themselves from hazard by accessing private water supplies, owning generators etc.

In a coevolutionary examination of vulnerability to coastal flood hazard in Vietnam, Adger (1999) identifies the historical progression of socio-physical periods of equilibrium and pays particular attention to the ways in which global climate change and market liberalism are re-shaping society and society–nature relations on this hazardous coast. These changes seem to be increasing overall human vulnerability to coastal flooding. More generally, and from a longer time-scale, the rise of urban ways of living and organizing can itself be thought of as an outcome of coevolution. As a coevolutionary process, urbanization is a mode of human organization producing new and unfixed sets of rules and constraints that shape the on-going interaction of humanity and the environment. Our interest is to examine how different forms of political organization in the city have shaped the capacity of local actors to move out of positions of vulnerability in relation to the environment, and the extent to which the rules shaping this capacity can themselves be changed to open more opportunities for coping with and mitigating environmental risk. A historical perspective will be needed to capture the thrust of coevolutionary change in the city.

Sustainable development and cities

> *'If there could be such a thing as sustainable development, disasters would represent a major threat to it, or a sign of its failure'* (Hewitt, 1995, p155).

Despite Hewitt's scepticism, the dominant discourse shaping the coevolution of urban spaces around the turn of the millennium has been sustainable development, and as components of this the ideas of participatory development and urban governance. It is incorporated here as a heuristic device for bringing together the different human and non-human elements that shape and are shaped by urbanization and risk.

Much of the literature on cities and development is limited by taking a weak sustainability approach (eg, World Bank, 2000). This sees cities primarily as engines of economic growth, where sustainable development is used to justify trends already well established in urban development. Support for the business-as-usual approach continues to be widespread, despite mounting environmental and social crises generated by the types of concentrated and extensive urban economic growth that result from this understanding of sustainability (Girardet, 1999).

The business-as-usual approach has been challenged by a more ecologically centred perspective of the urban ecology school (Hardoy, Mitlin and Satterthwaite, 1992; Girardet, 1999). This group criticizes the linear metabolism of cities, where flows of raw materials (food, water, chemical and human energy, inventiveness) are turned into products (political power, manufactured goods and services, social and biological reproduction) and waste. Goods are drawn in from increasingly distant environments to satisfy the urban metabolism. The distance from which goods are acquired and to which wastes can be sent is linked to the developmental stage of the city. For example, Mexico City's water metabolism draws from several different catchments. Through a system of canals, drinking water is drawn from up to 150km away (Connolly, 1999). Smaller and poorer cities will tend to draw on local hinterlands, the largest cities will draw upon a global market and contribute significantly to global environmental problems. The worst environmental problems are found in marginalized areas of poor or middle-ranking cities (recall the Payatas dump incident). Here local waste (rubbish, sewerage etc) accumulates together with waste from wider urban processes (industrialization, traffic) and even global trends (global climate change and sea-level rise) to create a treble burden of environmental risk for residents of these threatened places (McGranahan, Songsore and Kjellén, 1996; McGranahan et al, 2001). Add to this the greater susceptibility to natural disaster impacts experienced by those living in squatter settlements, tenement blocks or inner-city slums and the disproportionate weight of the environmental burden carried by the poor becomes clear.

The business-as-usual and ecological city approaches share two weaknesses. Neither adequately synthesizes the human and ecological imperatives of sustainable urbanization, and neither gives adequate weight to the social issues of poverty and human vulnerability (Pelling, 2001a). The fragmented vision of sustainable urbanization that these perspectives present allows gains in one area to generate losses elsewhere. A typical example is, as we saw above, for wealthy neighbourhoods or cities to export waste, simultaneously addressing local environmental concerns and causing more distant environmental degradation in low-income districts of the city or in the rural/global hinterland. Sustainable urbanization requires that urban systems be seen in a regional and global, as well as a local, context and that the components of urban development are viewed as an interacting whole.

The elements to be considered in such a holistic view of sustainable urbanization are shown in Figure 1.1. Five components are identified: social, economic, political, demographic and environmental. Some of the areas in which different sectors interact are shown, though there are many more that could be added. For example, the environment is linked to social development through local environmental quality and environmental justice – the ability of different social groups to access basic environmental goods, like shelter, and avoid the impacts of environmental hazards. This figure is useful in demonstrating the interconnectivity of the five components of sustainable urbanization and the need to place any policy to mitigate risk in the broader context of urban life as well as within larger regional and global physical and human systems (see Chapter 2).

There has been some criticism of the usefulness of this type of all-encompassing view of sustainable urbanization. McGranahan et al (2001) argue that in being confronted by a wealth of development issues and planning dilemmas, policy-makers are in danger of not seeing the policy wood for the contextual trees. This is a fair point, and there will always be a risk of sacrificing

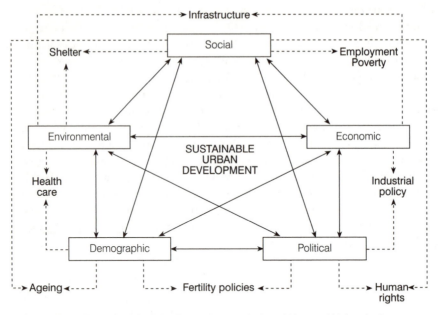

Reproduced from *Third World Planning Review* by permission of Liverpool University Press
Source: Adapted from Drakakis-Smith (1996)

Figure 1.1 *Sustainable urbanization: main components and indicative issues*

analytical detail when using such a broad framework. But the greater danger is to overlook the fundamental inter-connectivity of the different components that shape the coevolution of urban settlements, and their relationships with the wider regional and global human and physical environments. The urban system is complex, and we need to be cautious of falling into the trap of reductionism.

If identifying the components of a more sustainable urbanization is proving difficult, then operationalization is no less problematic. Moving towards sustainable urbanization requires:

> '*seeking the institutional and regulatory framework in which democratic and accountable city and municipal authorities ensure that the needs of the people within their boundaries are addressed while minimizing the transferring of environmental costs to other people or ecosystems or into the future*' (Satterthwaite, 1997, p1684).

Reorienting cities towards a vision of sustainability where environmental risk can be minimized places emphasis on the need for open and inclusive urban management set within a nested hierarchy of local, regional and international governance. Inside cities, municipal government occupies a pivotal position in its varied roles of service provider, community resource mobilizer, regulator, advocate and strategic planner. However, the capacity of municipal governments has very often been limited by financial and human resource scarcity and, especially in capital cities, by the capture of municipal responsibilities (and budgets) by central government (Stren, 1989). Strengthening municipal authorities whilst broadening the base of urban governance by including civil society and private sector organizations should be a central concern for policy-makers (Dillinger, 1994; Abbott, 1996; Schübeler, 1996). At the beginning of the 21st century some movement has been made in this direction, with international agencies and international non-governmental organizations (INGOs) as well as some national and city-level authorities prioritizing the institutional strengthening of city governments, urban poverty alleviation, family planning and community development. But such programmes tend not to be designed or implemented as part of broader integrated strategies for sustainable urbanization and risk reduction (Pelling, 2001b). Despite this, it is possible to identify examples of best practice, and selected cases are discussed below and in more detail in Chapter 4.

ENVIRONMENTAL HAZARD AND THE CITY

The disaster cycle in an urban context

What is known about the interaction of human systems with environmental hazards comes mostly from studies of rural natural disaster. These suggest that disaster shocks are discrete phenomena with a more or less well-marked beginning and end. They are also perceived as sequential phenomena, with each event playing a role in the shaping of subsequent risks, hazards, vulnerabilities and ultimately disasters (Mitchell, 1996). A disaster cycle results. Here, on-going pre-disaster preparedness activities are at some time interrupted by a disaster warning, followed by a disaster event. Immediately after the disaster is a short emergency phase, followed by progressively longer periods concerned with restoring basic services and physical, social, economic and psychological reconstruction. Reconstruction should dovetail into the next round of mitigation and preparedness work as systems learn from the event by adapting to reduce the likelihood of future events. This is of course an idealized model. In urban systems all phases of the disaster cycle may be experienced simultaneously in different parts of the city. This may be because more than one disaster is unfolding at any given time or because of different rates of response to disaster (communities may become isolated by disaster impacts, slowing their recovery). Discrete events often overlap, forming a complex mix of hazard types and disaster stages in any one place. From the perspective of impacted communities, Mitchell (1996, p31) quotes LaPlante (1988, p220) at length, and this is worth repeating here in anticipation of the discussions of community and grassroots actors which follow in Chapters 3–8:

> *'[T]he emergency phase, is typically a period of high consensus in the community, with much altruistic behaviour aimed at preventing or reducing human suffering. Next, activities that will return the community to normal functioning are undertaken and initiate the second period, called the restoration phase. When a semblance of normal functioning is achieved, activities aimed at permanence begin the reconstruction phase: families return to home, work or school and community rebuilding gets under way. Family and individual needs may come into conflict with community goals at this stage of recovery…*
> *[A] final stage … reflects activity at essentially the community level, called the … development reconstruction phase. During this time of second-stage community reconstruction, plans and actions decided upon during the earlier reconstruction are implemented.*

An important indicator of the capacity of a community or urban system to adapt to environmental hazards is the extent to which plans and actions decided upon before the disaster are reappraised. When time and political and financial resources are limited there is a danger that restoration and reconstruction are drawn out or never fully completed, exposing vulnerable individuals and groups to additional hazard, or that pre-disaster conditions are simply replicated.

The lack of a developed critical assessment of the social aspects of urban disaster is partly explained by the historical development of disaster studies, which has drawn greatly from examinations of mainly rural events, particularly floods and famines. By looking at the geography of environmental risk in this way, cities have been perceived as offering some security to these hazards, for example by providing access to food resources during a famine (Drèze and Sen, 1989) or as a place where resources are available for responding to rapid onset disasters. But cities are increasingly becoming the locus of risk (Mitchell, 1999). As early as 1994, Green (in Blaikie et al, 1994) commented that flooding, once a classic hazard of rural areas, was becoming a predominantly urban event. In 1993 Anton identified urban drought as an emergency problem for cities in Latin America.

In urban development there has been a contradictory tendency to exclude nature from analysis (Allen, Massey and Pryke, 1999). In urban areas, society is popularly perceived as being in control of a benign physical environment where temperature can be moderated, disease controlled, floodwaters channelled away and food easily accessed. The low priority afforded to environmental hazard is reflected in the dearth of information about hazards in many cities. Outside the wealthiest of cities it is unusual to find a database of identified hazard risk areas or populations at risk. Mitchell (1999) found this to be the case for several of the world's largest cities including Seoul, Republic of Korea, and Dhaka, Bangladesh, where despite hundreds of lives having been lost to floods neither city had collated information on hazard experience as a first step to mitigating risk. Where risks have been locally mitigated in cities they tend to have been shifted onto other populations and ecological systems. For example, sewerage may be piped out of some wealthy urban districts but is often received as river pollution by downstream peri-urban and rural communities (Hardoy, Mitlin and Satterthwaite, 2001).

Throughout this work the use of 'environmental' is preferred to 'natural' risk, hazard or disaster. This is because it is becoming increasingly difficult to separate the human and 'natural' causes of hazard and disaster events. Basic physical systems, from global climate circulation to local hydraulic regimes, have been influenced by human activity (IPCC, 2001). Smith (1984) called this process the construction of a 'second nature', where human intervention had created an increasingly modified natural world leaving few if any elements of it in a pristine state. There is a burgeoning literature on the human production of nature that supports this view (Peet and Watts, 1996; Bryant and Bailey, 1997; Braun and Castree, 1998). The recognition that human action has led to global climate change and accelerated sea-level rise makes it difficult to claim that any hydrological or meteorological hazard impacting on the city is entirely 'natural' in origin, although this claim is less valid for earthquake or volcanic hazard.

Catastrophic and chronic disaster

Work and writing on the urban environment tends to treat large, catastrophic events separately from apparently more trivial everyday hazards. Catastrophic shocks, such as flooding, hurricanes, earthquakes, droughts etc, win popular attention and are the concern of disaster studies specialists (Pelling, 2001b). Everyday hazards or chronic disasters are felt as long-term stresses associated with exposure to everyday risks such as poor sanitation, unfit housing or polluted air. Everyday hazards are less visible, and certainly less newsworthy than catastrophic events, and have been analysed in a somewhat fragmented fashion by diverse specialists including engineers, medics, land-use planners and urban sociologists. But chronic and catastrophic disasters are linked in many ways.

Figure 1.2 depicts the frustration experienced in Georgetown, Guyana, by residents having to cope with the inconveniences and health consequences of an inadequate drinking water supply whilst a dysfunctional drainage system leads to regular flooding in the city. Clearly, in this case at least, catastrophic and chronic hazards share root causes in a decaying urban infrastructure – an experience repeated throughout the cities of the developing world. But just how deep do these common roots go, and to what extent are shared patterns of risk generation amenable to common policy responses? This is a critical question for city authorities and funding agencies with limited financial resources. Some answers to these questions are offered in the following discussions. The everyday hazards that underlie chronic disaster (for example, daily exposure to disease pathogens) pave the way for catastrophic disaster by the incremental lowering of people's thresholds of resilience (Kasperson et al, 1996). At the same time, daily exposure to low levels of risk can have the perverse effect of reducing

Reproduced from *Social Nature: Theory, Practice and Politics* (Castree and Braun, 2001) by permission of Blackwell Publishing, Oxford
Source: Pelling (2001b)

Figure 1.2 *Everyday and catastrophic hazards in Georgetown, Guyana*

people's willingness to prepare for the possibility of catastrophic disaster, as risk becomes an accepted and normalized part of everyday life (Blaikie et al, 1994). Following catastrophic events, levels of resilience to both chronic stress and any subsequent catastrophic shock for individuals and groups are typically lowered. Indeed, in catastrophic disasters, the greatest potential for loss of life often comes not from the direct impacts of the hazard – collapsed houses or flying debris – but from everyday health risks following the dislocations caused by a catastrophic disaster, such as limited access to clean drinking water, lack of sanitation, insufficient access to food, warmth or shelter and social disorder. Frequent exposure to risk can lead to what Chambers (1989) described as the ratchet effect of vulnerability, where each succeeding event reduces the resources a group or individual has to resist and recover from the next environmental shock or stress. In cities the ratchet effect will be generated and felt by people having to live with multiple risk types – crime and violence, disease, unemployment, pollution and technological hazard – as well as environmental hazard.

Within disaster management, the need to integrate chronic and catastrophic disaster has been recognized, for example by the United Nations (UN) Healthy Cities Programme (WHO, 1999). However, the holism argued for by sustainable urbanization has not yet produced a synthesized policy approach to chronic and catastrophic disaster. The approach taken here is to broaden the standard conceptualization of disaster as catastrophe to include the chronic events rooted in everyday hazard. The distribution of both types of risk stems from unequal power relations between different social classes and residential districts in the city. Differential ability to access basic resources and services from the state, civil society and private sector shape the capacity of communities to avoid environmental risk. This is as true for risk from hurricane damage stemming from poorly constructed houses as it is for risk from diseases carried by vectors thriving in unsanitary neighbourhoods where garbage is left uncollected. The proximate environmental causes of catastrophic and everyday risks are also similarly associated with improper sanitation, inadequate drinking water provision and garbage collection, inappropriate housing construction and location, and insufficient education and health care (Hardoy, Mitlin and Satterthwaite, 1992). It is less important to separate the two final categories of risk than it is to understand the shared underlying processes that lead to human vulnerability overall. As the International Federation of the Red Cross and Red Crescent (IFRC/RC) argues, 'a city with good sewers, drains and rubbish collection is also much better able to cope with flooding. Well-designed and well-built homes greatly reduce risks from physical hazard, and from earthquakes, floods or cyclones' (IFRC/RC, 1998, p13).

OUTLINE OF THE BOOK

The body of this book is divided into three sections. Section I, comprising this introduction and Chapters 2, 3 and 4, sets up and then explores in detail an argument for the analysis of human vulnerability to urban environmental hazard based around the concept of adaptive potential. This theoretical debate is then grounded in Section II by Chapters 5, 6 and 7, which examine adaptive potential in three contrasting urban political contexts. In particular, the case studies allow us to appreciate the ways in which different aspects of the theoretical discussions can interact and affect one another in lived experience. These case studies and the theoretical debate are then synthesized in the final section and concluding chapter.

We have already introduced the concept of human vulnerability and situated it in broader debates and policy on sustainable development and the city. Chapter 2 takes this discussion of urban risk further through an analysis of the scale and nature of environmental risk faced by urban populations. The interactions between environmental hazard and disaster and urban evolution are explored. Chapter 3 examines the intellectual origins of vulnerability. To do this we need to travel outside of the urban studies literature and draw from studies of social vulnerability to environmental hazard in rural settings. Applying this work to hazards in an urban context is achieved through a discussion of adaptive potential at the local level. In Chapter 4 we take a closer look at the types of actor that make up systems of governance in the urban South. These include: the local representatives of global actors, such as INGOs and international financial institutions (IFIs), national governments, municipal governments, indigenous NGOs with national, city or local spheres of influence, and community-based organizations (CBOs).

The three case study cities, with populations ranging from 200,000 to 5 million, fulfil two purposes. First, they form a bridge in the literature on sustainable urbanization which has focussed on mega-cities with 5 million or more residents and tended to overlook smaller cities, despite these holding the majority of urban citizens in aggregate (Mitchell, 1999; Satterthwaite, 1999). Second, they represent examples of the reproduction of vulnerability and of adaptive potential under contrasting political–economic regimes. The first case study of a liberal democracy is set in Bridgetown, Barbados, one of the most highly ranked developing countries (UNDP, 2000). In Bridgetown, modernization and macro-economic growth have coincided with an undermining of community development and civil society, which in turn casts doubt on adaptive potential. The second case study is of a city that has passed through a centralized and so-called 'socialist' regime. Georgetown, Guyana, is an example of a post-socialist urban society where civil society and the private sector are both very weak and require building for adaptive potential to accrue, and where there is a tension between the long-term need to rebuild civil society to enhance adaptive potential and the desire for short-term mitigation efforts which overlook the deeper social roots of vulnerability. The third case study focusses on a country that has a history of right-wing government. Santo Domingo, the Dominican Republic, has a well-developed civil society, but one that is in competition with itself and the state. This has undermined opportunities for cooperation and constrained adaptive potential. In just three case studies it is not possible to capture the variety of state/civil society/private sector regimes that shape the reproduction of vulnerability throughout the global South, nor would it be advisable to try. However, this approach is useful in capturing the dominant political and economic fault lines and extremes of policy and action that are indicative of human processes leading to urban disaster which can be found to varying degrees of intensity and scope across urban societies.

In the final concluding chapter the theoretical discussions and case study material are brought together. An argument is made for social resilience as a concept that can move forward theory and policy on urbanization and disaster. Resilience incorporates the notion of adaptive potential as a response to human vulnerability and places politics (individual to global) at the centre of analysis and praxis on sustainable urbanization. Finally, some priority areas for further study and reflection are identified to encourage a broader discourse on urbanization and disaster.

Chapter 2

Cities as Sites of Disaster

INTRODUCTION

'The key fact and trend ... of natural hazards on development is the growth of large urban agglomerations' (Hartnady, 2002, p1).

This chapter outlines the scale and character of urban risk in so-called developing countries. The chapter is divided into three sections. First, data on urban growth and disaster exposure are presented. Second, the ways in which current urbanization processes can increase disaster susceptibility are discussed, and this is followed by an account of the economic and socio-political impacts of disasters on urban systems. The timeliness of such an investigation can be seen in Hartnady's statement, made as a contribution to the International Strategy for Disaster Reduction's preparatory discussion for the World Summit on Sustainable Development in 2002.

Research on urban disaster risk has so far focussed on mega-cities (variously defined as having 8 million (Nicholls, 1995) or 10 million (Hardoy, Mitlin and Satterthwaite, 1992; Thouret, 1999) residents), with themed editions of *Applied Geography* (1999) and *GeoJournal* (1999), and is dominated by a North American and Western orientation (see, for example, Sylves and Waugh, 1990; Berke and Beatley, 1992). There are some noteworthy exceptions (Main and Williams, 1994; Mitchell, 1999). But the trend in studies of disaster in developing countries continues to be a focus on large cities and their chronic hazards and risks (Hardoy, Mitlin and Satterthwaite, 2001; McGranahan et al, 2001).

'Urban' defined

Defining and delimitating urban areas, even in mega-cities, is difficult. Urban areas can be defined by their economic functions; where secondary (industrial, manufacturing) or tertiary (service) sectors dominate over the primary (extractive agriculture, forestry, mining etc) sectors found in rural areas, by population density or size, or simply by administrative region, where all land and activities lying within a metropolitan district become 'urban'. The use of socio-economic indicators is complicated by the extent to which apparently urban practices are found in rural areas and vice versa. Political/administrative urban boundaries have some utility in larger municipalities where jurisdiction over outlying rural areas may well lead to their marginalization. But again, for smaller settlements that might be included within rural administrative districts this method of definition does not help.

The approach taken here responds to the reasons why urban centres are important for vulnerability and hazard rather than sticking to any particular nominal category of what can or cannot be included in the study of urban risk. As Castells (1972, p11) noted,

> *'it is not by seeking academic definitions or criteria of administrative practice that one will achieve a valid delimitation of one's concepts; on the contrary, it is the rapid analysis of a number of historically established relations between space and society that will enable us to give an objective basis to our study'.*

To quote another formative influence on urban studies, 'The city is manifestly a complicated thing' (Harvey, 1973, p22). Given the overall orientation of this work towards a systems approach of risk, which acknowledges the non-linear nature of coevolutionary change in human and physical systems, the city is seen as a focal point for a wider complex of economic, social, political and environmental linkages and flows of power, energy and information. Because it is a focal point, place and context remain important as nodes through which power, energy and information flow and may be transformed. Indeed, it is contestation over patterns of distribution and transformation of these three flows that shape urban life and underpin geographies of vulnerability and environmental risk in the city.

URBAN GROWTH AND DISASTER EXPOSURE

The scale of risk

There is little doubt that urban areas are increasingly becoming sites of environmental risks for their residents (IFRC/RC, 1999). As an example of this trend, Hewitt (1997) noted that a survey of 650 modern earthquakes by Coburn et al (1989) found that barely 20 events involved over 10,000 deaths, but that in each case high and concentrated losses were found in cities. One of the most dramatic examples was the Tangshan earthquake, in China in 1976, which claimed between 250,000 and 800,000 lives. But why is it that urban areas, which were once assumed to be places of security from natural hazards, are now becoming places of risk? Is this future inevitable or can it be avoided?

Growth in urban disaster is superficially explained by the rapid spatial expansion of cities and a rapid increase in the proportion of national populations residing in urban areas at risk from natural disaster. The statistics for urban growth are impressive:

- In 2000, for the first time more than 50 per cent of the world's population lived in urban settlements.
- During 1975–2000, 52 million new urban dwellers were added each year, 87 per cent of these in developing countries. In 2000–2015, 65 million are added annually, 93 per cent in developing countries.
- Over the next two decades, 90 per cent of population growth in developing countries will be urban.

Sources: Clark (2000), Hildebrand (2001).

But population growth and urban sprawl are not satisfactory explanations alone. They hark back to a neo-Malthusian explanatory framework where population pressure is linked causally to environmental degradation and risk (Coleman and Schofield, 1986) and need to be unpacked. Around 60 per cent of urban population growth worldwide is due to natural growth, with migration accounting for only 25 per cent of growth in Africa and 34 per cent in Latin America. In Asia migration remains dominant, providing for 64 per cent of city growth (Brennen-Galvin, 2001).

Some African cities have seen a cycle of reverse migration. Men initially leave rural villages for the city, and in time women and children follow. Eventually – and especially under the harsher economic conditions of structural adjustment – able-bodied men return to rural areas to maintain hereditary farmland. This has resulted in a demographic profile for many secondary cities in Africa where women, the elderly and children are over-represented (Yacoob and Kelly, 1999). There are clear implications here for vulnerability to environmental hazard. This contrasts with cases where recent rural migrants are the most excluded and vulnerable. In Dhaka, Bangladesh, for example, the urban poor are mainly rural migrants whose lack of access to secure housing and livelihoods is compounded by the absence of familial support (Rashid, 2000). This underlines the importance of local cultural and socio-economic factors and the dangers inherent in any search for overly simple generalizations about urban vulnerability and risk.

The status of the urban political economy is also important in shaping geographies of urban disaster. This can be seen by comparing the effects of two earthquakes. In 1989, the Loma Prieta earthquake (7.1 Richter magnitude) in Santa Cruz, California, claimed 63 lives (Bolt, 1993). More recently, in 1999, the Marmara region of Turkey was struck by an earthquake registering 7.4 on the Richter scale, and 18,000 people were killed (Özerdem and Barakat, 2000). Differences in losses can be explained by the contemporary and historical development of these two regions. Strength in the Californian and US economies allowed buildings to be constructed or retrofitted to disaster-resistant standards, there was widespread cover from buildings insurance and emergency services were not overwhelmed. The weaker economies of Marmara and Turkey were not able to generate and direct sufficient surplus value for similar loss reducing strategies to be employed. As Satterthwaite (1998, p11), argues:

> *'the key problem [underlying urban risk] is not population growth alone, but a combination of the fast expansion of informal settlements, overcrowding or declining tenement districts, failure of city authorities to ensure sufficient water supply, sanitation, waste collection, health care etc, and the failure of city authorities to adapt their institutional frameworks in order to deal with rapidly changing city form and content'.*

Hewitt (1997) argues that the dense pattern of urban living also contributes to risk generation. Cities make up only 1 per cent of the land area of the Earth, but estimates suggest that they concentrate more than half of the world's population and the majority of its physical capital (buildings, infrastructure) (Potter and Lloyd-Evans, 1998; UN Habitat, 1999). Hewitt (1997) argues that concentration leads to urban vulnerability first through the increasing scales and concentration of energy or energy transportation routes and their proximity to residential areas. Second, living in crowded conditions increases risk through the likelihood of disease transmission, and congestion which constrains disaster relief. Third, cities are complex systems with many interactions between different elements – some less predictable than others. Fourth, during periods of political misrule urban populations can become targets for exploitation or repression.

The geography of urban disaster

Urban growth rates are highest in Africa and Asia, as Figure 2.1 shows. In 1990 Hardoy, Cairncross and Satterthwaite estimated that 600 million urban dwellers in Africa, Asia and Latin America and the Caribbean were already living in life- and health-threatening homes and neighbourhoods as a result of poor quality housing and inadequate provision of basic needs (Hardoy, Mitlin and Satterthwaite, 2001).

Increasingly, the world's largest cities are found in the global South: in 1950, five of the world's 15 largest cities (Shanghai, Buenos Aires, Calcutta (Kolkata), Bombay (Mumbai) and Mexico City) were in developing countries, while in 2000 only three (Tokyo, New York and Los Angeles) were in developed countries. Mapping the location of the world's largest cities in 2000 against zones of natural hazard (Figure 2.2) clearly shows the high exposure of these large urban settlements to environmental risk. Chester (2002, drawing from Degg, 1992, 1998; ODA, 1995; Steedman, 1995), reports that only 22 of the world's largest cities are unexposed to geological hazard, and that 86 of the 100 largest cities in developing countries are threatened. Much of the contemporary exposure of cities in Africa, Asia and Latin America and the Caribbean to natural hazard

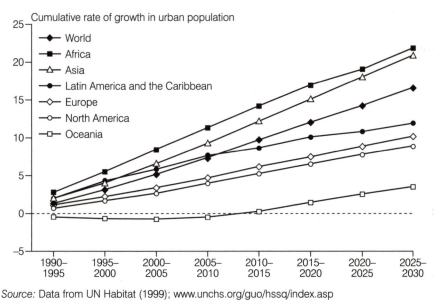

Source: Data from UN Habitat (1999); www.unchs.org/guo/hssq/index.asp

Figure 2.1 *Growth rates for urban populations by world region*

stems from their founding or expansion under European colonial control; this is discussed in Box 2.1.

Comparing Figure 2.2 with the distribution of urban disasters as reported by the BBC from January 1998 to December 2001 (Figure 2.3), we can see that whilst many urban agglomerations, such as Mexico City and Los Angeles, reported disasters over this short period, others such as Cairo and Bombay (Mumbai) enjoyed a relatively disaster-free period. Notwithstanding this, some general patterns do emerge. Perhaps the most impacted region was Central America and the Caribbean (Hurricanes Georges and Mitch, both 1998). Clusters of earthquake events are found in northern Turkey and Afghanistan, with cities in India and Bangladesh exposed to earthquakes, floods and droughts. In Southeast and East Asia, the Philippines, Taiwan and Japan appear to have the largest number of cities at risk from typhoons, earthquake and fire. In sub-Saharan Africa, cities are shown to be at risk from flood, drought and fire, and the high number of reported events from this region is noteworthy. This may be an outcome of the particular development constraints faced by this region – civil unrest, infrastructure decay and weak government. It may also be a reflection of the BBC's audience from Anglophone Africa. The data presented in Figure 2.3 should be viewed as an indicative snapshot of urban disaster rather than any more representative presentation. A three-year time span is a very short period and consequently many cities at risk will not have been identified.

Table 2.1 provides a glimpse of the large urban populations at risk in the developing world. This group includes most of the largest mega-cities included

---

Box 2.1 *The colonial roots of urban risk*

Many settlements are situated on coasts exposed to meteorological and hydrological hazards. For the majority of cities in developing countries this is a colonial legacy. From the mid-1600s to mid-1800s, a single port town emerged in many colonial territories as a node for trade and communication with the metropole, local administration and social control (Vance, 1970; Potter, 1995) These sites offered external powers access into the interior of colonial territories or provided fertile soils and plentiful fresh water for agricultural production (Satterthwaite, 1998). In the post-colonial period these cities have grown rapidly despite efforts at decentralizing urban systems, including the movement of capitals from the coast to interior locations (for example Dodoma, Tanzania, and Brazilia, Brazil) and the establishment of interior growth poles (such as Cuidad Guyana and Cuidad Bolivar in Venezuela) (Potter and Lloyd-Evans, 1998). The coastal cities most at risk from hurricanes and typhoons are those of South Asia, Central America, the Caribbean, Southeast Asia and East Africa (see Figures 2.2 and 2.3). Recent rapid onset disasters in coastal cities include flooding in Mozambique (2000), typhoons and tropical storms in Orissa (1999) and Gujarat (1998) in India, Hurricane Georges in the Dominican Republic (1998) and Hurricane Mitch in Honduras and Nicaragua (1998).

Decisions made during the colonial period have also placed cities close to areas of volcanic activity. Chester et al (2001) found that of the ten cities most at risk from earthquakes, seven are Latin American (Quito, Arequipa, Mexico City, Guatemala City, San Salvador, Managua and San José). Tucker et al (1994) estimated that by 2000 half of the urban dwellers in the world's 50 largest cities would live within 200km of faults that are known to produce earthquakes of Richter magnitude 7 or more. This is up from a quarter of a much smaller population in 1950 (Uitto, 1998). Some 90 per cent of the urban population exposed to volcanic and earthquake risk is located in developing countries. This pattern of interior colonial urbanization was typical of the Spanish territories in South and Central America and reinforced by the boom in agricultural commerce, especially in coffee, in the early/mid-20th century, which brought money to interior agricultural settlements (Swyngedouw, 1997). The exposure of colonial settlements to natural hazards is born out by the number of colonial cities that have suffered greatly from geological hazards. The original capital of Guatemala, Santiago, was destroyed by an earthquake in 1733. Jamaica's original capital, Port Royal, was destroyed by an earthquake and tidal wave in 1692. Perhaps the most hazard-prone city is San Salvador, which remains stubbornly at the foot of the active San Salvador volcano despite being destroyed by earthquake nine times between 1575 and 1986 (Pelling, 2001a).

---

in Figure 2.1 together with some other large and rapidly expanding cities (Delhi, Dhaka, Caracas).

There are, of course, hundreds of smaller settlements that are equally or more at risk from natural hazards (Cross, 2001). The total population of medium and small urban areas exposed to environmental risk is likely to exceed the total at-risk population resident in mega-cities. Recent research on disaster and mega-cities should not be uncritically projected onto smaller cities where political, economic, social and environmental contexts will differ.

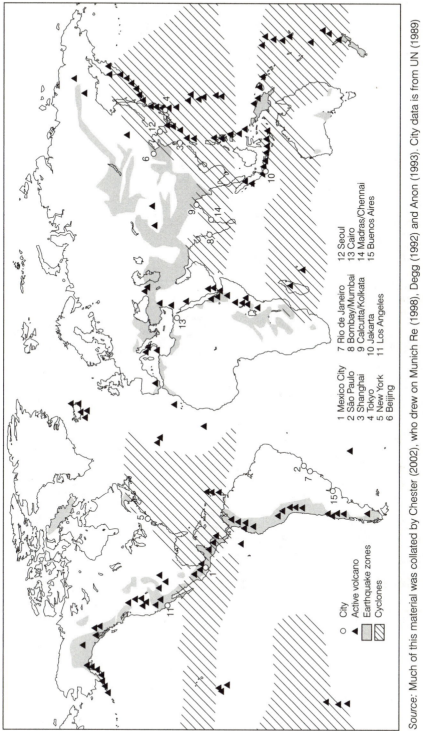

Figure 2.2 *World hazard zones and urban centres*

Source: Much of this material was collated by Chester (2002), who drew on Munich Re (1998), Degg (1992) and Anon (1993). City data is from UN (1989)

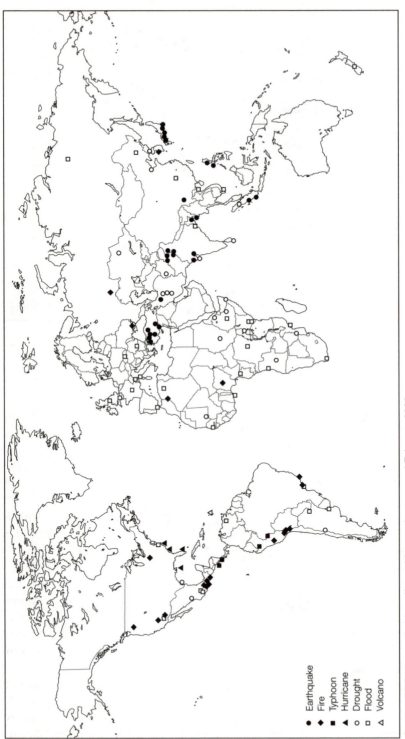

Figure 2.3 *Reported urban disasters 1998–2001*

Source: BBC Newsonline http://news.bbc.co.uk, accessed February 2002

Table 2.1 *Major cities at risk from natural disasters*

City or conurbation	Population 1990 (millions)	Population 2015 (millions)	Major environmental risks
Mexico City	15.1	19.2	Earthquake, pollution, subsidence, drought
Tokyo-Yokohama	15.3	26.4	Earthquake
Los Angeles	15.3	14.1	Earthquake, pollution
Buenos Aires	11.4	14.1	Flood
Calcutta (Kolkata)	11.0	17.3	Cyclone, flood, human waste
São Paulo	9.8	20.4	Flood, pollution
Jakarta	9.1	17.3	Earthquake, volcano, salination of aquifer, human waste, flood
Manila	8.5	14.8	Flood, cyclone
Delhi	8.4	16.8	Flood, human waste
Shanghai*	8.2	14.6	Flood, typhoon
Beijing	7.3	12.3	Earthquake
Cairo*	6.8	13.8	Flood, earthquake
Rio de Janeiro	5.6	11.9	Landslide, flood
Dhaka*	3.4	21.1	Flood, cyclone, human waste

* At risk from sea-level rise
Sources: Blaikie et al (1994), United Nations Social Statistics Office
un.org/Depts/unsd/social/main.html, UNPD World Population Prospects: The 1999 Revision,
Kreimer and Munasinghe (1992)

Environmental change and urban risk

Urbanization can be thought of as being reflexive, contributing towards its own increasing risk, through local, regional and global environmental degradation (Hardoy, Mitlin and Satterthwaite, 2001). Consumption of natural assets (trees for fuel, ground water, sand and gravel) and the overexploitation of natural services (water systems and air as sinks for sewerage or industrial waste) have modified the environment through deforestation and slope instability within and surrounding cities, the contamination and silting of water courses, the lowering of water tables followed by salt intrusion or land subsidence, and the loss of mangrove ecosystems with consequent coastal erosion. It is urban fringe settlements and inner city slums which most often experience the negative impacts of such changes. In São Paulo, localized environmental degradation was associated with 220 floods and 180 landslides in 1996 alone (Jacobi, 1997). The persistent re-urbanization of hazard sites, without any mitigation efforts, also adds to the impacts: in Rio de Janeiro, landslides caused 1000 deaths in 1966, rising to 1700 in 1967 (Alexander, 1989).

Changes in the land-use of urban hinterlands can also increase risk in the city, for example: modification of the city's bio-region (Haughton, 1999) through the deforestation of surrounding hill-slopes or the damming of rivers increases the risk of flash floods or landslides. Many losses to Hurricane Mitch,

1998, in Central America were in small regional towns which were smothered by mud slides or flash floods caused by destabilized, deforested slopes in adjacent agricultural areas (IFRC/RC, 1999). Similarly, efforts to control hazard in cities often pushes that risk onto rural communities. In Bangladesh, flood action plans are allegedly designed purposefully to direct floodwaters from Dhaka onto neighbouring rural regions (Huq, 1999). On a global scale, gaseous emissions from urban-industrial regions (principally in the North) which have driven global climate change may now be reflecting back onto cities (principally in the South) through potential increases in the severity of atmospheric hazards (floods, droughts, hurricanes and cyclones) and sea-level rise. The cost of improving sea defences worldwide to protect cities from a 1m rise in sea level has been estimated, at 1989 prices, to be US$103 billion (Turner, Kelly and Kay, 1990).

Another consequence of population growth is urban drought. In the early 1990s in Chennai (Madras) and Hyderabad, water was only available for two out of every 48 hours. In Chennai in 1993, water was only available every third day, and brought into the city by rail tankers from the nearest supply several hundred kilometres away. The failure to provide adequate water supplies for cities has large health impacts. In Delhi, some 34 per cent of the population are not served by water. In 1988 the urban poor suffered a cholera and gastroenteritis epidemic, with 643 deaths and 70,000 reported cases. Large cities are having to look far afield for sources of drinking water. Delhi has proposals to create reservoirs on the Ganges and Yamuna rivers some 260km distant from the city (Giles and Brown, 1997). Mexico City already exploits sources over 200km away. As cities become dependent upon increasingly distant sources for essential inputs, they also become vulnerable to environmental change in these regions. In 1991, the volcanic eruption of Mount Pinatubo caused mud slides that damaged the highway to the north of Metro Manila, blocking food supplies to the city (Solway, 1994).

Peripheral settlements at risk

The rapid supply of housing to meet rising demand without appropriate regulation can result in risk from sub-standard construction within the formal sector. This was the principal cause of high losses in the Marmara earthquake, Turkey (Özerdem and Barakat, 2000). In many cities it is common for the majority of urban residents to be excluded from the formal housing market because of economic poverty and inappropriate financial legislation that makes it very difficult for low- and middle-income earners to obtain loans to build or buy dwellings in planned developments. In Manila, informal settlements at risk of coastal flooding make up 35 per cent of the population; in Bogotá, 60 per cent of the population live on steep slopes subject to landslides; and in Kolkata (Calcutta), 66 per cent of the population live in squatter settlements at risk from flooding and cyclones (Blaikie et al, 1994). This pattern is repeated throughout the cities of the South. In Bangkok increasing intensity of land-use has resulted in the filling in of drainage canals and their conversion into streets that regularly flood (Mitchell, 1999).

The peripheries of expanding cities tend to grow most rapidly, with central districts growing more slowly or declining in population as non-residential land-uses take over. The population of São Paulo grew by 1 per cent per annum 1980–1991. However, within the city the central core lost 1.3 per cent of its population each year, while the periphery grew at an average rate of 3 per cent. In mega-cities, annual rates of peripheral population growth can reach 10–20 per cent when land invasions are taking place (Brennen-Galvin, 2001). In Rio de Janeiro, 1.6 million people have settled on peripheral hill-slopes, around garbage dumps and in flood-prone lowlands (Munasinghe et al, 1991). In São Paulo, 400 areas have been identified as being at risk from flooding, and an estimated 75,000 people are periodically affected, with 25,000 at high risk from landslides (Leitmann, 1991). Rapid colonization of these hazardous areas means it is not possible to keep urban risk maps or data on land-use and the housing market up to date. Decennial population censuses – the basic tool for planning infrastructure and service delivery – are unable to capture rapid expansion when the city might be re-shaped from one year to the next. Without reliable information the provision of infrastructure and services is difficult, even where financial resources and political will exist.

The expansion of urban areas is often a symptom of piecemeal urban development and a lack of strategic planning. Harris (1995) identified this process in Mumbai (Bombay) where, in response to changes in the global political economy, the city shifted its industrial base from import substituting to export orientation. This led to industrial relocation from the central city to highways extending beyond the city limits, catalysing massive population growth in the urban periphery. Some settlements reportedly grew to six times their original population. Similar, planned expansion in peri-urban development zones in El Salvador created human vulnerability and subsequently large losses during the 2001 earthquake. Migrant workers supplying labour to foreign-owned enterprises in the newly developed San Bartolo, El Pedregal, Olocuilta and San Marcos free trade zones were devastated (National Labor Committee, 2001).

Poverty and exclusion

The lack of adequate understanding and appropriate policy responses to ameliorate urban vulnerability to environmental risk is part of a broader failure to give sufficient attention to urban poverty in so-called developing countries in all its facets. There are two reasons why urban poverty has not been recognized as a priority concern and so been left off the mainstream of international development.

First, the use of poverty lines to indicate social exclusion has had the effect of artificially reducing the numbers of poor urban dwellers relative to the rural poor. Poverty lines identify the number of people who are unable to access a set of basic commodities measured in daily income. According to Satterthwaite (1997), World Bank poverty lines indicate that about one quarter of urban populations have incomes too low to meet their basic needs; in contrast, individual city studies based on more in-depth data suggest the proportion is closer to 50 per cent. There are a number of reasons for this mismatch. National poverty lines are normally set at a level equal to an estimated average cost of acquiring the basic needs for life (secure housing, subsistence food, clothing, basic education and health care). However, the costs of obtaining such necessities are often higher in urban than rural areas. Greater commodification in urban settlements means that housing, food and water may all have to be paid for, whilst they may be accessible without financial resources in more rural areas. The higher cost of urban living is not factored into national poverty lines. Even when urban poverty lines have been devised, they seldom take account of variation in living costs within a city or between cities. Costs of public transport, schools, health care, housing, basic services and so on are higher in larger, more properous cities. Within the same city, city centre households have access to employment but need to pay high rents, whilst peripheral locations have lower rents but the cost of transport into the city for work is high (Satterthwaite, 1997).

Second, until the 1980s many cities had only a relatively low level of poverty in contrast to impoverished rural populations, especially in Africa and South Asia. The international debt crisis and structural adjustment policies of the 1980s and 1990s hit hard on urban economies with poverty rising as a result. Failure to recognize the scale of urban poverty has contributed to the slow realization that many urban dwellers are vulnerable to disaster. The cycle of urban poverty, environmental degradation and vulnerability is perpetuated as much through indirect and secondary as through direct losses with disaster reconstruction often increasing international debt and reducing options for economic growth or anti-poverty policies (Anderson, 1990).

The debt crisis of the 1980s forced governments throughout Latin America, Asia and Africa to slash subsidies on food, light and transportation just when fiscal reform and restructuring of the public sector meant that urban unemployment and inflation were on the increase. These policies were disproportionately felt by the urban poor and middle-classes, whose livelihoods were put at risk (Briggs and Yeboah, 2001). The impact of these policies was perhaps most visible in the food riots of sub-Saharan Africa stimulated by the removal of subsidies on the price of food (Walton and Seddon, 1994). Poor people responded by putting more people (especially women and school-age children) into the labour market and by pulling back from long-term investments in children's education and housing improvement.

Partly as a response to insecurity caused by the debt crisis, structural adjustment programmes were introduced throughout the developing world by the World Bank and International Monetary Fund in the 1980s and 1990s. In Africa alone between 1980 and 1996, some 265 agreements had been made between governments and the World Bank/International Monetary Fund within

---

Box 2.2 *Structural adjustment*

Some principal conditionalities of structural adjustment

- Currency devaluation.
- Trade liberalization.
- A reduced role for the state.
- The elimination of state subsidies on goods including food and fuel.
- An increase in the export of primary products .

The impact of structural adjustment on cities

- *Slowing urban population growth.* As economic opportunities become more constrained and the quality of urban life deteriorates, rural to urban migration is reduced. Most of Africa's cities are examples. In more established urban centres, such as those in Latin America, in-migration is less important and growth by natural population increase may continue.
- *The rise of an informal economy.* People enter the informal economy in growing numbers, forced out by a contraction in public and private sector employment.
- *The urban economy contracts.* As formal sector activities decline the city's ability to generate economic growth is reduced.
- *Greater vulnerability.* As livelihood opportunities wither away, the costs of living increase and urban infrastructure and health and education services deteriorate. For those who were already marginal in society, the chances of escaping from poverty and vulnerability become even more remote.
- *Rising violence.* Crime and violence increasingly linked to drugs has spread amongst Latin American, African and Asian cities.
- *Mounting inequality.* Those with money are able to access safe living environments, education and health services and to insulate themselves from many of the impacts of structural adjustment.
- *Capital flight.* Money leaves the urban economy to avoid further devaluation and inflation.
- *Brain drain.* This weakens the entrepreneurial spirit of the city and sucks away those individuals who might otherwise have played key roles in governing or managing the city and country.
- *Urban food insecurity.* Agricultural production for export eats into production for meeting domestic needs. At the same time the cost of imported foodstuffs increases as a result of devaluation. This has been linked to the spread of urban agriculture and malnourishment.

Source: Riddell (1997)

---

the structural adjustment framework (Riddell, 1997). These agreements included conditionalities negotiated with national governments in exchange for loans. Box 2.2 summarizes the main types of conditionalities and the consequences of structural adjustment for cities and their inhabitants.

Structural adjustment has been clearly linked to rising urban poverty. In Mexico City the proportion of people below the poverty line increased from 59 per cent in 1988 to 66 per cent in 1992 (Garza, 1999). Gilbert (1995) studied the impact of debt and structural adjustment on poverty in Latin American cities.

He found that in Santiago and Panama rates of unemployment rose from less than 10 per cent in the 1970s to 30 per cent in the 1980s and 1990s. Not only were there less people in formal work, but the wages were reduced. In Lima, industrial wages had fallen by 1990 to 43 per cent of their 1980 value. With a declining formal sector, urbanites shifted livelihood strategies en masse towards a search for opportunities in the informal sector. Despite problems with defining the informal sector (Dierwechter, 2002) in some cities it is clear even to the casual observer that unregulated, small-scale entrepreneurial activity makes up a significant part of urban employment. De Soto (1989) classified 48 per cent of Peru's active workforce as informal. Whilst the informal sector has allowed many people to survive, few have been able to move out of material poverty. Evidence from Manila, Dar es Salaam, Guayaquil, Mexico City and Guadalajara indicates that households have changed consumption and dietary patterns in the direction of cheaper and less nutritious substitutes as a means of coping with the price increases and lower incomes caused by structural adjustment (Moser et al, 1993). Disaster impacts in developing countries are felt particularly strongly within the informal sector where productive assets such as housing, supplies and equipment are uninsured and the product of many years accumulation (Anderson, 1992). Informal activities are invisible to the analyst and are lost from disaster impact assessments. Their inclusion would dramatically increase the total economic loss to disaster.

Economic poverty linked to the informalization of the urban labour market has gone hand in hand with the collapse of public and private housing sectors in excluding growing numbers of urban dwellers from the formal housing market. Urban poverty has restricted housing construction and improvement in three ways. First, low-income households have not been able to invest in upgrading self-build units. Secondly, fewer houses have been built in the private sector as fewer people can afford to buy. Thirdly, as the public sector has retreated it has become less able to invest in housing and infrastructure programmes. Responses to contracting housing markets have included multiple households living in one dwelling and squatting. Gilbert (1995) identifies examples of increased household density in Bogotá and Santiago where more people have become tenants or moved in with kin in response to their exclusion from the housing market. Increased household density creates social stress and increases the transmission of communicable diseases. Squatting may relieve household density for some but uncertainty over household tenure and the absence of environmental and social infrastructure in squatter settlements increases exposure to environmental hazard. High-density living also increases the fire risk. In the Joe Slovo informal settlement in Cape Town, South Africa, seven large-scale residential fires were recorded between March 1996 and January 1997, in which 153 shacks were burned and 498 people displaced (Mehlwana, 1999 in Hardoy, Mitlin and Satterthwaite, 2001). In each case fires were started by individual faulty paraffin stoves or candles overturning but quickly spread from one dwelling to another.

The exclusion of low-income families from bank lending and mortgage financing forces people to turn to the high-interest loans offered by loan companies. This exacerbates economic poverty and reduces housing entitlements. The micro-finance and micro-credit schemes that have been operating to overcome parallel problems in rural contexts have yet to be transferred to the city to any large extent. However, even if finance was available it might not be spent on risk reduction. Retrofitting, relocation or housing insurance might be too expensive compared with the perceived benefits. Most income for poor individuals and households is utilized for daily survival, and the low frequency of risk of a natural disaster might not be sufficient to warrant a change in behaviour (Charvériat, 2000).

Resource scarcity for urban administrations and a burgeoning population that outstrips supply has been exacerbated in many cities by a failure to organize strategic urban planning that is accountable to and informed by open forms of urban governance. Despite being one of the largest cities in the world, Mexico City has endured many years with no effective urban planning. Garza (1999) links this to the structural adjustment experience, reflecting that the neoliberal vision of urban development propagated by the Western financial institutions fits easily with a presumption that the real estate market and not planning is the proper tool for determining land-use and urban morphology. A similar situation is found in Monterrey, Mexico, where a Strategic Plan for the Urban Development of the Monterrey Metropolitan Area, 2020, was only introduced in 1995. Public consultation on the plan is legally required but Garza (1999) argues that NGOs and other popular organizations were excluded and the planning committee has been captured by real estate interests.

On top of debt and structural adjustment, the necessity for large cities to compete in the global market has added to vulnerability in two ways. First, the footloose nature of global capital facilitates the shifting of risk from companies onto labour. This is seen amongst those people who are able to win employment in the formal sector but who nevertheless have to endure job insecurity, fluctuating incomes and a lack of unionization. Second, for cities in developing countries there is a pressure to capitalize on competitive advantages to attract foreign direct investment by turning a blind eye to poor employment practice, and for established companies to cut costs to maintain their market share. This is too easily translated into an erosion of worker and industrial safety, wider environmental management and social development. The huge human losses to a toxic gas leak in Union Carbide (India) Ltd's plant in Bhopal in 1984 can be explained by just such a cocktail of causes. In total some 3500 people were killed and 300,000 were injured. At the time of the disaster nearly 20 per cent of the city's population lived in slum housing, many in close proximity to the Union Carbide plant. The proximate causes of risk were a number of technical and management failures inside the plant, but these in turn were triggered by deeper causes rooted in Union Carbine's efforts to retain its position in an increasingly competitive marketplace for fertiliser (Shrivastava, 1996).

At the turn of the millennium not only is the magnitude of urban poverty in Africa, Asia and Latin America and the Caribbean being realized by national governments and international development agencies, but policy reliance on the economic reductionism of poverty lines has been improved by an appreciation of the multi-faceted nature of urban poverty (Lipton and Maxwell, 1992). This in turn has seen the beginnings of a shift away from anti-poverty strategies that focus solely on macro-structural issues such as interventions in labour and housing markets to a more nuanced agenda that builds on the varied ways in which poverty is experienced locally. This has given greater policy relevance to grassroots actors such as CBOs and to decentralized arms of the public sector and municipal government (see Chapter 4).

Urban planning

Inappropriate planning and legislation can exacerbate vulnerability. This is often an outcome of piecemeal approaches to development or inefficiencies in the administrative infrastructure. An example of the former comes from a study of disaster risk in Tanga, Zambia, where widows are denied any claim on household possessions following the death of their spouse (Charvériat, 2000) pushing female-headed households closer to vulnerability and household collapse. Here, for disaster mitigation efforts to be effective and equitable, there is need to consider legislative reform and support for female-headed households as part of broader programmes that might also include more traditional physical infrastructure interventions.

Most frequently however, disasters are linked to a breakdown or blockage in communication between scientists, politicians, emergency services and the public. In extreme examples, known risks are kept from the public domain or denied by government sources. The Chinese famine of 1959–1961 led to 26 million premature deaths whilst official news agencies reported record harvests. Motivations for cover-ups include a wish to prevent panic, and to maintain an attractive international image for foreign investors. More often information is available but simply does not get to those people who need to act upon it because of failures in systems of communication. The 2002 volcanic lava flow that destroyed 40 per cent of Goma, in the Democratic Republic of Congo, had been forecast by Mr Wafula, a local academic geologist (http://news. bbc.co.uk). The warning was not taken seriously enough by the international agencies Mr Wafula contacted. That Mr Wafula turned to international agencies itself indicates the lack of institutional capacity in Goma and Congo to respond to such threats.

That disaster interacts with many aspects of urban planning is clear. Box 2.3 describes how flooding in Rio de Janeiro in 1988 led to a more holistic strategy for development in the city's peripheral settlements.

Environmental degradation within the city often results in a multitude of comparatively small and localized disasters. Examples include local flooding,

---

Box 2.3 *Flood hazard and response in Rio de Janeiro*

In February 1988, three months worth of rain fell on Rio in less than 24 hours. The resulting floods and landslides left 289 dead, 734 injured, 18,560 homeless and extensive damage to physical infrastructure including roads, bridges, sewers, drains and waterworks. Vulnerability was linked to rapid urbanization in unsafe areas, leading to deforestation of steep hillsides and riverbanks, accelerated runoff and landslides, and to the poverty which forced people to live in such circumstances and which eroded human resilience to disaster impacts in the flood-prone Baixada Fluminense region to the north of Rio.

The disaster stimulated local government to undertake preventive measures to mitigate the effects of minor periodic floods and to improve the region's capacity to cope with the major floods that occur every 20 years or so. In 1988, the municipality of Rio created a special unit to coordinate activities and received financial support from the World Bank in one of its first loans to strengthen disaster mitigation works. The World Bank contributed US$175m to a US$393.6m flood reconstruction project. The project's central goals were to: improve emergency capacity to respond to natural hazards; rebuild basic infrastructure; institute engineering and institutional reforms to reduce exposure to future risk; help the state and municipal governments to develop flood prevention and mitigation programmes; and to make more public money available for maintenance of environmental protection infrastructure in Baixada Fluminense.

A key problem in meeting these goals was the institutional complexity of urban management in Rio, with agencies at the national and municipal level having a quick turnaround of management staff, and overlapping and unclear responsibilities.

Source: Munasinghe, Menzes and Preece (1991)

---

fires and landslides. These do not in themselves result in a significant enough loss of life or property to warrant national emergencies or the attention of the international press. However, when they are taken cumulatively – even across a single city in a single year – losses are often considerable. In São Paulo, localized environmental degradation was associated with 220 floods and 180 landslides in 1996 alone (Jacobi, 1997). Following major urban disasters, there remains a tendency to reconstruct the physical fabric of the city to a pre-disaster standard, thereby recreating physical vulnerability to future risk. In the more frequent localized disasters, reconstruction is more likely to go ahead without state involvement and without the assistance of international NGOs or bilateral aid. This both lowers the visibility of reconstruction efforts – many take place at a household level – and restricts the technical and financial resources available for reconstruction. The persistent re-urbanization of hazard sites, without any additional mitigation efforts, is a familiar consequence, which adds to future losses. In Rio de Janeiro, landslides amongst redeveloped favelas caused 1000 deaths in 1966, rising to 1700 in 1967 (Alexander, 1989).

Building securely

In 1993, 37 per cent of the total housing stock in Latin America and the Caribbean was judged by the Pan American Health Organization to afford inadequate protection against disaster and disease (PAHO, 1994). Insecure housing increases the immediate impacts of disaster – human death, injury, homelessness – and inadequate residential infrastructure (sewerage, garbage collection, drinking water, drainage) can prolong or worsen health impacts. The most insecure buildings may be the most recently constructed. Multi-storey buildings of between six and twelve storeys were the sites of the most devastation in the Mexico City earthquake (Degg, 1986). Poor location, weak design and inappropriate building technologies were critical in the collapse of multi-storey buildings in the Armenian earthquake (Kreimer and Munasinghe, 1992). Rapid modernization and the importation of building techniques and materials without the application of appropriate building standards are a recipe for disaster. Box 2.4 outlines the differential resistance of indigenous and non-indigenous building forms during earthquakes in the Himalayas.

The problem here is not a lack of building codes. Turkey, Taiwan and India are all recent big losers to urban earthquakes but have earthquake building codes. In some cases the codes are based on colonial regulations and may not be fully appropriate to local conditions. For example, Jamaica's use of British building standards has contributed to losses in hurricane events (Brown, 1994). More important is a general failure to implement existing building codes at the local level. Time and again this is flagged as a proximate cause of losses to urban disaster: recent examples include reports on earthquake damage in Turkey (Özerdem and Barakat, 2000) and Buju, India (www.anglia.ac.uk/geography/radix/gujarat.htm). Municipal authorities are normally charged with

---

Box 2.4 *Building form and disaster resistance in the Himalayas*

In three separate earthquakes affecting different regions of the Himalayas, vernacular housing has proven to be the most resistant to earthquake damage. In Kashmir, it was the Dhajji-Diwari houses built of wood and unreinforced masonry laid on weak mortar that survived the Srinagar earthquake in 1885. In 1905 when Himachal Pradesh was hit by the Kangra earthquake, it was the indigenous Kat-Ki Kunni houses that were left standing. Kat-Ki Kunni buildings are multi-storeyed, using wood bonding at vertical intervals both inside and outside mud masonry to give the structures flexibility for earthquake resistance. More recently, in 1991, and despite their age, it was the Pherols buildings that survived the Uttarkashi quake in the Garhwal Himalayas. Villages built using Pherols survived whilst adjacent villages with housing built from modern designs suffered great losses. As with Kat-Ki Kunni design, Pherols are multi-storey, utilizing wooden tie-bands to act as beams and timber columns as pins to hold the coursed-rubble masonry intact with the flexibility required to withstand earthquakes. Pherols also used long stones with flat surfaces to distribute the load vertically along walls, so minimizing the tendency of wall stones to push outward during a tremor.

Much of the skills and knowledge used to construct indigenous buildings in these regions have been lost with time. This, together with the prestige attached to modern housing design, has undermined the security of the whole region.

Source: Sharma (2001)

overseeing construction standards but are prevented from fulfilling their duty for several reasons. Internal constraints are perhaps greatest for smaller cities where land-use or development planning departments may be absent and responsibilities for overseeing construction standards become added to those of the city engineer or surveyor. In many cities, even these professionals may be absent and construction regulation is in effect non-existent. Clearly, the lack of sufficient human and financial resources at the municipal or city level is key to this. So are institutional cultures within departments where corruption distorts the oversight role. External constraints on construction regulation may be greatest in large and rapidly expanding cities where it may simply be unrealistic for limited numbers of trained staff to conduct comprehensive inspections of building designs, let alone make site visits. For cities where the majority of new buildings and conversions are made in the informal sector, the majority of developments are effectively invisible to the regulator. These problems perhaps represent one of the major impasses in reducing losses to urban disaster. In the long term, as Solway (1994, p162) argues, a city

> *'will be enabled to build to the appropriate standards and codes only when its own economy allows for the substantial urban planning and redevelopment that is needed to resolve the problems of poor infrastructure, housing, health and communications. Indeed, against such a bleak scenario, some would argue that there are no solutions of sufficiently low cost to enable significant progress'.*

Solway's pronouncement, speaking from the perspective of a civil engineer, is bleak. He is right to identify the urban economy as a fundamental barometer of a city's ability to withstand and recover from disaster. Given the unlikelihood of economic development reaching sufficiently high levels amongst the urban areas of the world to provide an incentive for institutional reform, the disappearance of corruption and informal construction in the foreseeable future, what policy alternatives do we have for addressing mounting urban disaster risk? A good place to start looking for answers is outside of those institutions that are currently seen as being the main players in attempting to manage urban disaster risk. This means looking in more detail at the private sector and at civil society actors. Especially in urban contexts where the predictability of risk is increasingly uncertain, what scope is there for these sectors to contribute to risk reduction in the city? In concluding his review of disaster and risk management in ten mega-cities, Mitchell (1999, p480) makes the following observations:

> *'The neglected approaches involve non-expert systems, informal procedures, non-structural technologies, private sector institutions, and actions taken by individuals, families, neighbourhood groups, firms, and similar entities... there is a lack of initiatives that jointly address different kinds of hazard, a slowness to integrate hazards management with other problem-solving urban*

programmes, and a failure to investigate other roles that hazard plays in the lives of urban residents.'

At the heart of these observations lies a recognition of the need for more awareness of the action of informal, or non-state actors. White et al (2002) argue along similar lines that future mitigation planning needs to include a greater involvement for community level actors and that any mitigation work should be placed within the broader context of community planning. This should not be seen as a call for shifting attention – and financial/technical support – from the public sector but as an argument for broadening the list of actors and institutions that so-called experts include in planning for disaster. In the end this list might more closely reflect the types of institutions that vulnerable individuals and groups interact with in attempts to deal with their own exposure to risk. Increasing the involvement of non-state actors in urban disaster mitigation has the potential to enhance resiliency in a number of ways:

- CBOs and NGOs can act as a means of transmitting information about risk and vulnerability.
- Being a collection of, usually, small horizontally structured and diversified organizations – compared to the municipality – CBOs and NGOs will continue to function as independent units, whereas public sector institutions may falter when communication or resource links are broken.
- Civil society networks offer an alternative to the private sector and public sector as a mechanism for at-risk groups to access the resources necessary to mitigate local causes of risk and vulnerability. Even where there is no net increase in resources in the city, by acting as an alternative distribution mechanism, individuals and groups excluded from established networks by being economically poor or politically marginalized will have an opportunity to overcome their exclusion.

There are a number of examples where civil society and private sector actors have already been brought into urban disaster mitigation, but scope exists for a much wider and deeper engagement. Exploring the roles and activities of different urban actors in disaster management is the aim of Chapter 4.

DISASTER IMPACTS

Economic effects

Neither the economic conditions that contribute to disaster risk, nor the economic consequences of disaster shocks are well understood for urban economies. In this section we deal with the economic impacts of disaster. Table 2.2 shows the types of impact caused by various hazard types.

Table 2.2 *Direct disaster impacts by hazard type*

Impact	Disaster trigger event					
	Flood	*Wind*	*Tsunami*	*Earthquake*	*Volcano*	*Drought*
Short-term migration	✗				✗	✗
Loss of housing	✗	✗	✗	✗	✗	
Loss of business production	✗	✗	✗	✗		✗
Loss of industrial production	✗	✗	✗	✗		✗
Loss of crops potentially leading to food price increases	✗	✗	✗		✗	✗
Damages to infrastructure	✗	✗	✗	✗		
Disruption of transport	✗	✗		✗		
Disruption of communication	✗	✗	✗	✗		

Source: based on UNDRCO (1991)

Disaster impacts in urban systems can be described as either direct or systemic. Direct impacts are the consequence of the initial disaster event, and are felt immediately as physical damage, especially to housing and physical infrastructure, and loss of life or injury. This phase of the disaster is often complicated by secondary technological or natural disasters; for example, an earthquake can trigger chemical fires or liquefaction. The death of up to 100 people in Goma, the Democratic Republic of Congo in 2002, was caused by the explosion of a petrol station that had been damaged by lava from the erupting Mount Nyiragongo. Risk from technological hazards is related to the development stage and size of the city. Larger and more industrially developed cities will have more sources of technological risk, but also tend to have better access to regulation and safety measures with which to contain risk and loss (McGranahan, Songsore and Kjellén, 1996). Direct impacts interrupt the flows of goods, services and information in and around the city and are the root cause of systemic impacts which are felt as instabilities in the political economy of the city. Perhaps because of this, as well as their high visibility, it is direct losses that have been the focus of mitigation effort.

The potential gain to be made from preparing for disaster to reduce direct losses can be seen in Jamaica. Following Hurricane Gilbert in 1988, 30,235 homes were destroyed. Losses in this sector have been blamed on a lack of preparedness in the physical planning and housing sectors. This is partly as a result of structural adjustment policies which encouraged poor maintenance of rental property and non-compliance with building codes (Ford, 1987 in Blaikie et al, 1994), and also because the National Building Code of Jamaica (1983) was inappropriately modelled on UK standards (Clement, 1990). In contrast to the housing sector, many small businesses were well prepared and were able to return to work quickly (Brown, 1994).

Direct impacts that cause damage to urban infrastructure networks are potentially the most destabilizing for the urban economy. This is a critical issue in the ageing colonial cores and rapidly expanding business and residential zones of many cities in Africa, Asia and Latin America, where basic infrastructure has been built without regard to appropriate construction standards (Solway, 1994). At times of disaster this can result in some parts of the city being isolated for hours, days or in extreme cases weeks before state agencies or services are re-connected (see Chapter 6).

Two types of systemic loss can be differentiated, and economists have labelled these indirect losses and secondary effects. Indirect losses are the costs of goods that will not be produced and services that will not be provided because of a disaster. Additional costs can be incurred because of the need to use alternative sources of provision and distribution for services to be provided. Indirect losses include losses of personal income in the case of total or partial loss of the means of production or livelihood (Zapata-Marti, 1997). The Philippines provide an example of an indirect urban loss, where low rainfall in 1989–1990 reduced hydro-electric power generation resulting in a decline in the annual rate of industrial growth from 7.4 per cent in 1989 to 2.5 per cent in 1990 (Benson, 1997). Sometimes indirect losses can be moved around the urban economy. This was the case in Kobe, Japan, following the 1995 earthquake. Here, major producers such as Toyota Motor Corporation and Kawasaki Heavy Industries used a 'just-in-time' stocking approach, where parts were manufactured on demand by sub-contractors. Following the earthquake, damage to sub-contractors threatened to hold back production and the major producers responded by shifting to new sub-contractors within a few days. In this way the just-in-time approach effectively passed risk on from the major producers to the sub-contractors, who had to cope with a double burden of disaster impacts and lost contracts. Many faced bankruptcy as a result (UNCRD, 1995).

Secondary effects are felt in the macro-economy. Because data is most accessible at the national level, these are most often used. Important indicators are gross domestic product (GDP), levels of indebtedness and monetary reserves. Secondary effects are normally felt during the calendar or fiscal year in which the disaster occurs but may spill over a number of years (Zapata-Marti, 1997). Larger, developed economies with sizeable foreign currency reserves, high proportions of insured assets, comprehensive social services and diversified production are more likely to absorb and spread the burden of disaster impacts. An example of large losses in an urban region that were contained comes from the Marmara earthquake in Turkey: direct losses were estimated at US$2b for industrial facilities, US$5b for buildings and US$1.4b for infrastructure, plus a similar figure for losses generated through lost production during the many months required for factories and industrial facilities to return to their pre-disaster production levels (Özerdem and Barakat, 2000). However, only seven months after the disaster, a down-turn in the rate of inflation and declining interest rates for government borrowing indicated that the Turkish economy had made a fast recovery (Pelling et al, 2002). In other cases, efforts to restore urban functions can be a drain on national development. This was the case in Mexico, where at a time of severe national economic problems recovery from the earthquake of 1985 hampered national development (Puente, 1999).

Technical difficulties in isolating the economic effects of disaster and a continuing focus by disaster researchers on rural areas have perhaps contributed to the delay in any serious study of the economic impact of disaster on urban economies, and this is now well overdue. Structural differences in cities will shape the extent to which direct losses force systemic impacts. In cities where fixed physical assets are most concentrated and where disaster response and infrastructure reconstruction are rapid, it may be that direct losses exceed systemic loss. Small cities may be especially susceptible to complete destruction in a single event, for example: a volcanic eruption and mud-flow in Amero, Colombia, in 1985 killed most of the city's 25,000 inhabitants (Hardoy, Mitlin and Satterthwaite, 2001). At a larger scale, there is potential for cities at risk that are central to the regional or global financial systems (eg Mexico City, Rio de Janeiro, Johannesburg, Bangkok, Manila, Seoul and Singapore) to spread the negative consequences of catastrophic disaster across the global economy with huge systemic loss effects. The 11 September 2001 attack on the World Trade Center in New York and the Asian financial crisis in late 1990s have already demonstrated the speed with which damage in one city can cause economic losses in others as investment and consumption patterns change. In 1987 a windstorm in southern England shut down the London Stock Exchange, and it has been argued that this event contributed to a subsequent international stock market crisis which was the largest since the Great Depression of the 1930s (Mitchell, Devine and Jagger, 1989).

Systemic impacts add burdens to those who have already suffered direct losses as well as widening the net of those affected. For urban residents, systemic economic effects may not be felt for some time as businesses re-structure, although in the short term unemployment or livelihood disruption is to be expected and may be prolonged. Of more immediate concern will be the containment of any possible disease outbreaks caused by delays in restoring urban water and sanitation systems. Other priorities should include efforts to maintain law and order to minimize social impacts through increased crime and looting and a search for necessary resource inputs (building materials, food, clothing, medical supplies etc) to control inflationary pressures on these essential goods which might otherwise be priced out of the reach of many urban residents. But systemic dislocations can also create opportunities. Most visibly, the construction sector will expand.

Socio-political effects

There is little research on the detailed performance of social and political institutions during emergencies in cities or on the political dislocations which may derive from disaster situations. Social change as an outcome of urban disaster comes about through disaster stresses weakening and fragmenting previously consolidated power blocks within the city, providing a space – perhaps only temporarily – for new social arrangements to operate. The dominant power block, through the national or city government, has an interest in preserving institutional integrity and social order. The propensity for any one city to move towards institutional fragmentation or consolidation will depend upon the pre-existing socio-political landscape: the political regime form, macro-economic scarcity, poverty and inequality and the administrative framework (Albala-Bertrand, 1993). The broader the social and cultural differentiation of society and the more their propensity to self-interest, the more important must be the political and administrative infrastructures to maintain cohesiveness. Freudenheim (1980 in Albala-Bertrand, 1993) in a survey of 89 disasters between 1972 and 1976, found that political problems were a regular   consequence.   The   most   common   problems   concerned acknowledgement of the disaster by the government of the affected country, the government's political interference with the response process, and corruption in the distribution of relief. Table 2.3 shows the socio-political reaction to disaster for selected urban cases.

At the heart of the political actions revealed in Table 2.3 is a tension between formal responses to disaster that come from, and so potentially give political power to, the state and its institutions on one hand, and on the other, informal responses that operate outside of established planning and social frameworks and potentially weaken the established socio-political order. Such responses may not have it as a goal to challenge the authority of the state or local social elite, but by operating outside of established norms they create an example of an alternative form of social organization that can stimulate subsequent critiques of the pre-disaster social system. As an example of this process, it is common in cities of the developing world for elite groups to use clientelistic linkages to control grassroots actors so that resources for infrastructure are distributed not by need but by support offered to the dominant social group (this could be centred on a political party, family or individual etc). Following a disaster, it is common practice for international assistance and aid supplies to be handed over to government agencies for local distribution. These goods have exaggerated importance during the period of scarcity following disaster, and it is likely that clientelistic relationships operating in the pre-disaster period are reinforced by the state's monopoly in goods distribution during recovery from disaster.

Increasingly, non-state actors use CBO or NGO networks to distribute aid not along lines of patronage but by criteria that may more closely respond to need (although, of course, non-governmental actors can also build up

Table 2.3 *Disaster and socio-political change*

Country, city	Date of disaster	Disaster trigger	Socio-political reaction
Turkey, Lice	1972	Earthquake	Discrimination against the minority Kurdish population was blamed for inadequate preparedness before and relief aid after the earthquake. Complaints were made by a Kurdish MP to the Turkish parliament.
Nicaragua, Managua	1972	Earthquake	80 per cent of houses were destroyed in this earthquake. The Somoza dictatorship diverted aid through its business interests, prompting popular revolutionary action that eventually led to the overthrow of the regime.
Guatemala, Guatemala City	1976	Earthquake	Described as a 'classquake' because of its high impact amongst slum dwellers, this event stimulated popular mobilization and land invasions which re-shaped the geography of the city.
Chile, nationwide	1985	Earthquake	A traditional civilian response threatened to undermine a weak dictatorship. The response was demobilized through repression and the state took over.
Mexico, Mexico City	1985	Earthquake	Inadequate state response. A highly organized civil society-led reconstruction programme emerged, unique in Mexico's modern history of authoritarian state control.
USA, Miami	1992	Hurricane	Broad interest coalitions formed assisting in the rebuilding of the city. These coalitions have not persisted but have created the potential for cooperation in local politics.

Sources: Albala-Bertrand (1993), Enarson and Morrow (1998)

patron–client relationships with beneficiaries). There is clear danger for elite groups in such activities that undermine their control of resources and basis of political power. In cases where the formal state response is politically biased (Turkey) or inadequate (Mexico City), informal responses can emerge or even come to dominate disaster relief, recovery (Chile, Mexico City) and reconstruction (Guatemala City). In some cases, informal efforts can become formalized when interest groups create coalitions with dominant political forces and seek to influence disaster response and reconstruction from within (Miami). In other cases, circumvention of formal administrative institutions and resistance to state disaster response is the aim (Mexico City). Both socio-political formulations can allow the emergence of political space for protest and for new social bonds to be formed that may continue to actively influence urban development beyond the disaster period (Mexico City). Where political differences between the cooperating groups are too large, collaboration may not last long beyond the disaster reconstruction period (Miami), but even here the experience is likely to have built up new trust between previously hostile social groups within the city. The state itself can also benefit from informal responses when, for example, the political function of party networks is adapted for relief distribution, or institutional weaknesses allow corruption (Managua). This suggests that it is in the interest of a parasitic governing elite to allow degeneration in the institutions overseeing disaster response (providing a space for corruption), whilst investing in formalizing local disaster response strategies (to prevent the emergence of potentially critical social actors).

Action by the state or municipal authorities is constrained in all but the most internationally isolated and authoritarian regimes (North Korea, China) by the countervailing actions of other political actors. These include location-specific actors such as CBOs, local NGOs and political parties; the local, national and international media; and international actors including international NGOs, foreign governments and international financial organizations (the World Bank, regional development banks), as well as private sector actors. The action taken by the representative of the Kurdish minority in Turkey is an example of countervailing pressure acting within the formal structure of the state. There is very little literature on the interaction of these actors in urban contexts with reference to natural disaster events.

SUMMARY

We are living in a largely urban world, with the most rapid urban growth taking place in Africa, Asia and Latin America. Set against this, disaster management continues to be seen mainly as a pursuit for practitioners of rural development. Linkages between urbanization and disaster are weakly theorized and as a consequence disaster mitigation is rarely integrated into urban development policy. Set within a broad coevolutionary framework, this chapter sought to outline the pathways through which environmental processes and change influence the geography of environmental risk in the city and its urban region, and how the features and processes of urbanization in Africa, Asia and Latin America and the Caribbean shape the social and spatial distribution of human vulnerability. Decision-making power is central to the distribution of risk but is also shaped by disaster events. The urban economy and the authority of its leaders are tested during periods of disaster when spaces can open for new kinds of economic and political organization. This could include the establishment of new business relationships, or grassroots organizations, or more negatively illegal activity and violence.

The demographic expansion of cities, increasingly fuelled by natural population growth, is a fundamental contributing factor to risk when it outstrips the capacity of the urban economy and the skills of urban managers to generate sufficient resources to offer ways of meeting the basic needs of a city's citizens. Relative population growth is most rapid in medium-sized cities and on the peripheries of large cities. It is here and in the inner-city slums that economic poverty and political marginalization are most likely to combine to produce households that are both exposed to environmental hazard and that hold insufficient resources to cope with any disruptions to livelihoods or ill-health that may result from such exposure.

The socio-economic and political consequences of disaster are shaped to a great degree by the pre-disaster characteristics of the urban economy and polity. Direct physical losses, whilst being visible, may not be the largest component of loss to the urban system. Productive activities and access to external markets can be halted or slowed for some time as telecommunications, transport links, resource inputs and labour supplies are interrupted. Disasters have the potential to create a moment of dislocation in the powers of the status quo. Social disruption can take many forms, from looting and lawlessness to more emancipatory activities where previously repressive state authorities are temporarily unable to exert control over local areas, and alternative forms of organization can spring up during periods of emergency response, relief and rehabilitation. It seems likely that coping at the local level following a major disaster will be enhanced if positive and inclusive social organization and leadership are already in place.

The useful contribution to risk management of such social infrastructure is a departure from established approaches to urban disaster policy that privilege physical infrastructure in disaster prevention. This is not to downplay the contribution to urban security made by engineering works or building codes, but rather suggests that disaster management programmes that omit a social reform component will be restricted in their scope and reach. The need to tie social and physical projects together is best exemplified by the absence of disaster proofing in many of the buildings in cities at risk. In many cases disaster codes are in place but have not been applied by self-builders or professional construction companies through a lack of knowledge or market pressures. Where state regulation and the market place have not worked, institutional reform offers another method for creating incentives for builders, architects, property owners and tenants to apply disaster proofing through retrofitting or in new-build projects.

Chapter 3

Social Vulnerability in the City

INTRODUCTION

'The many kinds of vulnerability in the urban environment can indeed only be understood with sophisticated information management systems. But it is to be hoped that the human element does not get lost in the race to acquire technology...' (Alexander, 2000, p103).

By focussing on technical and engineering issues in environmental service delivery, established approaches to urban environmental risk management tend to overlook or downplay political, economic and social forces. Such human elements of risk shape the mechanisms through which goods are distributed in society and people's entitlements or claims on resources with which to avoid harm and improve life chances. Recent innovation in urban risk management has included human characteristics at a relatively superficial level with, for example, housing tenure, construction form and population density distributions being incorporated into geographic information systems and associated urban risk maps (Trujillo et al, 2000). This is an example of a useful – but limited technology. As Alexander (2000) implies (above), the limits of management technology are in danger of being overlooked in a rush to provide policy-makers with clear recommendations – even at the expense of appropriateness. In relation to geographic information systems, Wisner (1996) notes that some key indicators of vulnerability – such as homelessness or individual psychological states – remain invisible to quantification, and are left outside of urban disaster mitigation policy.

It is the aim of this chapter to present a framework with which to assess the (re)production of human vulnerability and its reciprocal, resilience, and to trace the linkages between macro-, meso- and micro-level human characteristics and their roles in the shaping of experiences of urban environmental risk. There is relatively little theoretical discussion of urban vulnerability or resilience to environmental risk. The approach taken here is to build on work undertaken in studies of rural vulnerability and natural disaster. First we will review the evolution of the literature on environmental hazard in rural areas of Africa,

Asia and Latin America and the Caribbean. Livelihood assets found to be key determinants of individual and collective vulnerability are taken forward to help frame the examination of the political and social aspects of urban vulnerability.

A HISTORY OF HUMAN VULNERABILITY AND ENVIRONMENTAL HAZARD

Understanding hazardous nature–society relations was first attempted from the perspective of human ecology, which examined the behaviour of people responding to environmental risk stimuli. Burton and Kates (1964) described natural disasters as 'those elements of the physical environment harmful to man (sic) and caused by forces extraneous to him (sic)' (in Smith, 1992, p8). Such environmental determinism has directed the bulk of policy and research towards a preference for physical rather than social science analysis and policy recommendation in disaster management. There is much to be gained from physical science-based interventions, but without a social component practical interventions are in danger of ignoring differences in the influence of individual and social characteristics on susceptibility or response to environmental risk.

Responding to the lack of a critical analysis of human causes for environmental hazard, Hewitt (1983) championed a radical approach to disaster analysis, which drew on the Marxist tradition and dependency theory. It was argued that natural disasters should be seen as part of an on-going relationship between society and nature, not as one-off, extreme events taking place outside of development. This approach emphasized the importance of differences in social structures – like the macro-economy and national political regime forms – in the production of disaster. However, this focus on macro-structures of national and global politics and economics, such as aid flows and different phases of the capitalist global economy, underplayed human agency. The challenge today is to integrate agency and structure in examinations of the production of vulnerability, in specific places, whilst also acknowledging the importance of physical systems in generating hazard that can trigger disaster.

Figure 3.1 represents a more integrated perspective.[1] Environmental risk or humanitarian disaster with a natural trigger are the products of physical pressures in the form of environmental hazard, and human pressures experienced as vulnerability. Following from the work of Blaikie et al (1994), environmental hazard and human vulnerability are presented as the local outcome of progressions from root causes (global political economy, global climate change), via intervening dynamic pressures that link global or historical forces with the immediate conditions (a lack of institutions, rapid urbanization, local topography) that superficially indicate danger. Vulnerability is broken down into three components: *exposure, resistance* and *resilience*.

---

1 This model and its explanation were first presented in Pelling (2001b).

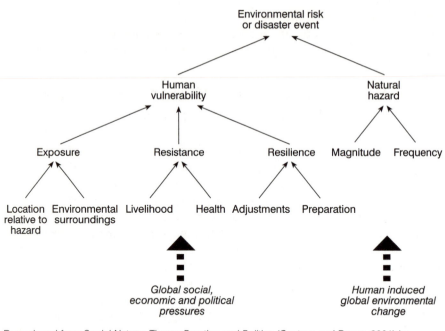

Source: Adapted from Pelling (2001b)

Figure 3.1 *The components of environmental risk*

Exposure is largely a product of physical location and the character of the surrounding built and natural environment. For example, a family living in ground-level, poorly maintained rental accommodation on a river bank and adjacent to a sewerage outfall will be highly exposed to flooding. The exposure component can be reduced by hazard mitigation investments made by individuals or households, such as building a house on stilts, or collectively through public–private social investment policy, such as the building of a wall to protect a community from landslides.

Resistance reflects economic, psychological and physical health and their systems of maintenance, and represents the capacity of an individual or group of people to withstand the impact of a hazard. If resistance is low then even a small hazard stress can lead to systems failure. The most successful efforts to enhance resistance will not directly target disaster vulnerability, but focus on the wider goals of economic, social and political inclusion.

Resilience to natural hazard is the ability of an actor to cope with or adapt to hazard stress. It is a product of the degree of planned preparation undertaken in the light of potential hazard, and of spontaneous or premeditated adjustments made in response to felt hazard, including relief and rescue. The most important policy options available to enhance resilience are those that shape formal or informal insurance mechanisms. Insurance is a key tool for use in spreading the economic costs of disasters across society and over time.

Exposure, resistance and resilience are all shaped by an actor's access to rights, resources and assets (Burton et al, 1993; Blaikie et al, 1994). Access profiles are in turn rooted in local and global political and socio-economic structures. Though the relationship between these components of vulnerability may not always be reinforcing, this is often the case, so that opportunities for resilience tend to be less common when resistance is already low and exposure is high, and vulnerability increases with each successive disaster event.

Before applying this framework to the urban context it is worth spending some time investigating in more detail the development of human vulnerability as a key subject for analysis and an object for policy intervention. To do this we need to return to the intellectual development of hazards studies and development economics that has taken place outside of the urban studies literature.

Vulnerability as exposure: technological and physical bias

Within the human ecology tradition, vulnerability was measured by exposure to hazard (Hewitt, 1983). For good reason, a physical science approach is often preferred by urban planners and political decision-makers. Engineering projects are visible and can unambiguously show the electorate and potential investors that the government is responding to risk, whilst social reform tends not to grab headlines and is a longer-term, slower process. Engineering responses are less likely to threaten the status quo in the city than social reform programmes, the aim of which is to extend the entitlements of marginal groups in the city by the redistribution of resources. But this does not mean that engineering responses are apolitical. They provide a source of income for vested interests in the construction business, in some cases including political leaders, and in this way contribute to the strengthening of existing power disparities in the city and nationally. India is an example of such collusion, where enormous amounts of money have been spent on river embankments despite their continued failure to prevent flooding (Pelling, 2001b).

The presence of physical hazard defences such as flood-walls or landslide-retaining walls has two effects on the social geography of the city. First, these investments encourage formal or informal development on hazardous sites. Whilst engineering responses provide much protection, there are many examples of cases where hazards have surpassed the threshold of safety provided by physical structures with very high human costs. Sanderson (2000) offers the example of squatters who have settled adjacent to the flood defences of the Yamuna River to gain access to work in the centre of Delhi. For more than 25 years these flood defences have only been partially effective with residents forced to evacuate at least once a year. Second, the presence of environmental infrastructure can increase the market value of protected land, which can result in low-income groups being replaced by middle- or high-income groups. This is most often the case when hazardous sites are located on desirable real estate land close to the city centre. This was the case in Mexico City, where initial reconstruction plans included the transfer of city centre land-uses from low-income residential to higher-income and business uses. Whilst the physical component of hazard analysis is undoubtedly critical, this approach underestimates the importance of socio-economic or political forces in shaping the production and distribution of risks and vulnerability.

Entitlements and vulnerability: bringing in the human dimension

Sen (1981) argued that the vulnerability of rural populations to famine was the result of structural changes in market exchange values, rather than a consequence of environmentally driven production failures. The rapid devaluing of individual or household productive capacities, relative to the costs of staple foods, resulted in the denial of access to food and so increased vulnerability to malnutrition and famine. A household's productive capacities were the result of its set of entitlements: labour, savings, land, cattle, goods, housing, and any state or social (community, NGO) support, eg subsidized housing, education or health services. Fluctuating economic returns from these household entitlements, in relation to the price of essential market goods (food, water, shelter), could be used to identify levels of household vulnerability.

This work was the first to look beyond environmentally determined factors and go some way to explaining how vulnerability was experienced differently by each household in the face of a shared environmental risk. It resulted in the identification of agricultural wage labourers and small-scale service traders as being the most vulnerable groups to exchange failure in rural society. In urban areas, amongst the key productive assets will be savings, material possessions and tools, labour and the dwelling. For low-income households, labour, tools and the dwelling will be most critical and are also the most liable to loss during disaster (Lewis, 1999b). Loss of these assets through environmental factors (or other shocks or stresses) will cause the income earning capability of the household to fall and lower the range of entitlements to which household members can make claim, making the household and its members more vulnerable to any subsequent everyday or catastrophic stresses or shocks.

The entitlements perspective – sometimes called the livelihoods or asset livelihoods approach – is central to contemporary understandings of vulnerability. Sen's argument was extended by Swift (1989), who proposed an analysis of household asset levels to identify vulnerability. During times of security, assets could be accumulated, or at least would not be eroded, and then during times of stress or shock these assets would be available to protect the household from hazardous impacts (eg malnutrition as a result of famine or indebtedness from loss of livelihood). Asset profiles act as informal insurance against future uncertainty (economic or environmental), and it is patterns of asset investment as well as their quantity that determine susceptibility to hazardous impacts: for example, amassing fixed assets in the same local area might not significantly reduce vulnerability to the impacts of large-scale physical hazards. Similarly, keeping surplus assets in money might not protect the household or family during economic inflation perhaps induced by an environmental disaster.

Scott's (1985, 1990) formulation of a moral economy built out of reciprocal social ties showed the importance of social claims as a means of accessing resources. Scott argued that access to basic needs such as food amongst the poorest in rural Asian societies was enhanced by their right to claim resources from more socially and economically wealthy individuals from the same local community. This observation led Scott to an understanding of the mechanism of basic needs distribution in rural societies that was influenced as much by the micro-politics of local social institutions (cultural norms as much as organizations) as the larger structural forces of the macro-economy and national development policy (Scott, 1985). Of course Scott's work was tied to a particular socio-cultural context but, nonetheless, it reinforces the need for examinations of resource distribution systems that underlie vulnerability/resilience to include an investigation of local social institutions.

The fundamental role played by social institutions in shaping entitlements has most recently been argued for by Leach, Mearns and Scoones (1997) drawing on field data collected from rural Africa. They saw institutions as mediators of people–environment relations, with institutions being 'regularized patterns of behaviour between individuals and groups in society' (Mearns, 1995). Two important findings were that institutions are dynamic over time, being built up or eroded by external pressures such as modernization; and that informal institutions – habits, cultural norms etc – need to be brought into development practice. Standard local development projects, it was argued, tended to see community organizations and groups as the focal point for action and intervention. Leach, Mearns and Scoones argued that this approach overlooked the underlying informal institutions that determine who participates in community groups (women, children, disabled, low caste groups, political and religious minorities etc). For the entitlements of the locally marginalized to be enhanced, attention needs to be paid to the cultural norms that lead to such marginalization within the local community. Thus, like Scott, the environmental entitlements group saw institutions as both formal organizations and cultural norms.

When considering the influence of social institutions on vulnerability and security we also need to consider the ways in which economic stores and investments will influence the range of social claims open to an individual, household or community. It is often observed, for example, that members of urban communities with greater stores and investment profiles also develop a wider and more influential social network on which to draw in times of crisis

(Pelling, 1998). The relationships between different kinds of asset are discussed in more length in the penultimate section of this chapter on adaptive potential.

The household is arguably the most fundamental institution and basic unit of social organization. Swift observed that poor households were constantly having to 'play off' expenditures on the immediate needs of household maintenance against the wish to conserve or invest assets against the possibility of future hazard events. Swift suggested that under prolonged pressure, household assets would gradually be exhausted. At this point a threshold would be reached: the household would become unsustainable as a social unit and collapse. This would occur even if wider economic conditions were improving. Exactly this kind of response to stress is seen in households where adult members succumb to terminal illness (the HIV/AIDS epidemic in African cities) leaving children in the care of grandparents or to fend for themselves (Young and Barrett, 2001). That households can fail in spite of wider economic conditions reveals how individual vulnerability operates with a degree of independence from structural conditions such as poverty. However, poverty and vulnerability frequently overlap, and it is the poor who are also vulnerable who will suffer the most from environmental stresses and risk.

Vulnerability as process not status: coping strategies

Like vulnerability, opportunities for coping with or adapting to hazards are influenced by livelihood, community structures, social groups, household, gender, age, ethnicity, historical time and physical/psychological health (Chambers, 1989; Burton et al, 1993). Though the relationship between vulnerability and coping is not necessarily reinforcing (for example, whilst age may increase vulnerability, experience can enhance coping), assets for coping tend to be less common when vulnerability is already high, resulting in the 'ratchet effect' of vulnerability (Chambers, 1989) where with each new hazardous event those impacted become more vulnerable to future events. A number of accounts within hazards studies have proposed models to examine forms of coping (O'Keefe, Wisner and Baird, 1977; Hewitt, 1983; Watts, 1983; Burton et al, 1993; Blaikie et al, 1994; Adger, 1996). Most are limited to short-term adjustments to specific hazardous events. Burton et al (1993) extend this by incorporating coevolutionary adaptation in biological and cultural systems in a four-stage model of increasing hazard severity and scale of adaptation.

In Burton et al's first 'loss absorption' stage, hazard impacts are absorbed without any tangible impacts or observed short-term adjustment. With close links to the cultural ecology debate of the late 1970s (Watts, 1983), the absorptive capacity of a society is conceptualized as being determined by its long-term biological and cultural adaptations (such as disease resistance and dietary norms or traditional land management systems), and also by less long-term incidental adjustments such as the architectural design of housing or urban morphology. Burton et al (1993) and Swift (1989) argue that the absorptive capacity of a society declines in rapid transitions from folk to mixed economies as traditional social supports are neither kept up in the face of capitalist incursions nor adequately replaced by welfarist support systems. In this understanding, coping capacity is tied directly to the form and penetration of the national/capitalist economy and associated processes of modernization, with rapid change being indicative of a disequilibrium in coevolving systems that is likely to produce human vulnerability.

This viewpoint perhaps partly explains the popular assumption that urbanization per se is a negative process, which inevitably erodes traditional coping strategies as rural migrants are dislocated to the city. Countries and urban regions are seen as being made vulnerable through their inability to generate the financial resources required to offset increasing vulnerability and hazard impacts (Burton et al, 1993). But capacity to manage risk should not be reduced to the size of the urban economy alone. The relatively rich city of Washington, DC is a case in point. Here, in August 2001, intense rainfall led to widespread flooding and blackouts, bringing the city to a standstill. Nick Bryant (2001) argues that national competition between the Republican Party (which dominates Congress) and the Democratic Party (which runs Washington) has cost the city in investment and disaster relief, creating what some have long described as a federal disaster area.

The second stage, loss acceptance, is reached once the negative effect of a hazard is socially perceived and losses are borne but not actively mediated. Whilst Burton et al associate lack of action primarily with the scale of perceived risk, this should also be seen as a product of the efficiency of political and scientific institutions, particularly as modern risks which may remain undetected without access to scientific technology spread out from the industrialized global North (Beck, 1992). Once vulnerable individuals or groups perceive that losses from a potential hazard will be greater than the costs of making adjustments to reduce vulnerability, the third stage, loss reduction, has been entered. This is the focus of most hazards research and risk reduction policy. The final stage, radical change, is reached once hazard losses can no longer be mitigated by local adjustments and major socio-economic changes are experienced, such as migration or land-use and resource-use changes. There is no steady continuum of movement from one stage of coping to another, and individuals and groups may be moving in different directions at the same time in response to the diversity of urban environmental risk. Ability to cope is determined as much by technological, political and social change as by the nature of hazard itself.

The broad view of coping adopted by Burton et al (1993) is useful because of its long temporal frame. However it offers less detailed insights into individual coping strategies. Adger (1996) identifies a three-tier hierarchy of coping strategies for rural societies. Each level of action represents an erosion of increasingly fundamental assets and a play-off between the immediate and long-term needs of household survival. These observations are also appropriate for characterizing urban adaptation:

- initial use of established insurance mechanisms (selling jewellery, loans);
- disposal of key productive assets (land, livestock or housing); and
- destitution or distress migration.

Both Adger (1996) and Burton et al (1993) see distress migration or homelessness as a final option. Whilst out-migration from smaller urban settlements following disaster has been recorded, there is a greater tendency to rebuild in situ. In larger cities with high volumes of in-migration, the movement of individuals or households away from a hazardous location may be compensated for by new arrivals so that the value of migration as an indicator of collective inability to cope is reduced in cities. This said, the movement of individuals between households is likely to take place before a household becomes unsustainable (Swift, 1989) and may be a useful indicator of a household under stress. Analyses will need to separate background movement of children and aged family members and the formation and dissolution of households as a 'normal' part of life-cycle changes from household changes resulting from external stress or shock.

Blaikie et al (1994) propose four generic types of coping mechanism which add more detail to the typologies of coping discussed above and which can be applied to the actions of actors from the individual to the state:

1   preventive strategies and impact-minimizing strategies (large-scale engineering schemes, warning systems or household adjustments);
2   diversification of production strategies (on the national scale this might mean promoting mixed cropping, and at the household level diversification of livelihoods);
3   development of social support networks (informal reciprocity or state welfare); and
4   post-event coping strategies (mechanisms for civil order or opportunistic livelihood strategies).

Again, this analysis is tailored to fit rural contexts but does indicate ways in which urban systems and citizens could reduce their vulnerability. Diversifying production may be difficult in a city whose productive sectors are increasingly constrained by global competition. But within sectors, diversification in raw material and component sourcing, investing in a skilled labour market and diversifying strategies for accessing the market could all raise resilience (see Chapter 1). Enabling individuals to get back to work or to re-establish a livelihood are essential if disaster is not to deepen structural poverty.

In this section's discussion of coping and vulnerability we have seen the importance of distinguishing between individual and collective vulnerability, and of breaking down the coping potential of individuals or groups to isolate the different pathways leading to capacities for resilience, resisting and recovery. Drawing on experience in rural development sociology, Chambers suggests that vulnerability and coping have two components: 'the external side of exposure to shocks, stress and risk; and the internal side of defencelessness, meaning a lack of means to cope without damaging loss' (Chambers, 1989, p1). This dialectical view of risk production reflects the view of Blaikie et al (1994) in recognizing the need to identify both the external (structural), and internal (agency) components of vulnerability. The next section looks at links between economic poverty and vulnerability.

LIVELIHOODS AND VULNERABILITY

'Norma Chavez, 25 years old and a mother of two boys and a girl, removes the rubble of what used to be her adobe house in Santo Thomás, 20km from the capital [San Salvador]. In her bits of free time, she continues to look for any belongings that might be used after the January and February earthquakes. Her house collapsed completely. Norma is a member of SETDESA, the union in Doall Enterprises where she has worked for four years. Doall makes clothing for Perry Ellis and Liz Claiborne [US-based multinationals]. "To think that I have worked so much and so hard, and we have never been able to leave poverty. But this is like taking a big leap backward. We are going from poverty to misery... but we have to keep up the struggle"' (National Labor Committee of El Salvador, 2001).

The account of Norma Chavez is taken from a press release by the National Labor Committee, an El Salvadorean advocacy NGO. It brings to life Swift's observation that poor households are constantly having to play-off poverty and vulnerability. Studying this relationship, Chambers (1995) suggests that poor households invariably choose to invest their resources in the immediate concerns of poverty over the longer-term investments required to raise themselves out of vulnerability. However, for the poorest of individuals and households such as that run by Norma Chavez, day-to-day survival consumes all available energies and resources. The ratchet effect – a vicious circle of economic poverty contributing to vulnerability, leading to losses from disaster shock, which in turn reduces the economic power of the household to resist future shocks – is clearly shown in this example. Sustaining livelihoods through periods of externally induced shock or stress has been recognized as the key to managing rural vulnerability (Chambers, 1995). Sustainable livelihoods are composed not only of assets, resources and claims. Thus political as well as socio-economic power is central to the reproduction of vulnerability.

The UK Department for International Development (DFID)'s Sustainable Rural Livelihoods Advisory Committee has devised an integrated framework encompassing vulnerability, access to livelihood assets and livelihood outcomes and recovery (DFID, 2000). Diversity in the sources of livelihood is seen to be the key in avoiding the ratchet effect of disaster. In urban contexts this approach remains novel and a long way from becoming a tool in mainstream poverty alleviation/disaster mitigation strategies. In a review of web-based resources on livelihoods, disasters and urban poverty conducted in September 2001, Sanderson found 'almost nothing on the subject of urban disasters and livelihoods' (2001, p3).

In addition to a focus on livelihoods, the local 'community' is increasingly being seen as a factor that shapes individual and collective vulnerability and a resource to build individual and collective resilience. The increasing number of small disaster events in cities and worldwide points to the utility and relevance of local place-based actors in vulnerability-reduction programmes. Again, community-based disaster management approaches have received most exposure in rural contexts, but guidelines can be applied to an urban setting. Box 3.1 summarizes the main elements of community-based disaster management guidelines drawn up by the Asian Disaster Preparedness Centre, Bangkok.

Livelihood and vulnerability in an urban context

Moser et al (1994) attributed the higher overall vulnerability of the urban (as opposed to the rural) poor to evidence that the social and economic support networks of low-income urbanites were less extensive than those observed in more traditional, rural societies. This section reviews the utility of livelihood approaches to understanding the pathways through which urban households experience and reproduce vulnerability. The work of three authors/groups of authors is discussed: Blaikie et al (1994), who proposed an asset vulnerability framework for households at risk, and a number of works including Moser and Sanderson, who have independently developed and applied livelihood asset models in cities. Through this discussion, the aim is to identify those most pertinent aspects of household asset profiles that shape livelihoods and consequent capacity to cope with risk in the city.

Moser et al's (1994) work highlights the contemporary vulnerability of the urban poor to changes brought about by structural adjustment. Three aspects of urban life and livelihoods which differentiate rural and urban experiences of vulnerability are identified. First, urban life is more *commodified* than rural life: obtaining goods in an urban economy nearly always requires money with only limited scope for households to survive outside of the cash economy by growing subsistence food, or harvesting water, building materials or livelihood inputs from common or open access environmental resources. Urban agriculture and waste recycling are two important exceptions to this, where resource entitlements may be held outside of the market (Allison et al, 1998). Second, the *complexity of environmental risk* is greater. This is especially true of overlapping risks associated with the household, workplace or neighbourhood and with pollution risks from industrial contamination of the air (Hardoy, Mitlin and Satterthwaite, 2001). Third, there is greater *social fragmentation* because of high

Box 3.1 *Community-based disaster management*

The features that are likely to compose a community-based disaster management approach are set out below:

- The focus of attention in disaster management is the local community.
- Disaster management activities revolve around reducing vulnerable conditions and the root causes of vulnerability.
- The strategy for vulnerability reduction is to increase a community's capacities, its resources and coping strategies.
- Disasters are viewed as unmanaged and unresolved problems of the development process.
- The community is the key actor as well as the primary beneficiary. Within the community, priority attention is given to the most vulnerable and their mobilization in risk reduction.
- The community participates in the whole process of disaster risk management, from situational analysis to planning and implementation.
- A multitude of community stakeholders are brought together to maximize the local resource base. Local organization is linked vertically with national- and international-level organizations to address the complexity of vulnerability issues.
- The framework is dynamic. Lessons learned from practice continuously feed into project planning.

As with any development intervention involving community actors, it is important to know who in the local area should be involved. There are dangers that social relations existing within the community may contribute to social isolation or inequality in access to public resources and this needs to be overcome – not entrenched – through a community approach.

Strategies for community-based risk reduction:

- Reinforcing people's existing livelihoods to increase or maintain current levels of production and income and so access to basic needs.
- Reinforcing people's coping strategies through diversifying livelihoods and the promotion of livelihoods that may offer some resistance to disaster shocks.
- Strengthening social and organizational support structures, which can act as a means of accessing basic needs in times of emergency.
- Seasonal cycles of preparedness to include weather reports, efforts to retrofit buildings and clean drains to improve resilience.
- Encouraging a shift from managing poverty to managing vulnerability. Whilst this may be difficult at an individual level, and could heighten local inequalities, at a communal level, tree planting or the training of local health workers or educationalists can reduce vulnerability for all in the long run.
- Enhance the human resources of community activists and leaders. Increasing local awareness of group leadership skills and of external sources of assistance can improve the effectiveness of local organizations playing a role in community-level development.
- Making health and sanitation services available at the local level. This can include lobbying for physical infrastructure provision or the resources to form a locally managed solid waste management service, and investment in human resources to provide local first aid. Everyday primary and child health and nutritional care and advice are also included.
- Conducting advocacy campaigns in the media and local and national government can help build a local spirit of solidarity and avert harmful external policies.

Source: Adapted from Yodmani (no date)

residential mobility and the loss of supportive social networks. There also tend to be more social problems in the city, such as crime and youth delinquency, that erode trust and potentially undermine social cohesion within communities (McIlwaine and Moser, 2001).

Moser's (1998) asset vulnerability framework identified labour, human skills, productive assets, household relations and social capital as the key assets shaping household vulnerability. This has tremendous resonance with Blaikie et al's (1994) asset framework approach to vulnerability to natural hazard. Here, household vulnerability is seen as an outcome of cycles of resource accumulation and expenditure. Whether or not a household can gain sufficient resources to maintain its members and offer sufficient buffering to prevent or absorb disaster losses is determined by the household's access to assets and decisions made about their use. Overlap between these two approaches should not be too surprising. Whilst the proximate causes of natural disaster and economic shock are different, they are both felt as a disruption to livelihoods and social networks, loss of material assets and a heightened risk of injury and illness.

A third livelihood-asset-based model, the household livelihood security model, has been developed by Sanderson (2000) and applied in urban vulnerability reduction programmes implemented by CARE International working with local partners in Angola, Mozambique, Zambia, India, Bangladesh and Madagascar. Sanderson's aim is to integrate poverty alleviation with measures for reducing risks from environmental hazards in the city. In common with the access approaches already discussed, it focusses on the household as a unit for the accumulation and management of resources. The model also acknowledges that attention to household coping needs to be undertaken in tandem with efforts to enhance the capacity and willingness of non-local actors with roles to play in poverty alleviation and risk reduction, such as municipal authorities and civil society organizations. Household livelihood assets are categorized as financial, physical, human and social.

Livelihoods and social capital

In an urban context, the livelihood asset models point towards labour, housing, possessions, tools of the trade and social networks as key resources for households in coping with vulnerability or moving out of poverty in the city. In the commodified economy of the city, where little can be obtained without access to money, labour becomes a critical asset. Any loss of labour power through illness or injury (or through a cut in the market value of labour) is likely to have a disproportionate impact on the urban poor, who are less likely than their rural counterparts to be able to turn to alternative sources of entitlement (transformation of common resources or claims on the moral economy). Similarly, any damage to productive assets such as the dwelling or tools of the trade can cause the abandonment of a livelihood, potentially pushing a household into debt and closer to Swift's point of household collapse. The existence of a moral economy in rural areas (Scott, 1985) provides the rural poor with, albeit contextual and limited, alternatives to a reliance on labour. Within urban households it is often women who experience the greatest burden of poverty. In India, 73 per cent of those below the poverty line are women and children (Amis, 1997). Women may suffer disproportionately when, as in India, they have fewer entitlements than men to household resources. Women also carry a greater burden of poverty when they are forced into the labour market as a household coping mechanism. Not only does this increase the work undertaken by women, who also have to maintain the household, but may breach social norms that had previously restricted women to home-based work (Peak and Trotz, 1999), burdening women with additional psychological stress.

Moser (1998) notes that whilst land has long been recognized as a productive asset in rural research, the importance of housing as a productive asset for the urban poor has received less attention. In her study of four cities, Moser (1998, p10) found that 'housing ownership was by far the most important productive asset of the urban poor... other productive assets such as sewing machines, radios, refrigerators, bicycles and motor vehicles were also identified'. This was especially so for home-bound women, although the success of home-based enterprises depended also on access to basic infrastructure and information. In Commonwealth, Metro Manila, one-third of households were engaged in some form of home-based production, accounting for half of total income. If we consider that housing is also a place for subsistence urban agriculture (Losada et al, 2000) and household reproduction (Kerr and Kwele, 2000), its critical role in shaping people's chances of survival or escaping from poverty becomes even more apparent. Those people without access to safe housing (the homeless, those living in slums, squatter settlements or cramped rental accommodation) will be amongst the most exposed to, and least able to cope with, shocks from environmental hazard, just as those who may have lost their housing through a disaster event will find it particularly difficult to recover. Housing is of course the biggest infrastructural loser to natural disasters (Lewis, 1999b).

The importance of social networks as a support mechanism for low-income individuals and households has long been noted in urban studies (Lewis, 1966; Lomnitz, 1977). Some of the more recent literature on social capital links social networks and organizations to a deeper level of trust and social norms (Fukuyama, 2001). In an urban context, reciprocity and inter-personal trust is often built on the need to develop new social networks in rapidly expanding peripheral settlements (Pelling, 1998). These often integrate newly formed ties with longer-standing networks based around kin groups or place of origin. Work in La Paz and Lagos has found strong ties remain between urbanites and their rural villages of birth (van den Bersselaar, 2001).

The relationship between vulnerability and social capital is dependent upon context. Individuals may hold latent social capital in relationships with many people, but only in selected relationships is social capital actualized and made manifest through cooperative relationships. Amongst marginal communities characterized by social violence and a lack of cohesion the number, variety and quality of social interactions is likely to be restricted and communal stocks of positive social capital will consequently be low. Under conditions of economic hardship, political intimidation or social violence individuals may withdraw from building up or maintaining widespread social networks and retreat into small but tightly knit social groups. Loss of interaction between groups (bridging capital) inhibits the flow of information, undermining trust (Evans, 1996). This has been identified as a weakness in building community cohesion and organization to reduce vulnerability in post-conflict societies (Colletta and Cullen, 2000; Goodhand et al, 2000), and in building democracy and economic development more generally (Putnam, Leonardi and Nanetti, 1993).

At times of stress, retreat into small social groups (bonding capital) minimizes risk and enhances coping in the short term by providing access to social and economic support between group members. Over the longer term, a lack of bridging capital weakens community coherence and adaptive potential. A lower intensity of on-going risk may act conversely to build up bridging capital, as individuals from different social groups cooperate informally to improve the living environment or more formally by forging community organizations. Such groups help build community coherence and may accelerate the development of local civil society. It is frequently stated that a disaster event brings people together, increasing bridging capital (Tobin and Montz, 1997). This may be the case during emergency response, but as goods start to flow into disaster-impacted neighbourhoods social networks tend to re-coalesce around old allegiances of race, caste, gender, religion or ethnicity. Following the Gujarat earthquake, international relief aimed at those most in need was distributed through local organizations. This is good practice, but a lack of local insight allowed some high-caste-dominated groups to capture resources that had been intended for lower caste victims (Disaster Emergency Committee, 2002). In this case, deeply rooted social allegiances based on informal social institutions of caste and built up strategically into formal organizations were able to distort the international disaster relief effort.

Work in the Caribbean has shown the great difficulty in building up bridging capital in the short/medium term as a mechanism for long-term community risk reduction (Pelling, 1998). Whist external interventions by NGOs or state agencies can support the creation of local organizations, they tend to be short lived once support is withdrawn. Such interventions fail to build lasting social capital. A more successful strategy might be to build upon existing social networks (Mitchell, 1999). Intervention strategies will be shaped by ethnic tension, cultural and political contexts, state structures, mixtures of traditional and modern organization and civil society–state relationships.

SOCIAL ADAPTATION AND AMELIORATING VULNERABILITY

The social component of adaptive potential

Whilst the contribution that can be made to individual vulnerability reduction through local economic development is significant, alone it is not sufficient to ameliorate collective vulnerability. Given the increasing number of people living in conditions of absolute poverty in cities of Africa, Asia and Latin America, the task of enhancing livelihood capacities to generate sufficient economic assets for all households to move out of poverty and vulnerability as individual units is daunting. In foregoing sections, the importance of socio-political assets and social development policy in complementing local economic development strategies to ameliorate vulnerability has been noted. The discussion that follows seeks to identify ways in which social assets can be categorized for use as indicators for individual or group capacity to confront vulnerability.

Separating socio-political assets from their economic counterparts should not be interpreted as offering the social as any fundamental source of vulnerability or resilience. As we have seen above, and in Chapters 1 and 2, the distribution of social assets is influenced deeply by access to economic and other resources, and visa versa. But in urban neighbourhoods characterized by economic poverty and dangerous living conditions, social and political resources offer a potential way out of collective vulnerability where past experiences of development planning have manifestly failed. The popular importance placed on accessing political and social influence as a mechanism for generating assets for neighbourhoods can be seen by the long history of land reclamation movements in Latin America (Castells, 1983) and the squatter settlements of Mumbai (Desai, 1995). Similar struggles over social influence take place at all scales, from the inter-personal to the inter-urban, and of course there will be individuals and groups who are excluded from social power networks just as they are from economic development initiatives. The aim is not to present the social as a panacea for vulnerability reduction in the city, but to use it as a lens to identify the potential as well as actual capacity of local communities to organize and confront their own vulnerability. Neither is this a call for the vulnerable to pull themselves out of positions of danger by their own bootstraps, but rather a mechanism to assess the potential held at a local level for exerting influence on the human structures that shape development and risk in the city.

Social assets are found at different scales in the city. They are held by individuals and households as social capital, which may be built up into developmental CBOs. Outside the community, a city's social assets are composed of civil society groups (CBO networks, NGOs, political parties etc) and developmental linkages between civil society groups and the public and private sectors. It is the number and character of these assets that forms the social dimension of a local area's or a city's capacity to adapt to perceived environmental risk. Existing capacity is likely to be underlain by potential social assets. These are links that are latent or dormant. It may be that individuals are reluctant to join community organizations for fear of political reprisals, or that a culture of competition and conflict between developmental NGOs and city authorities has made it difficult for supportive links to be formed. The extent of latent social capacity will be determined by the political history of a community, city and country. Building social capacity to confront disaster is all about realizing this potential.

The social dimension of adaptive potential can be broken down into two types of human response to environmental risk. These can be classified as *coping* and *institutional modification*:

1   Coping strategies mobilize social networks to directly reduce the likelihood of negative impacts of a hazard event, for example in Cali, Colombia, where local mitigation workers map hazardous areas and regulate further building (IFRC/RC, 1998).
2   Institutional modification aims to alter the institutional framework of a city, using political influence to create political space for at-risk actors to argue their case. For example: the Lebanese NGO Forum, which was established to give greater weight to the NGO sector and to promote coordination between civil society and the state in the Lebanon, and which has succeeded in coordinating relief efforts (Bennett, 2000).

Both coping and institutional modification have the possibility to change the physical and social structures of the city and interrupt the progression of vulnerability.

Coping and institutional modification can be further differentiated according to whether actions are purposeful (responding to stress produced by environmental hazards) or incidental (responding to background stress emanating from the political economy of the city). Table 3.1 shows examples of coping and institutional modifications, both purposeful and incidental, that an individual might undertake. The range of choices available to an individual or group will be constrained by developmental context – by access to entitlements and assets and by the institutional framework of the city.

Many development interventions will incorporate more than one kind of adaptive category. The categories are not mutually exclusive. The contemporary preference for integrated development policy is built on the understanding that local development should be holistic, simultaneously supporting the immediate concerns of coping and longer-term institutional modification (Wratten, 1995). Thus, non-local actors working within an integrated development approach seek to partner local community organizations, both as a mechanism to build local social capital and leadership resources (building institutional modification), and as a means of bringing local labour and knowledge resources into the project, enhancing project appropriateness and cost effectiveness (coping).

Table 3.1 *Adaptive potential*

	Coping mechanism	Institutional modification
Purposeful adaptation (environmental stress)	Build house on raised ground.	Join an NGO which is advocating greater access to environmental infrastructure such as garbage collection.
	Retrofit buildings to withstand hurricane or earthquake stress.	
Incidental adaptation (background stress)	Invest household resources in balanced food and health care for children.	Vote in municipal and national elections.
		Take part in community activities such as carnival.
	Maintain reciprocal relationships with relatives living overseas or with other community members.	Protest against corruption in city government.

Source: Pelling (2002). Reproduced from *International Development Planning Review* by permission of Liverpood University Press.

Of course, just as policy interventions can be used in attempts to strengthen helpful local institutions and build adaptive potential, wider political and economic trends can influence the integrity of local institutions. A study of adaptive potential to flooding in Vietnam (Adger, 2000) found that changes in the structure of the state and the growth of market and (quasi-)civil society institutions had shaped adaptive potential. Inertia in local state organizations had resulted in a failure to respond to changing environmental risk associated with sea-level rise. But this was offset by changes in the formal and informal institutions of civil society that offered a form of collective security mechanism through their ability to enhance livelihood resilience. Adger concludes that

> *'decentralization and privatization decrease opportunities for coherent collective action and often reinforce the uneven distribution of power over resources... The impacts of future climate change on Vietnam, for example, will be experienced by a more atomized social structure that will only exacerbate collective social vulnerability'* (Adger, 2000, p756).

Given the enthusiasm with which privatization and decentralization have been embraced in cities of the developing world, Adger's comments are more than cause for a little concern. It is to find opportunities for building adaptive potential amidst a period of institutional change in the city that we now turn.

Building adaptive potential

The retreat of the state and expansion of the private sector and civil society in cities worldwide has created an opportunity for new institutional forms and networks to be created that can enhance a city's ability to deal with vulnerability and environmental hazard. Within the institutional framework of a city, different actors command varied bundles of resources and skills. For example, CBOs will be best placed to organize grassroots involvement, NGOs can facilitate this and provide expert technical and organizational skills, the public sector and in particular city government can play a coordinating role by providing financial inputs and a legislative regime (Abbott, 1996; Bebbington and Riddell, 1995). There is scope for city governance regimes to go much further in vulnerability reduction than building regulation. More than this, not only is it important to recognize what actors can do alone; much depends upon the successful cooperation of different sectors and the possibility of building partnerships across sectoral divides (Fiszbein and Lowden, 1999). The same is true within a sector: lack of vertical cooperation between city and national government has been identified as contributing to high losses from flooding in cities as diverse as in Lusaka, 1989 (Mulwanda, 1993), São Paulo, 1995 (Jacobi, 1997) and Georgetown, Guyana, in 1996 (Pelling, 1997).

Structural change that redistributes power in the city is needed to reduce vulnerability. Elite groups at the local, city and national levels are likely to resist changes they cannot control. Resistance can be seen in bureaucratic foot-dragging, institutional inertia and by the co-option of non-governmental actors by political parties and the state (Desai, 1995; Adger, 1999; Pelling, 1999). For resistance to be limited and for cooperation to be built, trust needs to be nurtured between different political actors that in some cases may have historical relationships of conflict or competition. Trust needs to be built for partnerships to operate vertically (eg, between CBOs, local NGOs and INGOs) and horizontally in public–private partnerships and within communities so that adaptive potential can be maximized.

Social capital can be seen in formal partnerships and the local bonds that facilitate community organization. In the maintenance of local social capital, Moser (1998) argued that women play a disproportionately important role because of their gendered predisposition to share food, water, cooking or child care with other women. The status of social capital in a community fluctuates in response to changing urban conditions. In marginalized and vulnerable communities, social capital may be underdeveloped or counter-developmental, associated with systems of patronage or criminal networks (Desai, 1995; Hyden, 1997). Moser and Holland (1997) observed how increasing household poverty associated with structural adjustment in Chawama, Zambia, reduced the ease with which neighbours worked together, resulting in a decline in social capital. This suggests that the distribution of social capital within a city is likely to reinforce economic exclusion and political marginalization. However, it is argued here (and elsewhere, see for example Friedmann, 1996) that social capital is present in many vulnerable communities and that with a supportive institutional framework social capital can be transformed into social organization to build adaptive potential.

The possibility of strengthening social capital by building it into constructive social organization has been noted (Evans, 1996) and observed during the consolidation of informal settlements (Moser, 1996; Pelling, 1997, 2002). In most cases this transition is likely to be catalysed by an actor external to the community, such as a governmental community development department or a developmental NGO. Environmental hazards and disaster events can even be used as motivational tools to organize around. Berke, Kartez and Wenger (1993) report the successful construction of long-term social organization within a Montserratian community following an NGO intervention in response to Hurricane Hugo.

The responsiveness of individuals and communities to external interventions of this kind is critical if participatory development is to be positive in ameliorating social vulnerability. Wisner (1996) identifies as a priority the need to bring vulnerable groups into dialogue with less vulnerable neighbours and intervening agencies, and recognizes that the first step in this process requires local organization. However, Wisner (1998) also recognizes the difficulties of participatory approaches: first, a change of culture is required amongst city planners and disaster mitigation professionals to respect the involvement of vulnerable people; second, marginalized communities with high vulnerability are often unwilling or unable (because of constraints on people's time and energy) to become involved. In illegal settlements and even amongst renters, lack of security of land tenure also inhibits local organization and individual motivations to search for and adopt adaptations (Pelling, 1997).

CASE STUDIES OF LIVELIHOOD AND VULNERABILITY IN GEORGETOWN, GUYANA

The following two case studies draw from field research conducted in Georgetown two weeks after an urban flood on 12 November 1995. For background details on environmental risk and human vulnerability in Georgetown, please refer to Chapter 5, and for a more extended discussion of findings, to Pelling, 1997. The aim of this section is to provide examples of the ways in which different bundles of household assets can shape individual or household vulnerability to environmental risk.

Wendy Stewart's household: a failure to access safe housing
Wendy has lived in the same derelict and abandoned ground-floor flat with her nine children for the last ten years. Living in other rooms in the abandoned house and in a second abandoned building sharing the same small central courtyard are three other households. In all, 46 people live together here. The yard floods with every heavy rainfall, and when this happens rainwater mixes with household waste, sullage and sewage, which overflows from the broken sewer in the yard. Floodwaters frequently enter Wendy's house and her children suffer from diarrhoea, shortness of breath (possibly asthma) and colds. Wendy says that her biggest problem is finding affordable accommodation for her

family. Not only are private rents beyond her reach, but many landlords refuse to rent to families with young children. In response to this, over the last five years Wendy has twice cleared land in the squatter settlements that are growing on the outskirts of the city. In both instances she has been forced off the cleared land through intimidation from other, competing squatters. She feels that there is no option for a woman like her, with children but no man to support her, but to continue living in her house.

Wendy is clearly a motivated and able woman but is held back from moving out of vulnerability by a lack of livelihood assets. She lacks sufficient financial capital to enter the formal housing market, she does not have the political capital that might help in gaining a publicly rented dwelling, nor does she have enough social capital to enable her to self-build. As is too common, households that lack access to one kind of key asset often also lack access to other assets that could play a compensatory role if they were present.

Ina Campbell's household: navigating housing maintenance and flood management options

In 1985, Ina and her three adolescent children were allocated a government flat. Although the property was built around 1965, Ina does not think that it has been refurbished since. The property first flooded in 1988 and it now floods whenever it rains heavily. Although Ina has not suffered any direct economic losses from flooding, her children have suffered frequently from respiratory tract infections, including one diagnosed case of pneumonia. Ina also suffers from arthritis, which is exacerbated by the dampness of her house.

Ina has put a great deal of energy into trying to manage the flooding that affects her rented property. First she sought assistance from the government landlord in 1990 whose legal responsibility it is to maintain the flat. It was explained to Ina that the government had little money as part of a programme of structural adjustment so that it would be difficult to provide assistance. Ina was warned against making alterations to the property herself without permission. Ina subsequently tried to organize community action to clean drains as a way of preventing or reducing flood exposure. Unfortunately her neighbours, most of whom also frequently experienced flooding, were not interested in getting involved and this plan was short lived.

Finally, in 1992, Ina acted on her own behalf. Against formal tenancy regulations she bought some concrete and used it to raise the ground floor inside her house by 10cm. This seemed to help and when she had saved some more money in 1994 she built an 8cm-high path from her front door to her front gate. These adaptations have provided some protection from flood exposure but do nothing to mitigate flooding in the neighbourhood with subsequent exposure of health risks, nor damage to the wooden property from damp.

Ina's case shows what can be done by a determined family head with access to a modest level of financial capital. In this example, despite the absence of any useful political or social capital, Ina has protected herself, her family and their belongings from frequent flooding. This may offer some relief to the individual but does nothing to reduce flood hazard overall – and most importantly for those in the neighbourhood without the financial resources to protect themselves. Ina's actions can also be seen as one way in which responsibility for environmental risk and vulnerability management has been shifted from the government to the individual – this is to the advantage of the state, even when it is viewed as illegal.

SUMMARY

Chapter 2 identified the importance of the social infrastructure of a neighbourhood or city in reducing disaster risk. It was the task of this chapter to unpack the social dimension of vulnerability, to find out what it is that makes certain individuals more or less prone to the negative impacts of environmental stress or shock, and from this position to identify those attributes that might best be mustered to build resiliency in the face of future environmental hazard. An asset livelihood approach was taken. This borrowed from ideas developed in the study of environmental risk in rural societies. Here the susceptibility of an individual or group to environmental risk is understood to be an outcome of their access to economic, social, political, physical and environmental assets.

The asset profile of an individual or group shapes the likelihood of their being exposed to, but also their capacity to cope with, any negative impacts of environmental disaster. Vulnerability is closely related to economic poverty, social isolation and political marginalization, hence it is possible for policies aimed at reducing urban poverty, enhancing urban social cohesion and political participation to reduce vulnerability and build resilience at the local level. But this is not necessarily the case: efforts to maintain households during periods of poverty may require the expenditure of resources for immediate survival needs, preventing households from building up any stocks or stores of resources that could be called on in times of heightened need. Similarly, coping with disaster may require the conversion of productive assets – tools, the dwelling etc – into goods for exchange to fulfil immediate survival needs, thus undermining the household's asset base and setting back the household's chances of climbing out of poverty and vulnerability in the longer term.

In contexts of economic poverty where financial and physical assets are limited, it may be that social and political assets can provide critical levers for at-risk groups to mitigate their vulnerability. The concept of adaptive potential is used to describe actions that utilize social and political assets to enhance local resilience. Such acts can directly address perceived environmental risks or more indirectly seek to reconfigure the institutional framework of a city or local area.

Chapter 4

Urban Governance and Disaster

INTRODUCTION

This chapter introduces an actor-oriented approach where individuals or social units are the subject of analysis rather than the 'disaster moment' per se. Before discussing individual political actors, it is useful to outline the forces that shape the ways in which actors operate and interact. These forces are often referred to as institutional structures; they define the limits of rights and responsibilities for each actor, and the power that legitimates relative authority between actors. Of course institutional structures are (re)produced by actors, and so are themselves influenced by actors. Thus, whilst actors constitute the force that shapes institutional form, their behaviour is simultaneously constrained by institutional context (Giddens, 1993; Harriss et al, 1995). This makes it important to include both political actors and political context as subjects for vulnerability analysis. A number of wide-ranging socio-economic forces causing realignment in institutional structures have been noted in the literature, correlating with Blaikie et al's (1994) 'intermediate pressures' of vulnerability. These macro processes can perhaps best be summarized as the forces of globalization and localization. They link together local-level decision-making and production processes, and the macro-political economy (Bryant and Bailey, 1997).

Globalization has attracted much recent attention (see Germain, 2000; Scholte, 2000). Globalization points to the influence of new forms of non-territorial economic and political organization (Rosenau, 1997) with the emergence of inter-regional networks and systems of exchange and interaction (Castells, 1996). The example of Hyderabad, India, highlights the vulnerability of these global flows to local environmental hazard, here local floods have derailed attempts by civic authorities to market the city for foreign investors and undermined the city's aim of becoming a global high-tech centre (http://news.bbc.co.uk).

Localization (Samoff, 1990; Potter, 2002) refers to those processes that shift power downwards from centralized nation states to local actors, and can occur with government consent (decentralization and democratization) or without (grassroots action, urban social movements, everyday resistance). Although apparently working in opposing directions, localization and globalization are often intimately linked. For example, democratization and decentralization – movements towards localization – are both commonly cited elements of good governance conditionalities attached to structural adjustment agreements that, by their very nature, shift power away from the nation state under pressure from global institutions, the World Bank and International Monetary Fund (IMF) (Ferguson, 1995).

Since the mid-1990s, the good governance agenda, which cuts across localization and globalization tendencies, has placed growing emphasis on participatory development (see McIlwaine, 1998; Mercer, 2002; Mohan, 2002). It is argued that participation can enhance project efficiency and sustainability, and be a means of politically empowering local actors by increasing their stake in managing development. Despite this change in the discourse surrounding development, meaningful changes in the distribution of power are as yet few and far between.

Participation has been promoted at the global level through changes in funding strategy by the international donor community, where preference has increasingly been given to the funding of projects managed by civil society actors rather than the state (Mercer, 2002). But the funding strategy has itself led to a mushrooming of civil society organizations in cities of the global South, some more able to identify, represent and respond to the needs of the vulnerable than others. This has led many to criticize the effect that increased funding opportunities have had on the character of local developmental NGOs and CBOs (Mitlin and Thompson, 1995; Mosse, 1994). Involving the more marginal individuals and groups in participation is a challenging policy aim and calls for some reappraisal of present methods. At the heart of this policy process is the need for a redistribution of decision-making power. Clearly, any realignment of political institutions will result in some actors losing influence. It is not surprising that those actors currently holding the balance of power are reluctant to see reform of the status quo.

Information and power

The possession of information is central to power and planning in urban settlements (Ostrom et al, 1993). Information can be used to exclude groups from formal decision-making, it defines the ways in which political actors relate with one another, and is a means of legitimizing authority in decision-making. Freire (1985) shows how the masses of Brazil are excluded from participating in the shaping of society, and by extension the planning of their living environment, because of their exclusion from education and formal knowledge. Freire, and later writers, have also considered the possibility of marginalized groups constructing their own meanings for places, a process termed 'semantic resistance' (Fiske, 1989; Sahr, 1997). This can be seen through the action of hawkers, squatters or street dwellers who capture and reconfigure space designated for other uses by the city authorities.

Analysing the role of information can draw on work in institutional economics that starts with assumptions that decision-making is made under conditions of information scarcity, uncertainty, complexity and risk (for an overview see North, 1995). Decisions therefore take place within the context of bounded rationality. In this way, individuals who may otherwise have been perceived as acting irrationally in failing to reduce environmental risk in their living environments can now be seen to have acted rationally in uncertain and possibly hostile informational and political environments, and to have been risk-averse in a world of multiple-layered risks. In addition to individual decisions being made under information scarcity, joint outcomes which are dependent upon multiple actors are likely to be influenced by opportunistic behaviour. Opportunistic behaviour can range from petty bribery and conflicts of interest to grand-scale corruption and theft. The prevalence of opportunistic behaviour is determined by the institutional structures and cultural norms in which decision-making takes place and will influence the types of decision made and the distribution of resources in society before and after disaster strikes (Ostrom et al, 1993; Jordan and O'Riordan, 1995). It is to the influence of these stuctural forces on the actions of individual actors and the role played by individual actors in shaping these forces that we now turn.

POLITICAL ACTORS

International financial institutions

The World Bank and IMF are the most important international financial institutions (IFIs). The World Bank is funded principally by Northern nation states and provides financial and technical support for projects sponsored by governments in the global South. It is the largest donor in urban assistance and urban policy formation, with annual lending on urban projects in the 1990s reaching US$3b (Gilbert et al, 1996). The IMF has risen to prominence in the South since the 1970s through structural adjustment lending. Here loans are made available to governments only once certain conditionalities are met: originally macro-economic conditionalities such as streamlining the public sector (reducing the number of those employed) and privatization; in the late 1980s these were joined by political conditionalities (democratization, decentralization) and more recently by environmental conditionalities (Bryant and Bailey, 1997).

The World Bank's influence shapes the behaviour of other donors; its stamp of approval is used by bilateral donors as a sign of fitness in the recipient state, and without this lending is unlikely. Regional multi-lateral institutions, such as the Inter-American Development Bank and African Development Bank, also tend to follow World Bank lending strategy (Thomas, 1982; Gilbert et al, 1996).

The World Bank has received widespread criticism for its lending policy, which tends to support large-scale resource exploitation and technocentric environmental control projects (Hecht and Cockburn, 1989; Adams, 1990). This is true also in the field of urban development, where the World Bank has tended to support large-scale technocentric approaches to environmental risk, with investment in physical rather than social infrastructure. This has encouraged a dominant view of urban management that sees the root cause of environmental problems as financial scarcity, and the principal mode of amelioration as targeting IFI loans. This approach to urban management encourages inappropriate project design (as local participation is overlooked) and rent-seeking (as large loans are handled through government institutions with poor transparency and financial accountability).

Alternative institutional arrangements have been proposed (Hardoy and Satterthwaite, 1989; Hardoy et al, 1990, 1992; Ostrom et al, 1993; Mitlin and Satterthwaite, 1996; Pugh, 1996) where the focus would shift from macro to micro projects, from national to local financial agreements and from prescriptive to participatory methods of project management. This New Agenda in urban management (Mitlin and Satterthwaite, 1996) brings the focus of planning and management down to the local level and is already being practised through the action of grassroots organizations with the support of local NGOs and local government (Choguill and Choguill, 1996). Recent policy changes by the World Bank also show a convergence in rhetoric with the New Agenda through the support of limited participatory methodologies (Narayan, 2000), usually associated with structural adjustment social amelioration programmes and operationalized (Moser et al, 1993) through a national funding organization which works directly with grassroots organizations. The advantages of participatory methodologies as stated by the IFIs are an increase in fund efficiency through avoiding rent-seeking in centralized systems, and encouraging project sustainability through beneficiary involvement in planning, management and post-project maintenance.

Structural adjustment is led by the IMF and, through this, the IMF has a great influence on relations between other actors; for example, states are encouraged to reduce their financial burden by off-loading responsibility for service provision to local authorities or communities and grassroots actors through decentralization and privatization policies (McCarney, 1996). Many commentators have been highly critical of structural adjustment, which has tended to deepen political and economic dependency on the global North (George, 1992), and at the local level in urban settlements has increased social inequality and marginalization, reduced access to public services, and through de-regularized industrialization has been associated with increased health and pollution problems (George, 1992).

Overall, the impacts of IFIs have been indirect but powerful in shaping urban institutions and subsequent adaptive potential. The IFIs have been slow to respond meaningfully to calls for environmentally and socially constructive policies and have failed so far to address the identified requirements of the New Agenda in urban management. However, there have been some initiatives that

---

Box 4.1 *The World Bank's Disaster Management Facility*

Disaster is viewed by the World Bank from an economic perspective. Because urban areas concentrate wealth and human resources they are identified as priority areas for investment from the Disaster Management Facility. The World Bank is engaged in two types of lending with respect to disasters. First, lending for reconstruction following a disaster (over US$7.5b lent between 1980 and 1999). Second, proactive lending for mitigation to reduce disaster vulnerability (US$6.5b of loans have included some component of mitigation). Reconstruction lending has a longer history than mitigation; some 56 countries have received reconstruction funds, with projects implemented in both urban and rural areas. Projects concentrate on repairing infrastructure and management of the national economy through emergency import substitution.

Mitigation funding is more limited than reconstruction and, although many projects could be said to have included some component of mitigation, this has not until very recently been an explicit design feature of loan agreements. Mitigation funding is also less widespread than reconstruction; Brazil, China, Bangladesh and India account for 40 per cent of the mitigation portfolio, with 93 per cent of projects addressing either floods, forest fires or droughts. These are largely in a rural context, but have often included some support for the enforcement of land-use and building codes to avoid settlement in hazardous areas or in vulnerable structures.

There has not as yet been any independent review of the Disaster Management Facility but it has clear potential for facilitating a sea change in the way disaster mitigation is approached. By making disaster prevention and mitigation activities central components of future project loans, the World Bank could usefully put pressure on national planners to integrate disaster planning more fully with on-going development planning.

Source: Gilbert and Kreimer (1999)

---

are worth noting for their potential to contribute to the reduction in urban vulnerability to environmental hazard. Foremost among these is the World Bank's Disaster Management Facility, established in 1998 to provide a mechanism for feeding disaster prevention into development planning and to improve emergency response lending. The World Bank recognizes that rapid urbanization greatly increases disaster risk and has sought to integrate disaster management within its urban development project lending (Gilbert and Kreimer, 1999). Box 4.1 outlines the role of the Disaster Management Facility.

National government

Often, at the core of government inefficiencies lies a conflict of interest between the government's roles of protector of environmental assets and social welfare, and promoter of environmental and human resource exploitation to facilitate the extraction of an economic surplus (Walker, 1989). In the city this is expressed as a conflict between viewing the city as an engine for national economic growth or as a system for generating at least basic needs for its inhabitants at minimal cost to the environment. The nation state is often cast by INGOs, IFIs and grassroots actors as an obstacle rather than a facilitator of human development and environmental management objectives (Hurrell, 1994;

Pugh, 1996; Bryant and Bailey, 1997). These criticisms focus on the many institutional weaknesses inherent in the varied systems of government in the global South. National governments are frequently identified as having overly complex organizational structures, which reduce transparency in decision-making, produce contradictory lines of accountability and encourage corruption and rent-seeking behaviour (Ostrom et al, 1993; World Bank, 1997).

The state, however, continues to occupy a key position in environmental management and human development, being an intermediary between the local and the global (Hobsbawm, 1996; May et al, 1996). The UN, during the International Decade for Natural Disaster Reduction (1989–1999), placed primary responsibility for disaster reduction with nation states to 'encourage their local administrations to take appropriate steps to mobilize the necessary support from the public and private sectors' (UN in Twigg, 2001, p17). This said, national disaster management plans often omit urban settlements (Sanderson, 2000). Despite such claims for the competitive advantage of the state, its decline has been recorded in many countries, often, as noted above, a direct result of IFI-led restructuring conditionalities (Alfonso, 1997).

Central government is well positioned to coordinate regional or nationwide vulnerability reduction initiatives, which may or may not include an urban dimension. One such scheme, which has met with some success, was the Maharashtra Emergency Earthquake Rehabilitation Programme, launched in response to the 1993 earthquake in the Indian state of Maharashtra, which damaged 230,000 houses in rural and small urban settlements. The programme gained financial support from the World Bank and was managed by two national NGOs. It encouraged community participation at the village level, with beneficiaries consulted throughout the programme cycle, although the programme fell short of handing over decision-making responsibility to local groups. Whilst project managers were initially sceptical of the community participation process, they later came to recognize it as an effective tool for dealing with difficulties that arose during implementation. It is reported that for grassroots actors, involvement in the reconstruction process helped in overcoming trauma. The participatory process also opened many informal channels of communication between the people and the government, improving adaptive potential (Vasta, 1999).

Private sector

The private sector has received comparatively little attention in the development literature, partly because of the difficulties in defining its membership – as formal or informal, transnational or local, capitalist or indigenous – and partly because of the historical dominance of the state as a focus for research on the urban environment and social development. The private sector here is defined in its broadest possible terms, as all those activities that produce an economic surplus (excluding NGOs and grassroots self-help institutions). Including the private sector in analyses of urban change is becoming increasingly necessary because of privatization policies and the shrinking of employment in the public sector. These trends are the result of policies being promoted by structural adjustment. They act to redistribute decision-making in urban management through a delegation of power from national or local/municipal government to the private sector (Rondinelli et al, 1984, in Alfonso, 1997), and re-shape structures of urban (un)employment, access to economic resources and hence vulnerability amongst grassroots actors (Haggard and Kaufman, 1992).

Despite its failure to improve service provision for most low-income groups in urban settlements, the private sector continues to play an increasingly important role as a service provider, and examples do exist to demonstrate its capacity for enhancing urban service provision. Such successes appear to be limited to cases where natural monopolies do not exist (see Hardoy et al, 1990) and where strong and representative local/municipal government is capable of monitoring the private sector activity (Hardoy et al, 1990). Privatization without strong government allows shirking of responsibilities in the private sector, whilst privatization without representative and transparent government allows rent-seeking behaviour and encourages corruption and patronage in government (Ostrom et al, 1993).

Inequalities in access to financial resources between successful businesses and their workers are a potential source of tension during disaster. This is more so in the case of companies linked to foreign direct investment. Commenting on the Salvador earthquake of 2001, the National Labor Committee had this to say about local private sector inaction:

> '*Factories manufacturing for Gap, Nike, Liz Claiborne, Adidas and other US retailers have provided no help of any kind to their workers, in spite of the fact that approximately 30 per cent of their employees have suffered damages to their homes and in spite of the fact that damage to the factory infrastructures have been minimal*' (National Labor Committee, El Salvador, www.nlcnet.org).

Both DFID and the United States Agency for International Development (USAID) have funded initiatives to facilitate a greater role for the private sector in sustainable development, but as yet few private sector actors have engaged with disaster mitigation or vulnerability reduction in the city (DFID, 2000; Charles et al, 1998). At the macro scale, private sector finance is set to play a larger role in reconstruction after urban disaster as the increasing frequency of losses puts greater strain on national budgets and on the development banks. The high rates of interest charged by private sector lending institutions make the private sector prohibitively expensive at present. A World Bank initiative to cover a portion of debt services could enable governments to borrow at a lower interest rate over a longer repayment period, so opening up private sources of finance (Matsukawa, 2001). There are also possible roles for the private sector in regulating construction standards. A recurring theme following urban disaster is the failure of city authorities to regulate adherence to appropriate building codes. In some rapidly expanding cities where self-help construction is highly prevalent, insisting on building standards may make it more difficult for families to meet their basic housing needs of a minimal form of shelter. In other cases, tighter application of building standards is possible without penalizing the poor or putting undue pressure on public sector resources. Gulkan (2001), reflecting on the 1999 Turkish earthquake, suggests that planning and construction supervision could be transferred to the private sector. Firms could be established to monitor building design and implementation on behalf of the municipality, with costs being born by developers.

The media can be usefully brought in to increase popular awareness of risk and of promoting preparedness. One particularly innovative use of the media comes from the Pan-American Health Organization (PAHO)'s work in Central America, where radio was identified as the principal media used by low-income groups, and soap operas as the most listened-to programmes. PAHO has teamed up with NGOs to broadcast an educational soap opera before and during the hurricane season (Flentge, 2001).

In a global review of private sector contributions to disaster mitigation, Twigg (2001) found most documented cases were concerned with the USA,

Table 4.1 *Private sector involvement in disaster mitigation*

Name of initiative	Location	Description
Asian Urban Disaster Mitigation Program	Philippines	Corporate NGO manages programme of local-level capacity building for disaster mitigation.
Caribbean Disaster Mitigation Project	Caribbean	Creation of NGO in Dominican Republic with business representation on its board.
Corporate Network for Disaster Response	Philippines	Business involvement in support for coordinated disaster response and local-level mitigation.
East African Initiative on Disaster Management	E Africa	Two IFRC-led conferences to raise awareness and stimulate partnerships.
Hotel Safety Initiative	Caribbean	Partnership between the Royal & Sun Alliance, the Red Cross and hotels to improve disaster preparedness and response through staff training in return for lower premiums.
Insurance and Property Safety	Fiji	Tripartite partnership linking government-certified technical improvements against cyclone risk to reduced insurance premiums.
Public Information	Caribbean	Production and distribution of information by United Insurance to homeowners on how to make property more secure against hazards.
Technical Support	Turkey	Membership by Arup of a consortium to assess risk and design reconstruction/development programmes after an earthquake.
Technical Support	Solomon Islands	Technical support provided by Pacific Architects to local NGO training builders in low-cost housing.

Source: Twigg (2001)

Box 4.2 *Arup and earthquake mitigation in Turkey*

Arup is an international engineering company with offices in 32 countries. Following the Turkish earthquake in 1999, Arup joined with five other British companies to form the British Earthquake Consortium for Turkey (BECT). Coordinating this effort was the UK Department for the Environment, Transport and the Regions, which provided half the UK£1m budget: consortium members provided the rest. After discussions with Turkish authorities, BECT undertook a number of activities in Yalova province. Work undertaken included a study of local geology and seismicity, leading to the production of hazard maps covering the most densely populated areas. This in turn identified where hazard made it too expensive to rebuild. An outline town and transport plan was drawn up. Building on these technical plans, a reconstruction implementation plan was drawn up including detailed capital project outlines for civic buildings such as a university, a hospital, and water and solid waste infrastructures.

Arup seconded 20 staff to this project, including members from its office in Turkey who brought with them important local knowledge of building codes and regulations. A profit was available to Arup if the Turkish government released funds for capital projects, but in the end no funds were available and Arup did not make a profit. Arup's view was that such an outcome was not unexpected and, by entering into this collaborative work with this knowledge from the outset, expectations of the likelihood of winning capital work contracts had not been unduly high.

Sources: Twigg (2001); www.arup.com

---

with some evidence from the Philippines and the Caribbean. Table 4.1 presents a summary of Twigg's findings of private sector involvement with disaster mitigation in developing countries.

The small number of examples that Twigg could identify is immediately apparent from Table 4.1. More than this though, in most cases private sector involvement was minimal. The most active businesses were insurance companies and architects engaged with disseminating best practice in building construction. These sectors are well placed to successfully bring together business imperatives with socially constructive works. The absence of a more varied array of businesses engaged in disaster mitigation suggests that without government intervention, the private sector's potential for supporting mitigation is unlikely to be realized. The recalcitrance of business is explained by Twigg (2001) in terms of difficulties in measuring the effect of prevention programmes on local vulnerability to disaster, and a lack of readiness to build up the social capital and vision needed to overcome entrenched cultures of suspicion or conflict between the private, public and non-profit sectors.

Box 4.2 presents an overview account of a single initiative that involved partnership between UK-based private sector companies, the government of Turkey and the British government. It centres on the engineering firm Arup and its contribution to reconstruction efforts following the Turkish earthquake of 1999. The example shows what can be achieved when a company's corporate vision and organizational structure and the external enabling environment are supportive and open to private sector contributions. Unfortunately, as yet, these conditions rarely appear to coincide.

International and Southern NGOs

For the purposes of this study, NGOs are identified as non-place-specific organizations with interests in either environmental or developmental agendas. This includes organizations as diverse as nature conservation societies, women's groups, local Rotary Clubs and pro-democracy groups, but does not include more ambivalent interest organizations such as sports societies. Although it is recognized that sports groups constitute a part of the social capital of a community, they are not usually directly engaged in environmental or developmental debates (Putnam et al, 1993). Further differentiation needs to be made between those local NGOs that have evolved indigenously and local branches of Northern INGOs. Whilst these two orders of NGO often cooperate, their relative capacities and abilities closely reflect the strength and openness of the host civil society.

Disasters are often linked to failures in the dissemination of information from expert or non-expert sources that could have provided a space for mitigation, preparation or evacuation. Failures at the city level are sometimes a result of intelligence being collected at the national level not being connected with urban planners who could use this information to mitigate risk. The UN's World Earthquake Risk Management Programme has received this criticism (Solway, 1994). More recently, efforts by the UN International Secretariat for Disaster Reduction, the successor to the UN's International Decade for Natural Disaster Reduction, through the RADIUS project (Box 4.3) have operated at the city level, and local NGOs have played a key role in a programme that has linked them with public sector agencies, city authorities and the international community.

Local NGOs are plentiful in large urban areas but tend to be less common or even absent from smaller settlements. Local NGOs have a competitive advantage in that they are the best placed of the political actors to produce, accumulate and transfer knowledge in order to redress information asymmetries in local decision-making, and so promote empowerment and infrastructural sustainability, and weaken systems of dependency and patronage (Mitlin and Satterthwaite, 1996; van der Linden, 1997). In individual projects, noted advantages of infrastructure provision or environmental improvement by NGOs over the private sector or municipal agencies include cost effectiveness, increased transparency and accountability to beneficiaries, social capital formation and the strengthening of local democracy and government (Hardoy, Mitlin and Satterthwaite, 1992; Desai, 1995; Abbott, 1996; Pugh, 1996). In this way, NGOs are conceived as catalysts for a move away from hierarchical systems of urban government towards more resilient and inclusive systems of urban governance (Ostrom et al, 1993; Pugh, 1996).

Box 4.3 *The United Nations Risk Assessment Tools for Diagnosis of Urban Areas Against Seismic Disasters programme (RADIUS)*

RADIUS ran from 1996 to 2000 and had four components:

1   To develop earthquake damage scenarios and action plans in nine case-study cities from Africa, Asia, Europe and the Americas.
2   To develop practical tools for seismic risk management, which could be applied to any earthquake-prone city.
3   To conduct a comparative study to understand urban seismic risk around the world.
4   To promote information exchange for seismic risk mitigation at the city level.

The results have been disseminated amongst decision-makers and government officials, at the city and national levels, who are responsible for disaster prevention and preparedness. It is hoped that making this information available will reduce the threat of disaster by bringing seismic risk into urban planning decision-making and by providing some data to assist in emergency services planning. Doubt remains over the long-term impacts of the study. During the lifetime of the programme the UN reported that enthusiasm and commitment within case-study cities was generated, but it is not known whether this momentum has continued after the programme ended in 2000.

The case-study cities involved in the programme were: Addis Ababa (Ethiopia), Antofagasta (Chile), Bandung (Indonesia), Guayaquil (Ecuador), Izmir (Turkey), Skopje (Macedonia), Tashkent (Uzbekistan), Tijuana (Mexico) and Zigong (China).

Source: www.unisdr.org/unisdr/radiusindex.htm

Theoretically, urban systems resilience can be enhanced by NGOs as they act as alternatives to state or private sector-led channels of information and resources between the vulnerable and decision-makers. They can improve feedback to policy-makers and vulnerable groups about risks, vulnerabilities and opportunities for mitigation. As an additional component of the urban system they add capacity, and through their close links with grassroots organizations they are an example of a less hierarchical form of urban institutional arrangement. INGOs and NGOs play a key role in modifying the institutional structure of the city through advocacy and lobbying work. Their more direct engagement with the promotion of coping mechanisms can be seen to operate on at least three different scales. First, INGOs can form international networks for information and resource disbursement, often with national partners or chapters. The International Federation of the Red Cross and Red Crescent is perhaps the most well-known example of this configuration. Second, an INGO can have direct links with local partner organizations. CARE International is the best example in the context of urban disaster mitigation. Third, Southern-based NGOs can join wider associations of concerned organizations, perhaps also including private and public sector actors. La Red exemplifies this structure. Box 4.4 provides a brief description of the organizational structures and roles played by these different types of non-governmental organizations.

Box 4.4 *Networks, innovators and partners: three forms of INGO/NGO cooperation for disaster mitigation*

Networks: the International Federation of the Red Cross and Red Crescent (IFRC/RC)

The IFRC/RC has three main tasks: to coordinate international assistance from national Red Cross societies to disaster victims; to encourage and promote the establishment and development of national societies; and to act as a permanent body of liaison, coordination and study for national societies. Today there are national societies in over 175 countries that can draw support from the international network. Part of the federation's strength lies in its broad representation, with national societies in almost every country worldwide. This is an unparalleled resource for information exchange and training for disaster reduction.

The growing importance of urban areas as sites for disaster was recognized in 1998 with a special edition of the federation's annual report on urban disasters. The IFRC/RC is a humanitarian organization, but despite this it has promoted a conception of urban disaster that gives weight to disaster preparedness. Within this, urban governance is seen as key. Local government, it is argued, is the most important institution for reducing losses to natural and man-made disasters in urban areas.

Innovators: CARE International

CARE International was founded in the USA in 1946. Today, as one of the world's leading relief organizations, CARE International operates in 63 countries.

With funding from the UK's DFID, CARE International has commenced work to support the livelihoods of at-risk urban groups as a means of fighting vulnerability. Projects have been undertaken in Mumbai, Ahmedabad and Nepal. This is pioneering work and an example of innovation in the NGO sector that has wide potential for broad policy on urban disaster mitigation in the future.

Partners: La RED

Formed in 1992 and based in Puerto Limón, Costa Rica, La RED was formed as a forum to compare perspectives on social vulnerability. Today, La Red has expanded into a network of more than 100 affiliated individuals and groups from all over Latin America and the Caribbean. La RED continues to be involved in social research as well as information exchange and lobbying for social reforms as a way to reduce vulnerability and disaster risk. The DesInventar data set managed by La RED holds information on all disasters for member countries.

Sources: IFRC/RC (www.icrc.org/eng); CARE International, (www.careinternational.org.uk/index.html); La RED (www.desenredando.org/index.html)

Support for NGOs and wider civil society actors is not without its caveats. Almost all studies of NGO activity have used examples from large cities with traditions of civil society organization (SPARC in Bombay, ACHR in Bangkok, Asha Sadon in India, FUNDASAL in El Salvador), and it may be that in small settlements with less developed civil society, NGOs are less likely to find the political space required to organize or attract the resources to realize their potential advantages (Hardoy et al, 1992; Mitlin, 2001). The very success of NGOs has also been the cause of critical assessment; the institutional imperatives of expanding Southern NGOs produce conflicts of interest and distance professional NGO workers from the grassroots, reducing the inclusiveness and accountability that formed the basis of NGOs' competitive advantage over municipal and private sector service providers (Abbott, 1996; Pugh, 1996).

The appropriateness of partnership between NGOs and IFIs and the implications of such partnerships for a city's adaptive capacity needs to be questioned on two counts. First, there are doubts that NGOs have the institutional capacity necessary to manage significant increases in budgets and areas of activity. Second, an increased burden of basic service provision activity might be won at the expense of more progressive activities (Edwards and Hulme, 1996). These criticisms have led to a recent call for a greater involvement of government and grassroots actors in partnerships if NGOs and IFIs are to create truly beneficial relationships (Green and Matthias, 1995).

A second critical relationship is that between the NGO and local community partners. This vertical link can determine whether or not the experience of NGO involvement leaves the community stronger in human and social capital (critical outcomes if adaptive potential is to be enhanced) or creates a relationship of dependency upon the NGO. The way in which an NGO and partner community are brought together has a great influence over the nature of this relationship (Mitlin, 2001), as it influences the balance of power between the NGO and community. Desai (1995) shows how NGOs in Mumbai disregard power relations within the community, adding strength to existing power inequalities. Because NGOs are seen by community members as experts and as having access to funding and other resources, it is often too easy for the NGO to impose its own agenda for development on the community (Pezzoli, 1993). This is a classic case of efficiency over equity. More can be achieved in project terms if the NGO takes a firm lead in identifying and managing the project objectives and tasks, but a failure to engage community members in these critical activities misses the opportunity to transfer technical and personal skills, and so build up local human and social capital (Gazzoli, 1996).

The Guayas chapter of the Ecuadorian Red Cross is a good example of the kinds of local strengthening activities that can be facilitated by a non-governmental network. Since 1988, the Relief and Disasters Programme of the Guayas Red Cross has worked in five marginal urban communities in Guayaquil, with cooperation from the Spanish Red Cross and the municipal council. Some 100 families have been trained in risk management, environmental health, community leadership and health education with several participants reportedly going on to train others in their community (Ojeda, 2001).

An area of NGO activity that has not yet been fully developed in urban areas, and that offers a good chance of enhancing local adaptive potential, is micro-finance. Micro-finance and other kinds of informal saving groups are useful mechanisms for low-income individuals and households to overcome the impacts of accidents or illness. It is not yet clear how far a micro-finance scheme will be able to help absorb the losses of a more widespread disaster when many of the members of such a scheme might simultaneously be in need of credit, and unable to repay loans (Pitt, 2001). Micro-finance has been seen to be useful in rural contexts, where it has reduced risk by allowing diversification of livelihood away from agricultural production. Micro-finance may also provide a mechanism for households to incrementally improve the integrity of their dwelling and progressively invest in enhancing its physical resilience to potential disaster shocks or provide a mechanism for households to join together to obtain basic environmental infrastructure such as piped water (Mitlin, 2001), which will reduce risk more directly.

Local/municipal government

The capacity for local or municipal government to contribute to building resiliency is greatly determined by its organizational structure and relationship to national government (Solway, 1994). Until recently the significance of local and municipal governments has been downplayed and failings were generally discussed in terms of budgetary shortfalls and skill shortages, rather than questioning basic institutional configurations and relations with other political actors. The new agenda in urban governance makes local government a more prominent actor. It occupies the optimum institutional position to oversee privatization of local public services, facilitate grassroots and NGO participation, liaise between grassroots actors and the state or other sectoral actors (Gilbert et al, 1996; McCarney, 1996), and to strengthen the engagement of urban citizens in the democratization process. The case study in Box 4.5 shows the enhanced resilience that came from local authorities working with community-based actors in disaster mitigation in the Philippines. This agenda is contingent upon a redistribution of power and access to resources for environmental and human development between actors in the city (Mitlin and Satterthwaite, 1996). Because of this it is likely to be met by challenges from established and powerful interests and actors, particularly those whose authority or influence lies in central government (Rodriguez and Winchester, 1996).

As was noted above, decentralization associated with structural adjustment programmes (SAPs) is often experienced as an offloading of responsibilities from the national state to local authorities. Of the 75 developing countries with populations greater than 5 million, all but 12 had initiated some form of transfer of power to local government as a result of SAPs by 1995 (World Bank, 1995, in McCarney, 1996). This is not always good news. Wisner (2001) identifies decentralization from central to municipal government of responsibilities without adequate financial support as an underlying factor in the 2001 earthquake in El Salvador. When the earthquakes struck,

---

Box 4.5 *Local governance and community resilience in the Philippines*

Experience from the Philippines has shown that involvement of citizens in disaster management enhances local coping capacity. It also strengthens local capacity by institutionalizing the participatory principle in local governance.

In the Philippines, national, regional, provincial, city/municipal and local/village governments and officials are legally required to organize disaster coordinating councils (DCCs). In most cases local authorities do not receive any dedicated funding for this and, partly as a result, most DCCs are little more than organizations in name alone. Where DCCs are most effective they have encouraged citizen participation. An example of success comes from Talba, a small settlement in central Luzon.

The settlement was threatened by flooding from a nearby river. During periods of risk, municipal and local authorities kept in close contact, but otherwise the DCC was not functional, it had no members and officials did not know how to operationalize the structure. An NGO with experience in disaster management was requested by a health service NGO working in Talba to assist in training and setting up a disaster management group, which became known as the Barangay Disaster Response Organization. This group shared information with the local government-supported DCC, but both were separate organizations. In 1995 a flood destroyed the settlement. At this time the government communication system failed, and it was the parallel community system that provided sufficient warning and organized evacuation. The Barangay Disaster Response Organization also augmented the delivery of health services and during reconstruction secured the provision of water, electricity and health services.

In the example of Talba, the local government and community disaster organizations complemented each other. The local authority was open and prepared to work with a citizens' organization instead of perceiving it as a rival.

Source: Asian Disaster Preparedness Centre (www.adpc.ait.ac.th/infores/adpc-documents/zen-citizens.pdf)

'*only a handful of the country's 262 municipal governments had any professionally trained staff... Since opposition parties are strong in many of the elected municipal councils, the ARENA-dominated national government simply does not wish to devolve power and capacity, although it makes the appropriate sounds about decentralization to please the donors*' (Wisner, 2001, p264).

The deleterious effects of this mismatch between financial resources and functional responsibilities are often exacerbated by a reluctance from the state to admit to the limits of local government. This is a necessary position from which to seek partnerships to share the burden of service provision

If strengthening local government is seen as the way to reduce vulnerability, Sanderson (2000) sounds a note of caution. He argues that strengthening urban planning legislation can result in poor people's increased vulnerability if it results in their eviction from informal settlements. Indeed, improvements in building standards regulation and enforcement in rapidly growing cities in the least developed countries will rarely assist the most vulnerable who live in illegal and unplanned settlements. A less controversial role for municipal government is to utilize its links with overseas governments, national governments and local government networks. This is particularly useful in large cities with more than one municipality or in small cities with limited non-governmental capacity. Such networks could provide a rich resource for transferring information and skills to enhance local adaptive potential. In the Mexican state of Veracruz, the Solidarity Programme of the Mexican Social Security Institute has been working with the Civil Protection Directorate of Veracruz State and the Office of Foreign Disaster Assistance of USAID to train municipal officials in charge of disaster response from those parts of Veracruz most at risk from natural disaster. Some 90 officials have been trained and they will act as trainers to build capacity at the local level (Velásquez, 2001).

Grassroots actors

Grassroots actors cover a wide range of social institutions: individual social entrepreneurs, households, kinship groups, informal social networks, CBOs and networks of CBOs (Pugh, 1996). There are similarities with local NGOs as a rule of thumb, but grassroots actors are at the lowest level of social organization: they are local, and defined spatially rather that sectorally. Grassroots actors are prevalent in most cities. With so many CBOs, it is not surprising that there is a great heterogeneity in their form and function. Mitlin (2001) identifies eight common motivating forces explaining the origin and maintenance of such organizations: kinship, ethnicity, trade union involvement, support from city-based federations of community organizations, support from NGOs, religious organizations, political parties and the private sector. With such diversity in support, the aims of community leaders within such groups and of their backers in the wider polity of the city will be diverse. Some will be more active in pressing for positive change in the local community than others, and some may even be looking to capture community support for the gain of external actors, such as political parties potentially undermining adaptive potential. Box 4.6 describes the Asian Urban Disaster Management Program, an example of grassroots actors working with NGOs in urban vulnerability reduction.

The advantages of grassroots actors are similar to those of local NGOs: they hold local knowledge (of local social norms, customs and organizations, of local environmental characteristics and of local needs and wants) which is necessary for successful project planning (Ostrom et al, 1993); they are able to convey information between local residents and other political actors, correcting information asymmetries and reducing dependence on extra-local actors for decision-making (Desai, 1995); and, through the facilitation of more meaningful involvement of local residents in development projects, they have the capacity to enhance local social development. Cross (2001) cites the urban population as a key resource for cities during times of disaster. He uses Mexico City as an example: following the 1985 earthquake, up to 1 million volunteers joined to

---

Box 4.6 *The Asian Urban Disaster Mitigation Program*

The Asian Urban Disaster Mitigation Program (AUDP) is organized by the Asian Disaster Preparedness Center in the Philippines and is funded by USAID. The programme was initiated in 1995 and has eight local partners. These are NGOs working in urban disaster mitigation in Bangladesh, Cambodia, India, Indonesia, People's Democratic Republic of Laos, Nepal, the Philippines and Sri Lanka. In each country the local organizing institution has engaged with grassroots actors to facilitate community-level disaster management planning. The country-level projects are at different stages of completion. The two examples below indicate the kinds of activities that community groups have successfully been involved with.

The town of Ratnapura, Sri Lanka, is subject to a number of hazards. Community-level planning has focussed on developing a methodology for identifying hazards and determining potential losses. Outputs of the project have included the constitution of a Disaster Management Council, guidelines for building construction in disaster-prone areas and a Disaster Management and Mitigation Plan for Ratnapura.

CARE Bangladesh is the implementing agency for projects in Gaibandha and Tongi. Both projects aim to enhance local resilience to flood hazard. The project aims to improve the capacity and skills of the communities to manage the risks and apply mitigation skills in the urban areas.

In general, AUDP local projects include a large training component. Training sessions are seen as a key opportunity to pass on best practice generated by other community projects and, more generally, to facilitate increased awareness of the importance of local actors and their capacity in mitigating environmental risks. In this way, both the coping and institutional modification aspects of adaptive potential are being addressed.

Sources: Asian Urban Disaster Mitigation Program (www.adpc.ait.ac.th/audmp/audmp.html); Asian Disaster Preparedness Center (www.adpc.ait.ac.th/default.html)

---

help in rescue operations. The need to reassess grassroots action in a hazards context is noted by Blaikie et al (1994):

> '[W]e believe too little attention has been given to the strategies and actions of vulnerable people themselves... They form support networks, develop multiple sources of livelihood systems... People learn rather cynically, yet realistically, not to rely on services provided by authorities' (Blaikie et al, 1994, p14).

There is a growing consensus that grassroots actors should be involved in programmes to reduce vulnerability to environmental hazard. It is argued that through involvement in decision-making, grassroots actors will become more politically empowered (Friedmann, 1992) allowing institutional modification. IFIs and donors argue that grassroots involvement promotes feelings of ownership in the local community for new infrastructure, and that this prevents vandalism and encourages maintenance amongst the local community, thus prolonging the lifetime of physical infrastructure. These priorities have converged on the same broad social mechanism (Gilbert and Ward, 1984a; Abbott, 1996) but their contrasting political orientations need to be considered in understanding the ideological framing of urban risk management and how this ties in with the broader and deeper politics of development.

Certainly the involvement of grassroots actors is required if the partnerships that lie at the heart of the New Agenda of urban management are to take hold, and this requires a significant extension of the planning community and an inclusiveness in decision-making. This, however, is likely to meet with resistance from local authorities and political parties, whose domination over urban development is facilitated through the maintenance of relationships of dependency and patronage and through institutionalized cultures of rent-seeking. But successful examples of urban institutional reform do exist. Hardoy and Satterthwaite (1989) document experiences in Rio de Janeiro where CBOs, local government and an INGO (UNICEF) have cooperated on a series of projects to improve housing and health. Moving towards such inclusive planning mechanisms requires open political space. There are those settlements, particularly within nations that have experienced strong centralized control and have only recently commenced the democratic transition, where civil society is narrowly defined, and where community organizations (and local NGOs) may be absent. In these instances strong, representative local government is essential for the initial promotion of horizontal community linkages, and there may be a role for community facilitators (Mitlin and Satterthwaite, 1996) to act as catalysts to encourage such links to develop. Box 4.7 presents a case study of the Citizens' Disaster Response Network. The network includes local organizations and CBOs from across the Philippines, all engaged in disaster mitigation but also in working towards an alternative approach to disasters and development that seeks to avoid the weaknesses of the dominant government-based system. A similar grassroots-based movement with national scope can be found in India (Disaster Mitigation Institute, www.southasiadisasters.net/index.htm).

Information asymmetries and unequal distributions of power are as prevalent within community structures as between the community and other political actors. There has been a tendency to ascribe roles to the community (a source of local knowledge, a source of cheap or free labour, a resource to shape for infrastructural maintenance) rather than first asking how a community is structured and which groups are most likely to experience the costs and benefits of participation. Whilst this implies a wish to accelerate development, it can also be seen as a means of minimizing 'beneficiary' resistance to projects (Desai, 1995), and implies that, despite rhetoric to the contrary, community participation may be shaped less by local conditions than by government or donor policies (Gilbert and Ward, 1984b).

In many low-income settlements that face environmental risk, very few people actively participate in CBOs. Mean proportions of resident participation in community organizations based on studies conducted in Commonwealth (Philippines), Cisne Dos (Ecuador) and Chawama (Zambia) are 14 per cent for men and 21 per cent for women (Mitlin, 2001). Since a component of

---

Box 4.7 *The Citizens' Disaster Response Network, Manila*

After the Mount Mayon eruption in 1984, an ad hoc coalition of organizations under the umbrella of the Support Disaster Victims Campaign coordinated the response. More than 1000 families were assisted by this initiative. The success of the campaign and a wish amongst its participants to push forward agendas for change at the national level led to the formation of a more permanent Citizens' Disaster Response Center (CDRC) in Manila. The CDRC consulted and linked up with counterparts from regions where disaster risk and human vulnerability were high, forming the Citizens' Disaster Response Network (CDRN). Thirteen regional partners are currently active. The CDRC acts as a communications hub providing technical assistance and capacity building to regional partner groups and working in advocacy and funding. Local knowledge of risk and vulnerability is the primary resource of the regional centres, which act as first points of contact with vulnerable communities and people displaced by natural disaster or civil unrest.

Whilst the Marcos dictatorship was overthrown in 1986, the Citizens' Disaster Response Network remained critical of government development priorities, arguing that the factors generating vulnerability to disasters had not been dismantled:

- Government relief and rehabilitation were marred by corruption.
- Relief was used to further political agendas and to foster dependence on political patronage.
- Government responses to the food and medical relief needs of disaster-affected areas was insufficient, partly due to the misappropriation of funds.
- Distribution of relief and rehabilitation aid was hampered by bureaucracy and favouritism.
- Assistance was inappropriate for the emergency needs of those affected.
- Lack of coordination among government agencies resulted in duplication and gaps in service provision.
- Political will and a programme for disaster preparedness were lacking.

To identify ways forward, national conferences have been convened under the CDRN, culminating in the publication of a citizenry-based development-oriented disaster response framework. The individual projects supported by the CDRN are too numerous to mention here; for more information refer to www.adpc.ait.ac.th/pdr-sea/cbdo-dr/cover.html.

Source: Heijmans and Victoria (no date)

---

vulnerability is social isolation, it is possible that unless directly compensated, the most vulnerable will also be those least represented by community organizations. The differences in participation rates between men and women also add weight to the observation that women tend to be over-represented, and men under-represented, in the membership of grassroots organizations, and that access to grassroots organization is constrained by income and pre-existing social capital (Weinberger and Jütting, 2001).

More fundamental criticisms come from Gilbert and Ward (1984a, 1984b) and Desai (1995, 1996), who use examples from Bogotá, Mexico City, Valencia and Kolkata (Calcutta) respectively to show how community participation can be turned on its head and become a means by which the state, or local political brokers, can subvert local initiatives and manipulate local people. It is argued that participation needs to be bottom–up, inclusive and have representative leadership. Inclusivity is perhaps the hardest problem to resolve, particularly in those societies without a history of public involvement in decision-making or in deeply divided communities (often communities that experience environmental vulnerability: migrant communities, transitional inner-city or squatter settlements) (Anzorena, 1980, in Desai, 1996). Leadership issues are the result of a paradox: to be representative and accountable, leadership must be deeply rooted in the local community; however, to gain resources to pursue a community's wishes leadership must have substantial linkages with external institutions. It is through this paradox that community organization is laid open to capture by external forces, and in this way community participation can become a mode of social control.

There are two mechanisms through which community organizations can be captured by external political actors: co-optation and patronage. Both have the effect of prolonging dependency upon external political actors (Everett, 1989). Co-optation is the result of a formal agreement between community leadership and external political actors (often the dominant political party). Patronage systems are less formal arrangements based on personal exchanges between actors of unequal power. The weaker partner (community leadership) benefits by improved access to influential decision-makers; the dominant partner (political party) benefits from commanding the loyalty of partner actors (community leaders) who have been made dependent upon it (Desai, 1995). Patronage is a system whereby communities (through their leaders) are at least able to have some voice and influence in decision-making, which is achieved with the minimum of political exposure on the part of the community. This is compatible with the risk-aversion strategies used by marginalized groups (Ostrom et al, 1993; Desai, 1996), which have to balance the perceived costs, risks and benefits of direct participation (if they have the option) with the patronage route.

Community leaders occupy a strategic position, liaising between the local community and other partners. A basic requirement for leadership in contemporary systems is access to sufficient socio-economic resources. Leadership involves time away from income-earning activities and possibly transport and hospitality expenses (Verba, 1978; Desai, 1995). In this way the urban poor are marginalized from the very decision-making procedures that seek their inclusion, which in turn acts to exacerbate socio-economic differentiation within the community. In addition, leadership requires access to information and an awareness of politics. Leadership positions can also be less accessible to women, the young and old or minority ethnic and low-caste groups (Verba, 1978) because of religious (Callaway and Creevey, 1989) and cultural (Everett, 1989) norms. Leadership can also be seen as a coping mechanism. As Blaikie et al (1994) show, individuals have differing resource profiles, which translate into differing capacities with which an actor may have control over his/her own life chances. In this way leadership as a coping mechanism is only open to specific groups within society.

A final dynamic force available to grassroots actors, especially those trapped in systems of patronage or co-optation, is resistance. Grassroots resistance can be overt, public and declared (such as petitioning, demonstrations, riots, boycotts, land invasions and strikes) or covert, private and hidden (such as poaching, squatting, vandalism and linguistic resistance) (Scott, 1985, 1990; Pred and Watts, 1992). Minh-ha (1989) suggests that silence should also be perceived as a form of hidden resistance; silence indicates a refusal to participate and so becomes active, not simply a sign of indifference or apathy. In societies with little open political space, the intra-politics (Scott, 1990) of hidden or everyday resistance can act as signifiers of protest and hidden dissent amongst the politically and socially marginalized. These actions may or may not indicate a trajectory towards increasingly organized and overt protest and social movements. This differentiation between public and private forms of resistance has also been noted by Giddens (1984) who distinguishes between 'front regions' and 'back regions'. Front regions are spaces of open conflict but also surveillance, whereas back regions allow concealed expressions of discontent.

Reflecting the novelty of its approach, there is limited documented experience of projects targeted at reducing vulnerability through grassroots actors. One key lesson gained from work in Central America is the need to move beyond one-off community-level interventions into building long-term relationships between local and extra-local organizations. PAHO (2001) reports that the Italian government had invested in the establishing of local emergency committees but that many committees quickly fell apart because of a lack of follow-up efforts designed to maintain community interest. Despite this criticism, the concept and value of local emergency committees remained in the community, even if the organizations themselves had lapsed. This suggests that even where organizations no longer function, a community memory for the principles of disaster preparedness and first response may still enhance local adaptive potential.

In its own efforts at strengthening local adaptive potential in countries affected by Hurricane Mitch (1998), PAHO (2001) worked through its network of community-level health centres to promote local disaster preparedness with community members involved in key decision-making roles. Obstacles to this process were conflicts between local political leaders and between local government and community groups if they were identified with competing political parties. At times, government officials tried to marginalize community groups, seeing them as adversaries or competitors for political or financial capital. The wider political context also made a difference. In Nicaragua, with its tradition of local social organization, community groups overcame partisanship, creating the most inclusive local disaster preparedness organizations identified by this project, which also included Honduras, El Salvador and Guatemala.

Similarities with PAHO's work and the Guayas Red Cross initiative are striking. The tying of local disaster preparedness work to established networks of community health volunteers has proved successful in both cases.

From actors to partners?

A focus on actors could be seen to imply that resilience rests with individual organizations. But, as many of the examples of good practice have shown, partnerships are important. There are many different kinds of partnership. At the most basic level, partnerships simply denote some kind of joint initiative, perhaps between two organizations of a similar type, say two NGOs or two CBOs, or between two or more organizations of different types, say a partnership between a private sector business and a community-based group.

The notion of power is critical to the functioning of partnerships (Fowler, 2000). Partnerships will falter and may even produce counter-developmental results if one actor dominates (Fiszbein and Lowden, 1999). It is the additional energies and outputs or synergy (Evans, 1996) derived from a coming together of different resources that gives partnerships a potential advantage beyond actor-centred projects. But power asymmetries between partners can undermine adaptive potential in the short term by distorting projects, and in the longer term by creating ties of dependency and weakening local accountability. Figure 4.1 shows the types of resource that different actors can bring to a partnership. It also goes some way to explaining why partnerships are vulnerable to domination by certain actors.

Typically, money, technical expertise and status flow down the hierarchy from global to local organizations with proof that an agency is engaged with more local actors, and some local project knowledge flows upwards. It is in such circumstances that groups can become captured and donors are allowed to drive local development agendas. However, if these potential problems are planned for, partnerships can be rewarding and equitable, with lower-order actors learning the skills necessary to approach new partners and play an increased role

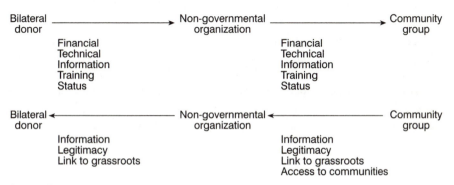

Source: Based on Lister (2000)

Figure 4.1 *Resource flows between partners*

in management should they wish, and with higher-order partners sharpening the relevance of their project funding (Fowler, 1997; Edwards and Hulme, 1996). Successful examples of partnership include the projects of CARE International in cities of South Asia and Africa and the support for national societies from the IFRC/RC. At a global level, partnership can be seen in the ProVention consortium, which has brought together policy researchers from the World Bank, the private sector, the IFRC/RC and independent and university research institutes to share information and spread awareness of innovation in disaster risk management (www.proventionconsortium.org).

SUMMARY

If vulnerability to environmental hazard is partly an outcome of the distribution of power in the city, then what types of actors are engaged in urban politics? This chapter identified six broad categories of political actor: IFIs, national government, the private sector, international and Southern-based NGOs, local or municipal government and grassroots actors. Each type of political actor has a competitive advantage that it can bring to fighting vulnerability in the city. For example: IFIs have access to capital; national and municipal government can oversee the provision of basic services, regulating when necessary; and grassroots actors have local knowledge and energies to help sharpen local mitigation interventions.

Whilst it was useful to discuss political actors individually here, in the city they seldom act alone. Fulfilling adaptive potential tends to be facilitated when many political actors work together, and this is reflected in the New Agenda of urban development policy, which has partnership as a central tenet. Collaboration between actors – particularly when grassroots actors are involved – can provide opportunities for learning how to access resources and build self-esteem with which to claim rights to resources for local risk reduction. But neither partnerships nor grassroots actors should be viewed too romantically. Power lies in relationships, and when partnerships are built on unequal relations of power development outcomes are open to bias. This is as true for relations between local organizations and non-governmental or state actors as it is for relations between men and women, the young and old, or different ethnic or religious groups at the local level. Despite this danger, partnerships and the participation of grassroots actors offer considerable opportunities for building local resilience in the city, and without them vulnerability reduction is unlikely to become an integrated part of participatory urban development.

Section II

The Case Studies

Case Study Selection

In order to identify the potential for public action to reduce vulnerability and losses to urban disaster we need to follow the social relations that shape opportunities and constraints for such action on the ground. This is the goal of the three case studies presented in this section of the book. The three case-study cities each highlight the constraints and opportunities for local action to confront vulnerability in contrasting political systems: a liberal democracy in Bridgetown, Barbados; a state in transition from a so-called socialist regime in Georgetown, Guyana; and a state in transition from an authoritarian state regime in Santo Domingo, the Dominican Republic. The methodologies used to collect and analyse data from the case study sites can be found in Appendix 1.

Bridgetown, Georgetown and Santo Domingo have a number of important attributes in common which allows for comparative analysis:

- they are national capitals;
- they share histories of colonial settlement;
- they share post-colonial histories of dependency upon North American and Western European states; and
- they are exposed to catastrophic hazards (hurricanes and flooding) as well as everyday hazards (access to basic services and safe housing).

But set against these general similarities, the cities differ markedly in their post-colonial political development paths and in their citizens' vulnerability to disaster. It is this difference that provides an opportunity to examine the effect of political regimes on public action and the formation of adaptive potential to avoid disaster.

The key characteristics of each case-study city are shown in Table II.1, and will be expanded upon within each case study, so we do not need to dwell on them here. However, it is worth reviewing the table as an aid to a comparative reading of the case studies.

Reflecting on the preceding three chapters, and reading Table II.1, points to five key issues that need to be considered in making a comparative assessment of public action and adaptive potential in these cities: length of democratic rule, post-colonial regime form, urban scale, the extent of urban poverty and dependency, and the city as an arena for national politics. These issues are outlined below and should be used as a guide in interpreting the case studies.

Table II.1 *The case studies*

	Georgetown	Santo Domingo	Bridgetown
Political regime			
Date of independence	1966	1844	1967
Post-colonial political regime	One party 'socialist' state, racialized	Authoritarian, neo-patrimonial, right wing	Multi-party democracy
First free and fair post-independence national election*	1992	1996	1971
Status of civil society	Repressed and undeveloped	Conflict with state but vibrant	Limited human capital, co-opted
Vulnerability indicator			
City population (1991)	275,000	5,000,000	150,000
Annual urban population growth rate	1.5%	3.5%	1.2%
Proportion of city population below the poverty line	29% (1994)	38% (1997)	8.7% (1997)
UNDP National Human Development Index rank (1999)	99	88	29
Hazard indicator			
Principal catastrophic hazard risk	Flooding (21 city floods 1990–1995)	Hurricanes and tropical storms (>50/100 years)	Hurricanes and tropical storms (>5/100 years)
Everyday hazard risk	High: decayed environmental infrastructure	High: inadequate environmental infrastructure	Low: adequate environmental infrastructure

Note: * In the present period of democracy. Earlier periods included free elections in Guyana in 1967 and in the Dominican Republic in the 1980s. Barbados has had uninterrupted free elections since 1951.

Length of democratic rule

Each case-study city is currently administered under a democratic system of government. Democratic government is defined simply as the presence of regular free and fair elections. Of course, for a democracy to function meaningfully it requires more than regular free elections, which are used here as an accessible comparative indicator of political regime-form change through time. The length of democratic rule has varied considerably between the case studies; Barbados has the most extensive history of democracy reaching back to democratic local rule within the British colony in 1951. Both Guyana and the Dominican Republic have had more recent shifts to democracy, Guyana moved from a so-called socialist model with free and fair elections in 1992, and the Dominican Republic emerged from an extended period of authoritarian rule with free and fair elections in 1996. The length of formal democratic rule is used as a basic indicator of the strength with which norms of democratic governance are likely to be found within each political system at the grassroots, and within institutions of the public, private and civil sectors. Well-functioning democratic systems are expected to be less constrained by clientelism and patriarchy, they should have more transparent public decision-making, and they may tend towards encouraging partnerships between civil society, the private sector and the public sector.

Recent post-colonial regime forms

The contemporary relationship between civil society and the state is greatly shaped by recent events. In Barbados, a continuum of liberal democracy tied to healthy rates of economic growth have legitimized a strong state that is dominant in almost all spheres of public life, and a corresponding weakness in civil society as a space for critical political action. This is quite the opposite in the Dominican Republic, where a long history of authoritarian patrimonial rule has concentrated power in the person of the president, and where civil society has emerged as a powerful site for dissenting voices and actions. In Guyana, centralized planning following a socialist model of government has led to the repression of the private sector and civil society, and this is still very evident in the weaknesses of these sectors compared to the state, which is itself undergoing a period of legitimacy crisis with racially partisan political parties failing to deliver macro-economic stability or meet basic human rights.

Urban scale

Scale is often overlooked in analyses of urbanization, and this is a mistake. Scale affects the quantity of resources (financial, physical and human) flowing through a city and the amount and type of waste that is produced. Smaller cities are less likely to accrue the resources necessary to support comprehensive local government and are also less likely to attract the large-scale industrial complexes and informal housing settlements that shape the environmental hazards of the largest cities. In absolute terms, the greatest losses to environmental hazard are found in mega-cities with populations in excess of 5 million. Santo Domingo is such a city. Its large size, high population growth rate and poverty shape not only the extent and character of vulnerability but also the city's adaptive potential. But the majority of urbanites do not reside in such large cities, and both Georgetown and Bridgetown exemplify the production of vulnerability in smaller urban centres, though from very contrasting developmental perspectives.

Urban poverty and dependency

The close relationship between poverty and vulnerability was discussed in Chapter 3. Access to economic resources affects governmental and public action. Both the quantity and quality of economic resources are important. For city authorities, money to provide basic services is likely to come from local rates, government subventions and donor aid. For civil society, money may come from grassroots fund-raising, but is also more likely to come from government or donor support. Particularly for large projects or programmes, city authorities and civil society actors are reliant upon attracting external financial support. This dependency opens local actors up to the conditionalities that donors or national government can attach to grants. This is a key mechanism through which local communities are linked into national, regional and global developmental agendas. In the case studies, the influence of successive global donor agendas can be seen, ranging from colonial and military interventions in the early–mid 20th century, to the SAPs of the 1980s and 1990s, and to the participatory paradigm from the mid-1990s onwards.

The city as an arena for national politics

Whilst the case studies have been selected because they differ in scale and political orientation, they are all capital and primate cities. This is useful for our examination because of the political importance of capital cities, which are often the focal points of national politics and symbols of national pride and identity. It is often in capital cities where the greatest disparities in wealth and poverty are to be found. Similarly, it is here that development initiatives are often most prominent and political protest is most marked. Capital cities are not representative of all cities, but they exemplify many of the tensions found in other cities: political tension, trade and aid, global/local linkages, environmental degradation, fiscal mismanagement and financial scarcity are writ large in these focal points for national pride and development.

Chapter 5

Maintaining Civil Society in a Liberal Democracy: Bridgetown, Barbados

INTRODUCTION

A mature and active civil society is often regarded as a cornerstone of liberal democracy. Civil society can act as a check on the power of the state, as a place for the socialization of democratic norms, as a training ground for future political leaders and as an arena for the working out of development projects that complement, supplement or are an alternative to the state. The necessity of a vital civil society as a key component in the progression towards democracy is frequently remarked upon by political scientists. It is ironic then that in the world's mature democracies there should be a crisis over the health of civil society and the condition of social capital (Putnam, 2000). Barbados fits this pattern well. With over 50 years of stable democratic government, it is the third-oldest parliamentary system in the world. Yet, as cultural and economic modernization have taken hold, popular participation in the democratic process and support for civil society has begun to wane. The challenge under such conditions is how to maintain a healthy and constructive civil society that can contribute to efforts to confront human vulnerability at the local level.

In this chapter, a background discussion of the political economy of Barbados is presented first, together with some comments on the nature of risk and the scope and scale of human vulnerability in Bridgetown. Adaptive potential is then assessed with reference to state and civil society actors engaged in reducing losses from everyday and catastrophic environmental hazard. A detailed case study of an inner-city low-income neighbourhood called the Pine is then used to examine in more detail the contemporary factors that shape the kinds of social capital found in vulnerable communities, and the extent to which local stocks of social capital and local organization are being utilized to enhance resiliency to shock and stress in Barbados.

DEMOCRACY FROM ABOVE: THE BARBADIAN PATH
TO DEVELOPMENT

Between adult suffrage in 1951 and 2002, 11 elections were held in Barbados, none with any disputed transfer of power. Public unrest is not common, but neither has popular protest been suppressed by the state. The most recent mass public protest in Bridgetown, in 1991, involved a march of 15,000 trade unionists critical of structural adjustment austerity measures that had led to the forced redundancy of public sector workers. Outside of the formal political system, political debate is active in an independent national press and through popular radio phone-ins. Despite these positive indicators, the proportion of the electorate voting in national elections fell from 73 per cent in 1976 to 61 per cent in 1994. Duncan (1994) called the low turnout of 1991 a watershed, with 37 per cent of the electorate declining to vote. Perhaps most worrying for the future of participatory democracy in Barbados, it was 18–28 year olds who were least likely to have voted in 1991. The winning party appeared to have been chosen 'as the least undesirable of the partisan offerings to the electorate' (Duncan, 1994, p79). Rising voter apathy has been linked to the consolidation of political parties in Barbados, so that from the 1966 general elections onwards Barbados has become an increasingly partisan two-party state. Political consolidation has intensified with the election of the social democratic Barbados Labour Party (BLP) in 1994 and 1999. The BLP appears to have made the strategic decision to offer posts to leading individuals from opposition political parties or key civil society organizations. Whilst maximizing the human skill base of the state, this policy opens opportunities for the state to capture alternative development strategies and undermine the capacity of political opposition and civil society, thus weakening democratic competition over the long run.

There is no local government tier in Barbados, with planning decisions for Bridgetown being taken at the national level. Urban planning is governed by the Town and Country Planning Act, which established the Town and Country Planning Advisory Committee. In 2000, an Urban Planning Commission was set up by government to head an urban renewal programme. Successive governments have not attached a high priority to either the environment or community development in the rush for economic modernization. This is reflected by the frequency with which these departments have moved between various ministries. For example, between 1984 and 1995, the environmental portfolio was assigned to eight different ministries, and between 1971 and 1996 the community development portfolio was moved between ten government agencies. Despite this unsettling background, the number of local community centres provided by the state has increased from 15 in 1982 to 28 in 1995 (Government of Barbados, 1996).

In the absence of local government, members of parliament (MPs) elected to represent the interests of their constituency occupy a critical position between citizens and the state. They are the first point of contact for citizens with problems. Constituents frequently berate or praise their MPs in the press over their ability to secure investment in local services from the central government budget. This ability is more important than party affiliation in many constituencies, offering a countervailing force to political partisanship, but creating ties of patronage and dependency between communities and individual MPs. A letter to the *Daily Nation* newspaper from a resident of St Philip shows how much weight is put on MPs to deliver goods to the community, and how in this context communities are reluctant to take up self-help themselves:

> '*I write on behalf of the residents of Pounder Road, St Philip. We the constituents of the above address lack proper representation by politicians... For too long, we the residents have been complaining in vain about the state of the roads with its potholes, which have become a great menace to pedestrians and motorists, especially when rain falls. Lest we forget, the X [vote] is mightier than the sword*' (*Daily Nation*, 31 August 1998).

No register is kept of the number of NGOs operating in Barbados. However, CBOs, which include all kinds of local interest groups, are registered with the Community Development Division. In 1998, 160 CBOs were registered in Barbados, with 55 in St Michael, the parish in which central Bridgetown is located (Community Development Division, 1998) (see Figure 5.1). The majority of organizations are sports oriented, with fewer than ten local development groups in all of Barbados. There is no umbrella network for civil society organizations. In addition to the low density and lack of developmental orientation amongst civil society, the government of Barbados is a key funder of the most well-known heritage conservation, environmental and women's NGOs in the country. This can be interpreted as offering a means of support for independent civil society organizations as well as providing a mechanism for exerting government influence on individual organizations and the sector as a whole. The biggest gaps in civil society are the lack of developmentally oriented organizations and the reluctance of young people to join local organizations. In a review of 17 local interest organizations, it was noted that:

> '*It appears that in joining the groups, the youth do not see the group as satisfying their needs beyond sports and religious activities. The non-sporting persons were not easily attracted to the groups*' (Nurse, 1997 p27).

In 1997, the government of Barbados organized a series of 16 parish meetings to hear people's views on poverty alleviation. The discussions also shed light on the status of civil society and its relationship to the state in Barbados. In every meeting, some reference was made to the loss of community ties in recent years and the need for poverty alleviation to work through CBOs rather than the public sector, which was perceived as being overly bureaucratic, having an anti-

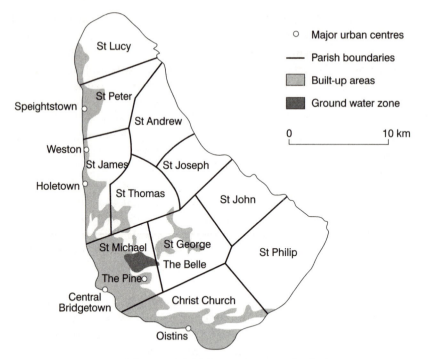

Figure 5.1 *Urban settlement in Barbados*

poor culture and being open to political influence. The final report identified special concerns amongst participants, including the limited involvement of community-based actors in poverty alleviation:

> '[I]n Barbados, members of government perceive NGOs and CBOs as enemies, therefore it is difficult for needs and priorities articulated by these organizations to be recognized or fulfilled. In addition, the movement in Barbados away from local government and towards centralized government has led the population to expect that government will provide everything – it can not' (UNDP, 1997, p11).

Although, in rhetoric at least, the state does acknowledge that bringing community actors in could be a way of avoiding bureaucratic weaknesses:

> 'avoid delays and problems resulting from bureaucracy either by reducing the bureaucracy or by working through [civil society] institutions' (UNDP, 1997, p4).

When government agencies have responded to the global push for greater local participation in development initiatives they have expressed disappointment in the lack of community-level response, but have stopped short of questioning the underlying citizen–state relations that have produced this outcome. Commenting on problems faced by two government-sponsored natural resource management studies, Smith (1997) notes that their public participation components have encountered difficulties in mobilizing people: 'This is largely due to the fact that the whole idea of community participation in the development planning process is new to Barbados. It has even been said that there are less grassroots NGOs found in Barbados compared with neighbouring Caribbean islands' (Smith, 1997, p11).

It is unfortunate that, at a time when a consensus is emerging in the government and public sector that participation is a good thing, community organization appears to be at a low point in Barbados. Duncan (1994) hints at the negative impact of rapid modernization on Barbadian society when he identifies a social crisis in Barbados: 'the social fabric appears to be disintegrating into an alarming and persistent outbreak of crime, child abuse, drug abuse, poor service and inter-personal relations, absence of restraining standards and rampant consumerism' (Duncan, 1994, p86). He ties this social crisis to the discrediting of national political authority, corruption and political patronage, undermining of established religion, the spread of unrewarding employment and increased population mobility. What remains, and what has been overlooked, are the more informal ties between individuals and households in local areas that might form the basis for a rejuvenation of more formal organizations if the incentives are right.

SOCIAL VULNERABILITY AMID ECONOMIC DEVELOPMENT

Barbados is classified by the World Bank as an upper middle-income country. From the 1960s onwards, tourism has been the dominant economic sector. There is little agriculture for domestic consumption, and as sugar lands have gone out of production they have fallen idle or been converted into tourist uses. Despite a period of recession from 1989 to 1991 and the introduction of stabilization policies in 1991–1992, the national economy has recovered, with gross national product (GNP) per capita in 1999 of US$14,353 and a Human Development Index Rank of 31 (UNDP, 2001). However, income inequality has remained high (Gini coefficient of 0.46 compared with 0.49 for Latin America, for 1986), with 8.7 per cent of households living below the poverty line of US$2750 (Thomas, 1995). More than 20 per cent of the workforce is unemployed. Unemployment is disproportionately affecting youth, women, urban dwellers and retrenched public sector workers over 50 years of age, all of whom have been identified as being especially vulnerable to poverty.

Barbados has a stable population, but one that is ageing: in 1960 only 6 per cent of the population was over 65 years, by 1995 this proportion had doubled (PAHO, 1998). Some 92 per cent of people of pensionable age are eligible to receive a state pension, the highest level in the Caribbean. However, the family

Table 5.1 *Assets for urban areas and for all Barbados*

Asset	Urban (per cent)	All Barbados (per cent)
Dwelling tenure:		
house owned	66	76
private rental	21	16
government rental	10	5
rent-free	3	3
Sewerage:		
toilet linked to sewer system	3	1
septic tank	62	65
pit latrine	34	32
other	0	1
no facility	1	1
Head of household in employment	59	61
Household insurance	25	25

Source: 1990 Barbados National Population Census (Statistical Service, 1993)

remains the primary source of support for the elderly. Some 6680 women are lone heads of households (9 per cent) and are vulnerable to social isolation and economic poverty. Notwithstanding this, women are major actors in the Barbadian economy with female labour force participation above 40 per cent (Coppin, 1995).

Indicators for access to health, education and social services suggest that Barbadians enjoy amongst the best facilities in the Caribbean. Life expectancy is 75 (highest in the Caribbean), infant mortality is 9 per 1000 live births (lowest in the Caribbean), the leading causes of death for children under five years are conditions originating in the peri-natal period, congenital anomalies, pneumonia and AIDS. This indicates that public health hazards are generally well contained but, as the dengue fever epidemic of 1995 showed, still a potential source of risk (PAHO, 1998). Adult illiteracy rate is 2 per cent, with Barbados having the highest expenditure on education and health as a proportion of GDP in the Caribbean, with a five-year average of 5 per cent for education and 7.2 per cent for health (UNCSD, 1997).

Urban Barbados centres upon Bridgetown, with linear coastal development to the north and southwest and a more rural hinterland to the east. In 1998, two-thirds of the population lived within a quarter of a mile of the coast. To reduce flood risk, new construction must now be set back by at least 30m from the high-water mark, and the Prevention of Floods Act allows the removal of structures and the construction of physical structures as needed to prevent or control flooding. The majority of urban houses are owner occupied (66 per cent in the 1990 population and housing census), with little government provision since the 1980s (see Table 5.1). However, increasing house and land prices (partly a consequence of foreign investment and competition for limited land) have meant that 55 per cent of the population are currently unable to afford buying or building a house (Government of Barbados, 1996), increasing pressure for greater government intervention. This has contributed to the recent phenomena of squatting. Squatting sites are often largely populated by labour migrants from St Lucia and St Vincent. The integrity of the Belle water catchment area, which is a source for about two-thirds of the drinking water in Barbados, is under pressure from 450 squatter households (Division of Housing, 1998).

ENVIRONMENTAL HAZARD

The Barbadian environment is being increasingly stressed by urban growth and modernization in the agricultural and tourism sectors. Whilst 94 per cent of households are connected to the piped drinking water system (PAHO, 1998), access to adequate amounts of safe drinking water is being threatened by contamination due to the expansion of urban areas into water reserves and by continued high rates of extraction from the freshwater aquifer. The renewable freshwater yield of 45.2m gallons/day is exceeded by extraction rates of 48.6m gallons/day in the public sector alone, with demand growing annually by about 4 per cent. Barbados is defined by the United Nations as a water-scarce nation. Severe drought was recorded in 1894 and 1978. Best estimates for the effects of global climate change suggest that greater extremes in rainfall will increase the likelihood and severity of both flooding and drought.

The environmental costs of intensive economic development are perhaps most visible in coastal ecosystems which are contaminated by urban and agricultural runoff and outflows of human and industrial waste (Brewster, 1992). The degradation of coastal coral reef and mangrove communities not only erodes the eco-tourism base and biodiversity of the island but weakens a key line of natural defence for Barbados against coastal flooding. Property damage caused by the erosion of sand beaches on the urbanized west and south coasts is an on-going problem (Cambers, 1987) which is likely to be exacerbated by greater storminess and sea-level rise associated with global climate change.

There is a long history of urban flooding in Bridgetown linked to failures in urban management. The Urban Renewal Programme cites four main problems: first, the inappropriate design of drains which no longer serve all the built-up area; second, the use of gravity drainage which limits the time when storm water can escape to low tide; third, the dumping of household refuse in drains which reduces flow capacity; and fourth, the construction of buildings next to drains which impedes maintenance (Government of Barbados, 1998). In 1970, heavy rains caused multiple flooding across the island killing three people and making 200 people homeless (UNDP, 1990); in 1995 the calypsonian De Great Carew was killed and 18 families made homeless during a flash flood in Weston, to the north of the urban corridor, with a cost of 4.8m Barbadian dollars (B$) (Advocate, 1995a); in October 1998, 30 people were made homeless as a result of storm water flooding (*Daily Nation*, 1998b).

The greatest source of catastrophic disaster risk comes from hurricanes. Barbados is at risk from June to November. From European settlement up to 2001, Barbados has been directly hit by three hurricanes: in 1780, when 4000 people died; 1831, when 2000 people died; and in 1955, when 57 lives were lost and 688 people made homeless (UNDP, 1990). Many more hurricanes have passed to the north of Barbados, and these near misses can also produce hazardous conditions. For example, Hurricane Gabrielle, 1989, passed 66km to the northeast but still produced wave heights in excess of 3m, leading to extensive flooding, beach erosion, property damage and vegetation loss, with waves reported to reach 40m landward of the mean high-water mark (Nurse, 1989). Barbados is also at risk from tsunamis and has been classified as being at moderate risk from earthquakes.

Total risk is growing with investment in oil and hazardous chemicals industries. Any additional risks must be played off against gains to the national economy both in terms of increased revenue and diversification in the economic base, both of which have the potential to reduce vulnerability overall. Despite this, the potential for complex disasters that may be triggered by human error or a natural hazard has grown with these new industrial developments. In addition to storage and plant facilities, transportation of oil and chemicals in coastal waters and on the roads has become increasingly frequent. Small-scale industries also contribute to environmental risk and degradation, especially through the dumping of waste into abandoned drinking water wells with subsequent risk of pollution of the water aquifer. Increasing volumes of solid waste and the limited land area available for dumping, the use of asbestos in public housing and high chemical inputs in agriculture are similarly of concern. High vehicle numbers have increased the risk of death and injury for pedestrians, cyclists and vehicle users alike, with 19 road deaths in 1998, up to 1 October.

DISASTER MITIGATION AND RESPONSE CAPACITY

Household insurance cover is available in Barbados. The minimum value of a house which can be insured is B$25,000. This excludes low-income house owners and squatters, who are doubly at risk: they live in the least resilient structures which are most prone to disaster damage but do not have insurance cover with which to offset disaster losses. For those households that can afford cover, the spiralling cost of insurance premiums has reduced its desirability. Between 1990 and 1994 there was a 400 per cent increase in the cost of household premiums for hurricane insurance (Government of Barbados, 1996). Although premiums have since been lowered, they remain well above 1990 levels.

New construction in areas prone to flooding has been legislated against. Flood risk zones are identified in the 1998 National Land-use Plan and the Flood Prevention Act, and can be used to prevent construction in these areas.

Unfortunately, the majority of these zones have been settled for many years. An opportunity to reduce physical vulnerability has been missed through the absence of enforceable housing construction standards in Barbados, although a new building regulatory body was proposed to government in 1998 (Government of Barbados, 1996). The physical vulnerability of Barbados's housing stock is indicated by the frequency with which people have been rehoused following beach erosion or flooding. In 1989, 31 households were rehoused from Speightstown (*Advocate*, 1989). Rehousing is typically a drawn-out process: in the Speightstown case this took five years to complete. There have been claims that money designated for flood relief has been used to buy votes, for example following flooding in St Peter in 1984 (*Advocate*, 1997).

The state is the principal actor in vulnerability reduction and in disaster response led by the Central Emergency Relief Organization (CERO). Formed in 1940, CERO has been successful at the national level, lobbying for its inclusion on a number of government committees and is a statutory consultee in any large development application, including the recent oil storage facilities discussed above. Partnerships with the private sector have been cultivated with representatives from the Barbados Chamber of Commerce on the National Disaster Committee and a special Media Sub-committee. Perhaps because there has not been a natural disaster in Barbados for more than 50 years, popular sentiment does not view hurricanes, drought or earthquakes as serious threats (CERO, 1998). One of CERO's strategies to make people aware of disaster risk has been to involve the local media. Television, radio and newspaper space is often dedicated to messages on disaster preparedness and mitigation, especially in the run-up to the hurricane season. The media has been criticized, however, for presenting hurricanes as a curiosity and an excitement during normal programming, which undermines the more serious message CERO is trying to convey.

CERO places great emphasis and resources into organizing community-level disaster preparedness. A network of local District Emergency Relief Organizations (DEROs) was set up in 1978 based on an idea first developed in Kenya. Each of Barbados's 28 electoral districts has its own DERO. The DEROs are community-run groups acting as local points of contact for residents, coordinators for small relief operations and as a pool of skilled persons in disaster preparedness and first aid. In many ways they fill the role that would have been played by local government, and indeed a similar system is run in Jamaica through local government offices. During everyday hazard events, local groups should be first to respond and should be aware of the location and needs of vulnerable individuals.

Local social capital and adaptive potential

In 1990, a review of disaster management in Barbados noted that some of the DEROs existed only on paper. In 1998, 12 local groups were registered but only six were active, with Bridgetown being particularly under-represented (CERO,

1998). Amongst the groups, there is a reliance on the central administration, with DEROs tending to relay requests for assistance on to the CERO rather than responding themselves; a symptom perhaps of a broader popular deference to central government. Findings of the 1990 report suggested that weak DEROs were a function of a lack of remuneration for members, lack of support from CERO and a lack of equipment and training. With the exception of remuneration, these issues have since been addressed by CERO, with little improvement in community participation. Several reasons for the inactivity of DEROs were given by DERO members, community leaders and officials from CERO. Some are specific to the DERO network, others suggest a more general malaise in social development:

- People simply do not feel that disaster preparedness should be a priority concern in their daily lives. It has been 50 years since Barbados experienced a nationwide disaster.
- Citizens tend to see environmental problems as being the responsibility of government. However, in disaster preparedness and immediate response, the state will be less efficient than local actors; reliance on the state is misguided in this instance and reduces local resilience.
- Historically, working-class people would look towards labour unions or MPs rather than community-based groups to represent their interests, reinforcing the belief that problem solving is best undertaken by actors external to the local community.
- Rapid material development in Barbados has enabled the privatization of leisure time, and a withdrawal of individuals from public space and community-based activities. One DERO member commented on the social changes that have followed material advancement, recalling that 'when I was young community activities were the best form of entertainment after work or school, now people prefer to stay home'.
- People increasingly identify themselves though their professional or political concerns and personal interests, rather than their place of residence, and this is reflected in group membership, with professional associations growing as local community associations decline in popularity.
- With social and technological modernization and economic prosperity, residential mobility has increased. The flow of individuals and families to and from international destinations for short or long periods of migration, together with the growth in commuting, has strained family and friendship ties and diluted communities.

CERO's director sums up the main impediments to building local resilience to disaster as: a lack of awareness of natural hazard, a lack of district preparedness groups, and a lack of community feeling. This all points to the need for incentives to encourage a greater involvement of citizens in community-led disaster preparedness planning. Underlying this need is the deeper observation that whilst social ties between households and neighbours at the local level – local social capital – may be present, they are not built up into developmentally oriented local organizations, such as DEROs. In Barbados, it seems that many people choose not to call on neighbours for help in times of emergency and instead, in the absence of local support organizations, rely upon CERO. This is exemplified repeatedly following local hazard events such as houses blowing off their foundations or local floods. It could be that local support networks are in place but that people prefer to seek help from the state, partly out of a sense that this is their right to claim. However, this is not the interpretation of CERO's director, who judges reliance upon centralized organizations like CERO to be indicative of a crisis in self-reliance within society. This is a tendency that could place severe limits on the coping capacity of individuals, communities and, by extension, the nation, should widespread disaster strike (CERO, 1998).

Non-governmental organizations and adaptive potential

There are few non-governmental actors with direct interests in community-based environmental hazard or vulnerability reduction. The only national NGO that claims disaster preparedness and response to be amongst its core concerns is the Barbados Red Cross Society. Formed in 1960, it is independent of government but collaborates with CERO. Symptomatic of the low levels of activity in Barbados's civil society, it has only 40 volunteers and no local branches. The group has little revenue and has not been able to make an impact at the community or national levels. It has a policy of promoting hazard preparedness but is unable to conduct community outreach due to funding constraints. Its most important contribution is in relief work: for example, in 1997 food hampers were given to 126 families who were victims of house fires. The national society also has reciprocal agreements with other Caribbean Red Cross societies that could be activated in times of emergency.

At the national scale, Barbados's stable political economy has attracted a number of regional civil society and inter-governmental institutions. This has established the presence of a cadre of skilled professionals in disaster mitigation and the heightened visibility of Barbados at the regional level. The Caribbean Disaster Emergency Response Agency (CDERA) (www.cdera.org) is just such an institution. Formed in 1991, it has 16 member states from the insular Caribbean, the Guyanas and Central America. CDERA acts to promote disaster preparation through the support of national disaster agencies, a role played by CERO in Barbados, and to coordinate international response following catastrophic disaster.

In a national review of civil society organizations completed as background research for this publication, three groups were identified that had gone some way to coupling community development with environmental issues and so offering scope for enhancing adaptive potential. These were the Future Centre Trust, the Abyssinian Youth Group and the Cornerstone Project. The leadership for all these organizations was either expatriate or had experienced long periods of life overseas in the UK, the USA or Jamaica. This reiterates the limited capacity of indigenous civil society leadership in Barbados, but also shows a positive outcome of the high population mobility found in this country, which has otherwise been identified as contributing to the erosion of community cohesiveness.

The Future Centre Trust (FCT) is a follow-up project run by the organizer of the NGO Forum of the UN Conference on Sustainable Development in Small Island States held in Barbados in 1994. It enjoys support from prominent and influential Barbadians. The principal aim is environmental education. Whilst the educational mission is being accomplished admirably, the FCT has experienced substantial problems in attracting grassroots interest. The project is seen by many as being a middle-class, expatriate or white Barbadian concern. Its director is a white, British expatriate, and although he is a well-known local figure and has been resident in Barbados for over 30 years, he is still viewed by many as an outsider. FCT has experienced particular problems in stimulating youth membership. Partly in response to this, FCT is planning to adopt a local economic trading scheme (LETS) as a first means of providing some payback for volunteer workers. Volunteers will provide labour or skills that will then be traded for cash or in kind (for example, organic produce) with FCT.

Those practising Rastafarianism claim that the religion promotes communitarianism and environmentalism, both qualities that could add to local adaptive potential. Two Rastafarian groups were identified that had translated these ideals into positive action. The Abyssinian Youth Group was founded in 1994 following the UN Conference on Sustainable Development in Small Island States, and in 1997 won the Ministry of Health environment award. It occupies 5 acres of land farmed organically for subsistence and for profit. The group has six members, all young men under 30 years of age, and an elder who heads the project. The elder, Ras Ibo, was born in North America and spent 15 years in Jamaica before settling in Barbados. The project has succeeded in building local social cohesion by mobilizing unemployed male youths, but has not yet gained the full trust of external organizations. Association with Rastafarianism in this case has been a burden for the organization, which has not been able to gain any training or financial support.

A second Rastafarian enterprise is the Cornerstone Project, managed by six members of a Rastafarian community, the Theocratic Government of His Majesty Haile Selassie I Churchical Order of the Nyhbinghi. The project occupies 3 acres of land. In 1994 farmers from the religious community were invited to the UN Conference on Sustainable Development in Small Island States. As a result of this exposure and of the possibility of funding from the United Nations Environment Programme (UNEP), in 1997 the group put together a project proposal which received a United Nations Development Programme (UNDP) Global Environment Facility Small Project Grant. The project has, however, been plagued by managerial problems which have resulted in little being produced despite the funding support. In response, members have attended business management classes run by an NGO, Pinelands Creative Workshop, funded by the Government of Barbados as part of a national poverty reduction campaign.

There are important linkages between these three projects and Pinelands Creative Workshop. A focal point for their formal establishment was the UN Conference on Sustainable Development in Small Island States. This shows the positive influence that such talking shops can have by exposing local social entrepreneurs to the ideas and experience of groups worldwide, and by creating an informal environment for networking amongst innovators within civil society. Whilst each of these projects has made a positive contribution to resilience by both building local social capital and enhancing the local environment, their outputs have been limited. There is no indication that these groups have acted as models for subsequent initiatives. Conversely, they have met with continued barriers to success, most importantly a failure to engage with the wider Barbadian society and to develop the management skills needed to sustain the projects over the long term.

Relationships between citizens and the state in Barbados clearly have a great impact on shaping the extent to which grassroots actors have been able to build up adaptive potential to environmental risk. In the following section we turn to a detailed case study of a low-income at-risk community in Bridgetown, and examine the opportunities and constraints that shape local adaptive potential.

THE PINE COMMUNITY

The Pine is on the eastern edge of Bridgetown (see Figure 5.1). The first residents were rehoused here from rural settlements in St Philip and St James as a consequence of flooding in the 1940s. Later public housing and a small middle-income private sector enclave development in the 1980s have added to the area's social heterogeneity. There is no squatting in the neighbourhood and all houses are linked to sewerage systems, drinking water and electricity networks, and are served by the city refuse collection service. Maintenance of public housing and physical infrastructure is the responsibility of a number of government agencies, most importantly the National Housing Corporation. The Pine returns a single MP to parliament but has shifted between the two dominant political parties and appears to value good service to the community above party loyalty.

A coral ridge dissects the area and is a source of flood risk during heavy rain. Storm water is drained by wells dug into the coral but these are often blocked by garbage or overgrown. Despite 77 per cent of residents being tenants of the state, maintenance of public housing had not been sufficient to prevent degradation of housing stock in the neighbourhood. The two most severe problems for public health have been the overflowing and leaking of sullage and sewerage waste water pipes, and the use of asbestos in dwelling construction. This was reflected in the most important environmental problems identified by respondents. Starting with the most frequently identified problem they were: inadequate maintenance of public space (which was seen as a health hazard), housing conditions, mosquitoes, garbage dumping, road traffic, flooding, garbage collection and sanitation.

The Pine has a population of 5000 and is one of the poorest areas in Bridgetown. This can be seen in Table 5.2, where 41 per cent of households are shown to have at least two dependants for every economically active member. Perhaps because the houses were state built and so have a minimum of two living rooms, internal densities were not high, with only 26 per cent of households having more than two people to each living room, reducing vulnerability to public health hazard. However, some vulnerability did arise from the large proportion of households with members over 65 years of age (22 per cent), who may be particularly susceptible to public health hazards and the impacts of natural disaster. This also suggests that any community-based approach to risk mitigation in the Pine would do well to include mechanisms for identifying where vulnerable older people live, their everyday needs and needs in times of disaster. Simply knowing where vulnerable old people live could enable home visits or help evacuation during hurricane warnings.

The community can be sub-divided into three social/spatial groups. First, the majority of residents are low-income; second, a relatively high-income enclave of privately owned housing; third, a low-middle-income group living in more recently constructed public housing located in the south of the Pine. Despite such social heterogeneity (to say nothing of the heterogeneity within these three groups) most people were long-term residents, providing the opportunity for social capital accumulation between households and across social/spatial groups, and potentially to provide a mechanism for mitigating vulnerability. The mean length of residence in the Pine was 20 years, and the mean length of residence in the present house was 18 years.

Perhaps surprisingly, given the high mean lengths of residence, informal social contact between residents was low (the lowest of the three case studies presented in this volume). Only 65 per cent of respondents had spoken to a neighbour on the day they were interviewed. Informal community activities were still reported: a third of respondents had painted houses with or shopped for a neighbour, and just under a quarter of respondents had cleaned the street or played sport with a neighbour. But membership of formal organizations was low. Church groups were the most commonly supported (48 per cent), although most churchgoers attended churches outside the Pine. The low number and small memberships of local interest groups contrast with the comparatively high proportion of respondents who were members of a political party (29 per cent). There was also a high level of knowledge about political issues: 89 per cent of respondents knew the name of their MP. This suggests that national politics was perceived by residents of the Pine as a principal mechanism for

Table 5.2 *Vulnerability and risk*

Variable	Indicator
Household asset profiles	
Economic resources	Workers/dependants ratio of 1/2 or more, 41%
	Rooms/residents ratio of 1/2 or more, 26%
Education of household head	Primary, 14%; secondary, 74%; tertiary, 12%
Overseas remittances	84% have relatives overseas, 29% receive remittances
Household structure	Common law, 8%; married, 21%, visiting, 9%;
	single, 54%; divorced, 5%; widowed, 2%
Demographic profile	Generations present: 1, 17%; 2, 54%; 3, 28%; 4, 1%
	Households with members aged less than five years, 26%
	Households with members aged more than 65 years, 22%
Dwelling tenure	Government landlord, 77%; own, 18%; private landlord, 5%
Length of residence in Pinelands	Mean, 20 years; 25% less than 10 years
Length of residence in house	Mean, 18 years; 25% less than 8 years
Ranked environmental problem	Overgrown public space, housing, mosquitoes, garbage dumping, road traffic, flooding, garbage collection, sanitation.

Note: All values are for positive responses. See Appendix 1 for data collection methods.

effecting change in their quality of life. High voter turn-outs at the last election support this conclusion (Table 5.3). The most important community association in the Pine is the Pinelands Creative Workshop (PCW), which has worked within the community for 30 years. The deep integration of this local organization into the lives of people living in the Pine was reflected in the high levels of awareness respondents had of PCW: most people had heard of the group and knew what it did. Just under a quarter of respondents had also been a client of one of PCW's services. Few people had attended disaster preparedness or crime prevention meetings, despite the range of public and civil society agencies that had organized these events. This again suggests a lack of community orientation amongst residents.

Community organization

When the Pine was first established in the 1940s, there was no community infrastructure, such as a community hall or youth club. The Pine soon gained a reputation as a poor quality living environment associated with crime and delinquency. The first community groups were formed in the 1960s and succeeded in constructing the Pinelands Community Centre, the Golden Rock Day Care Centre and a senior citizens' home. In 1975, the Pinelands Development Council (PDC) was formed out of a number of local organizations with the aim of coordinating work among local groups. In 1978

Table 5.3 *Social capital and adaptive potential*

Variable	Indicator
Informal social support	
Did you speak to your neighbour today?	65%
Do you exchange food with neighbours?	35%
Where does your closest friend live?	Pinelands, 34%; same house, 32%; Christ Church, 10%; Bridgetown, 10%; other parish, 16%; overseas, 2%
Communal activities:	
Cleaning the street	24%
Painting houses for Christmas	33%
Shopping for a neighbour	33%
Playing sport with a neighbour	23%
Clean public spaces	29%
Local community group member	
Member of a church	48%. 3% in Pinelands; 81% in Bridgetown; 6% in Christ Church; 10% in another parish
Member of a sport club	7%
Member of a community group	11%
Member of a *sou sou* (saving circle)	29%
Member of a political party	29%
Participation in elections	
Vote in last national election	80%
Client of civil society services	
Heard of PCW	96%
Know what PCW does	77%
Seen a PCW show	35%
Been a client of PCW	21%
Been to a disaster preparedness meeting	6%
Who organized the meeting?	CERO, 2%; work, 2%; PCW, 1%
Been to a crime prevention meeting	4%
Who organized this meeting?	Police, 2%; MP, 2%; youth services, 1%; PCW, 1%
Social distress	
Do you feel worried about crime in Pinelands?	39%

Note: All data are for positive responses. For notes on data collection methods see Appendix 1.

the PDC organized a series of dance and drama workshops which inspired the creation of the Pinelands Creative Workshop (PCW). The PCW soon took on the responsibilities of the PDC and, as other community groups were disbanded over time, the PCW has remained to become the principal local developmental organization in the Pine.

Today, the PCW is a unique institution in Barbados and is the most successful CBO in the country. PCW has evolved over the last 20 years and has diversified into a community business providing cultural shows for tourist events and cruise ships, which funds its programme of local social welfare and social development. Since 1997 it has also been brought into the national arena as an intermediary NGO managing a national urban poverty alleviation programme. Its principal role in this is to identify and work with building capacity in developmental community groups across Barbados and to provide management training for community businesses.

The organization has adopted a business model of management. Initially, leadership was elected and running costs for the organization were generated from membership fees. However, in 1987 the group decided that holding elections every two years was counter-productive, creating division, opening the group up to political capture and disrupting programmes. At this point leaders were made permanent and membership fees were abolished. A UNDP study identified this model and PCW's leadership as major factors in the success of PCW (UNDP, 1998a). Leaders feel that a key component in the organization's longevity has been its political neutrality. This has allowed residents of all political colours to support PCW, while at the same time the PCW has attracted support from various political administrations and government agencies.

PCW has three full-time paid staff working on community development programmes. All are recruited from and live within the Pine. This has been an important mechanism through which PCW has built social cohesiveness within its host community. A wide-ranging outreach programme has also proven a useful tool in developing skills, trust and community pride (UNDP, 1998a). In its community outreach work PCW has targeted youth (through sporting, dance and drama outreach), the elderly and extremely poor (through its meals-on-wheels service), young entrepreneurs (through business training and micro-financing) and students (through a fellowship scheme and work training placements). PCW has also been active beyond the local community by consulting with less developed community groups and new leaders.

The PCW operates a DERO comprised of a network of 31 street officers. These officers identify vulnerable people (aged, disabled) and sources of hazard (trees, blocked culverts and frequently flooded areas). This information can then either be acted on by the street officers themselves, or fed centrally into the PCW for more formal action, such as lobbying government for housing repairs or including an elderly resident in PCW's meals-on-wheels service. The street officers also distribute information and provide local training in disaster preparedness. PCW and CERO have a close working relationship resulting in a number of unsafe dwellings being improved, the cleaning of drains in flood-prone areas and training in local disaster preparedness. Somewhat in contradiction to the decline in activity nationally amongst the DERO network, PCW has found that the local disaster response unit has been a useful way of bringing a wide range of residents together and identifying people's environmental concerns, and that it has offered a mechanism for developing social capital at the street level. This experience has prompted PCW to recommend registration as a DERO as a way to mobilize support to other community organizations hoping to strengthen a community base. A community group in an adjacent low-income district of Bridgetown has taken up this advice and will be the first new DERO group to be registered for many years, going against a trend in declining DERO activity. This also suggests that one way of increasing activity amongst the DERO network may be to more closely integrate DERO groups with any other local development groups that may exist.

The PCW also builds resilience to environmental hazard through its everyday lobbying of government departments responsible for basic service provision. Negotiating with public officials to reverse decisions to disconnect power from households that have been unable to pay bills, or complaining about delays in housing repairs are its stock-in-trade. PCW also lobbies the government over more strategic issues affecting the environmental quality of the Pine. At the time of this investigation, for example, PCW leaders were lobbying the National Housing Corporation to have asbestos roofing removed and road traffic calming measures put in place. A final way in which PCW has been successful in confronting vulnerability has been through its meals-on-wheels scheme. Some 77 seniors are supported through this scheme, which delivers meals twice weekly. Food is donated by restaurants, retailers and wholesalers in Bridgetown. Raising and collecting donations, cooking and distributing food is undertaken by volunteers (Pelling, 1998).

The major constraint on PCW has been relationships with public agencies that at times have become confrontational. For example, in 1996, PCW complained to the Attorney General that funds allocated to it and other community groups from the UN Drug Control Programme were being held by the government (Grant, 1998). Similarly, during a dengue fever epidemic in 1995, repeated calls for assistance from the Sanitation Service Authority to clear garbage and plants from public space were not replied to, despite PCW having 'established environmental committees which will oversee the area once we get the necessary help from government departments. Residents will do the maintenance themselves, we just need assistance' (*Advocate Newspaper*, 1995b).

Perhaps the greatest constraint on PCW is a lack of human resources. Given PCW's policy of recruiting staff from within the Pine, there has been a problem in identifying people for middle-management responsibilities. A number of very able and dedicated staff exist within the organization, but they are already overburdened. A recent additional pressure on management staff has been the secondment of leaders to advisory positions within the government. In October 1998, Hamilton Lashley, a key community leader involved in PCW and its predecessor, the Pinelands Development Council, and from 1994 the MP for Pinelands, joined the government as an advisor on poverty. The director of PCW joined the Ministry of Social Transformation as an advisor in poverty alleviation in 2000. Whilst both appointments are well made and both men are experts in this field, it remains to be seen whether the impact is negative or positive for the PCW and the Pine community as a whole. In a wider perspective this could also be seen as a continuation of the administration's tendency to offer leaders from civil society or opposition parties roles within the government. This does allow such individuals access to national policy-makers, but it also runs the risk of capturing the agenda of civil society and opposition political groups, undermining the authority of potentially critical voices from outside the ruling party.

SUMMARY

Of the three case studies presented in this volume, Bridgetown, Barbados, is perhaps the most complex. The non-linearity of development outcomes can be seen in the inability of Barbados to reduce risk despite its recent economic growth. At the national, city and local levels, exposure to environmental risk has increased through a post-independence economic modernization project that has degraded the environment. At the same time, development has generated an economic surplus, much of which has been invested by the state to provide basic environmental infrastructure and services to enhance security. An example of this contradiction in Bridgetown comes from the difficulties urban planners have in resolving the illegal settlement of the Belle water aquifer conservancy. Because the squatters do not have access to sanitation they present a risk to the aquifer, which supplies drinking water to most of Bridgetown. In a water-scarce nation like Barbados, contamination of such an environmental resource could have wide-ranging consequences – over and above the more immediate public health risk. The state has the resources to supply sanitation to the squatter community, which would remove the wider public health risk, but at the same time provide an incentive for yet more squatters to invade conservancy land.

There are signs that open democracy in post-colonial Barbados, which has gone hand-in-hand with economic progress, is suffering from a crisis of participation. This was first identified in 1991 from a decline in the proportion of votes cast by the electorate in national elections. Young people were the least likely to vote. Whilst this is a cause for concern in itself, it is linked to a deeper malaise in the Barbadian polity which has seen popular participation in civil society organizations wane and a degradation of local social capital, as individuals' leisure time has become privatized and places of residence are no longer a focus for community. The failure of the DERO network is an example of this kind of loss of adaptive potential that can accompany successful macro-economic development. One way beyond this impasse may be to consolidate place-based community activity. This opens up the possibility of tying DERO functions onto more general community development organizations, such as youth or women's groups.

At the national level, disaster mitigation and preparedness is taken seriously by the state. The CERO is in many ways a model organization that has been well integrated into the workings of government and has links with the private sector. Again though, it is the absence of a strong civil society and the lack of incentives for grassroots actors to participate in disaster preparedness that is the biggest single barrier to further vulnerability reduction. Individuals turn first to state organizations or their local MP rather than to self-help solutions. During times of disaster it is likely that the state and its agents may not be able to function and so the capacity of communities to recover from disaster will be shaped largely by the capability of local institutions.

It is difficult to see how a population that has seen the state bring in economic development and a stable democracy can be weaned of its dependency. This is particularly the case when the lifestyles and cultural tastes that have accompanied modernization have tended to erode social ties and foster individualism. But examples of good practice in community-led environmental risk reduction do exist under these conditions. The example of PCW has survived and remains strong, with an independent source of income and a multitude of links into different groups which make up its host community in the Pine. From its origins in the 1960s, this group has grown to the point where its role as a local advocate and social development organization has been added to by its new role as a national-level actor in poverty alleviation. This is certainly an exciting development for PCW. However, a note of caution should be sounded. In following the global trend for participatory urban governance, the offer for closer partnership between PCW and the government of Barbados could undermine the very foundations that have allowed PCW to operate so effectively for so long. In coming closer to the government, PCW is in danger of loosing its independence, and in taking on the role of a national-level actor in urban poverty alleviation it is in danger of losing sight of its origins as an organization that has come out of the people of the Pine and which aims to support improvements in the quality of life for those who live in the Pine.

A final contradiction is the organizational strength of PCW given the apparently low levels of formal social capital that were observed in the Pine. There are a number of explanations for this. First, it may be that PCW has grown to monopolize local formal organization so that any individuals or groups wishing to participate in local developmental work tend to do so through PCW rather than on their own. If this is the case it may be a force for enhancing the inclusivity and representativeness of PCW and the effectiveness of local organizations, which would be strengthened by being able to access the human and physical resources of PCW. Second, this contradiction also suggests that the survival of CBOs like PCW may not be contingent upon local reserves of social capital as they were defined in this study. This in turn weakens the common assumption that local organizations are a good surface indicator of social capital, and suggests that formal organization and informal or cognitive forms of social capital can operate independently of one another.

Chapter 6

Post-socialism and Barriers to Building a Civil Society: Georgetown, Guyana

INTRODUCTION

'The agents of change are not here' (Becker, 1999).

'Politicians fan the flame of bitterness amongst the people' (Blair, 1999).

Under state-centred models of development, civil society is viewed at best with scepticism and at worst is brutally repressed. A minimum degree of freedom of association is necessary for civil society organizations to flourish and this has been sadly lacking from many developing countries that have chosen a state-centred development path. Under such conditions, the potential for local community action to reduce disaster vulnerability or loss are limited. However, in the wave of democratization that has swept over the global South since the 1990s, many former centralized regimes have begun to adopt democratic norms and procedures. In this chapter we ask, have such reforms been sufficient to open up political space for non-state actors to confront disaster vulnerability?

Guyana's experience is presented here as a case study of the kinds of barriers to building a civil society that can inhibit resilience to environmental hazard. These barriers are indicative of a country that has passed through a centralized and so-called 'socialist' political regime form. Contemporary weakness in civil society and capacity to manage environmental hazard are presented as an outcome of development history (summed up by the intellectual flight that Becker observes), as well as a product of contemporary structural barriers to social capital and civil society formation (Blair's 'flame of bitterness').

A background discussion of Guyana's developmental history is presented first together with some comments on the nature of risk and the scope and scale of human vulnerability in urban settlements. Georgetown's adaptive potential is then assessed with reference to state, municipal and civil society actors engaged in reducing losses from everyday and catastrophic environmental hazard. A detailed case study of an inner-city low-income quarter, Albouystown, is then used to examine in more detail the contemporary barriers that shape the kinds of social capital found in vulnerable communities.

A LEGACY OF MISTRUST: GUYANA'S DEVELOPMENT HISTORY

Shortly after independence in 1966, Guyana embarked on a path of so-called 'cooperative socialism', resulting in an increasingly centralized and radicalized political regime. This regime lasted until the late 1980s, by which point Guyana's economy was in crisis and physical and social infrastructures were on the brink of collapse (Ferguson, 1995; Thomas, 1995). Political repression and the state control of production meant that social capital and civil society were undeveloped and the private sector was stifled. The dominant structures and styles of government policy-making and project management fostered grassroots dependence on vertical lines of clientelism with national political figures. The dominance of the predominantly Afro-Guyanese People's National Congress (PNC) and the marginalization of the predominantly Indo-Guyanese People's Progressive Party (PPP) deepened the racial character of national and local politics. This was reinforced by the racial division of labour (Afro-Guyanese, public; Indo-Guyanese, private) and settlement patterns (Afro-Guyanese, urban; Indo-Guyanese, rural).

Free and fair national elections were held in 1992 and 1998, and local elections in 1994. However, in 1999, the postponing of local elections at the request of the opposition PNC indicated the continuing fragility of Guyana's democratic transition. Some macro-economic recovery was experienced, associated with an SAP, which was reintroduced at this time. But enhanced macro-economic stability was paid for in increased inequality, poverty and environmental degradation. The costs have been high.

In 1992 the Indo-Guyanese-backed PPP came into power and has retained the presidency to date. Despite this change, there has been only a little deviation in the pattern and culture of local and national politics. The continuing racial bias in politics (to which the main opposition parties also contribute), partisan decision-making in the public sector and foot-dragging on constitutional reform have constrained the evolution of the democratic principals of citizen participation and fair inter-party competition. This has also caused a blurring of the divisions between and roles of public sector and civil society, with key actors in government holding influential positions in developmental NGOs and CBOs (UNDP, 1996).

Guyana's electoral system is based upon proportional representation. There are elected local and national governments, and an intervening layer of regional government appointed by the national government. Importantly, at the local level the electorate can vote only for the party of its choice, with individual representatives appointed by officials from the national party. Given the racial bias in voting, accountability for members of local government points towards the national party organization rather than the local electorate. Indeed, local and regional government have historically acted as arms of top–down central government control rather than as the means of representing local communities. The six largest settlements, including Georgetown, elect a city council and bypass the regional tier. Since 1994, Georgetown City Council (GCC) has been led by Hamilton Green's minority opposition party Good and Green Guyana (GGG), with the ruling party PPP and main opposition party PNC also well represented on the city council.

Despite a rapid increase in the number of nationally identified NGOs, rising from 300 to 780 between 1992 and 1998 (UNDP, 1998c), civil society continues to be weak. Most NGOs are fragile institutions, led by one or two key people. NGOs are reactive rather than proactive, responding to the news agenda and funding opportunities. Weaknesses in civil society, and the slowness of change in government and the public sector, are partly explained by a lack of human capital in Guyana. Many of those individuals who might otherwise have pushed for reform in Guyana have migrated overseas. Consequently, despite popular acknowledgement of the problems of racism and centralized control that pervade many of the institutions of Guyanese life, the agents of change who could orchestrate a move beyond this impasse appear to be missing or silenced.

Some 96 per cent of civil society organizations define themselves as service or development-based, such as parent-teachers associations, religious groups, youth clubs and neighbourhood development associations. This contrasts with the low numbers of groups concerned with advocacy or political reform. The disproportionate representation of non-political groups is indicative of the top–down process through which many groups have been formed. Many have been generated from opportunistic responses to calls from government for local leaders (often from established political groups) to form 'non-political' community development committees to access funds from national-level funding bodies targeting community-sponsored development, funded principally by the Social Impact Amelioration Project (SIMAP) (World Bank) and the Basic Needs Trust Fund (Caribbean Development Bank). The former was established in 1993 to fund projects aimed at ameliorating the social impacts of structural adjustment, the latter funds small bids from community-based groups for infrastructure rehabilitation. Most active community-level organizations continue to rely on these funding sources, or on larger NGOs, and few have become self-financing (Pelling, 1998).

The small number of reliable NGOs and representative CBOs has confounded the work of international donors. Responding to the New Policy agenda of the mid-1990s and beyond, non-state actors were increasingly the target of development aid provided by international organizations such as the Caribbean Development Bank (CDB) and the Canadian International

Development Agency (CIDA). These international organizations are under pressure to show their disbursement of development funds through civil society actors and have consequently sought out organizations to fund. Critically, these disbursements were not supported by coordinated programmes of training in project management, financial accountability or leadership and without putting in place mechanisms for the verification of the representativeness or political neutrality of non-state actors. The result has been a high failure rate for community groups and a reinforcing of established structures of power amongst elites at the local level (Pelling, 1998). Both these outcomes allow vulnerability to persist in the face of increased funding for projects ostensibly designed to enhance local-level resilience and support the democratic transition.

In a review of the non-governmental sector, the UNDP (1998c) identified three key technical problems that have hindered growth. First, there is a lack of human skills to source and administer project funds, with only the most visible and well-connected organizations benefiting from increased civil society funding by international organizations. Second, there is an inability to meet the high cost of officially registering as non-state organizations: again, it is the smaller and less well-skilled organizations that are at a disadvantage. Without registering it is difficult to obtain international funding. Third, the enabling environment is poor. In particular, there is no umbrella organization to represent non-state actors at a national level. Recognizing these weaknesses encouraged CIDA in 1997 to shift from the direct funding of non-state actors to fund a Building Community Capacity Programme. Under this programme, CIDA provides training in management and financial accounting as well as exposing leaders to less centralized and more democratic and inclusive models of leadership and priority setting. The programme is working with 20 NGOs, including the Guyana Red Cross (CIDA, 1999).

URBAN POVERTY AND HAZARD

In 1993, 29 per cent of Georgetown's residents fell below the poverty line. This proportion reportedly decreased to 16 per cent in 1999 (UNDP, 1999b). As with all poverty-line data, these figures should be viewed with some scepticism. Un(der)employment and informality are rife in Georgetown, and the number of illegally constructed households has escalated rapidly in the last ten years (see Table 6.1). Both these more qualitative indicators suggest that the formal economy is unable to sustain Georgetown's population. Whilst decreasing proportions of Georgetown's population may meet the economic criteria to be classified as economically poor, a large number, perhaps the majority of residents, are 'getting by' more than they are 'moving on'. Housing costs in Georgetown are high by Guyanese standards, accounting for 13 per cent of total household expenditures; this is almost double the national average (UNDP, 1999b). Despite this, Georgetown's housing stock is of low quality: 80 per cent of dwellings are wooden, 90 per cent have zinc sheet roofs and 33 per cent are over 24 years old. Few dwellings have been adequately maintained over the last two decades due to declining incomes and absentee ownership. Most households rent from a private landlord (46 per cent) or are owner-occupiers (43 per cent), 5 per cent rent from the state and 6 per cent live rent-free (1991 housing census). Squatting on state-owned undeveloped and abandoned cane plantations is increasingly common. These lands are prone to flooding and residents are made vulnerable through a lack of basic infrastructure and health services (Pelling, 1997).

Despite the central role of the state in planning and managing development, the public sector is weak. A lack of sufficiently trained personnel, reliable data for planning and economic and infrastructure resources has led to the absence of strategic policy and a crisis management approach to environmental infrastructure provision. Sea defences and storm drains lie at the heart of urban Guyana's flood prevention system but often receive maintenance only after a break or blockage has resulted in local flooding. In Georgetown, overlapping responsibilities and unclear lines of command between national and municipal authorities further weaken the system of infrastructure delivery: for example, the provision of drinking water in Georgetown is the joint responsibility of the national-level Guyana Water Authority and the Georgetown Sewerage and Water Commissioners (GS&WC). Such constraints jeopardize the provision of drinking water in Georgetown. Although the proportion of yards or houses with water connections is high (about 90 per cent in Georgetown), water quality is low. Water is contaminated by asbestos from piping, as well as by sewerage and untreated water sucked in through cracked pipes during the frequent periods of low water pressure.

Further health risk comes from dysfunctional sewerage and solid waste collection services. About 10 per cent of households in Georgetown share a toilet, many pit latrines and septic tanks are in disrepair and the central Georgetown sewerage system is in urgent need of rehabilitation. Only about 9 per cent of residents have a regular garbage collection service. Solid waste accumulation is a health hazard. Clogged drains are a main cause of local urban floods. Public service provision is 'in such a dilapidated state that it is beyond repair or requires urgent and comprehensive rehabilitation' (World Bank, 1992, p15).

Bad management and degraded infrastructure have also made Georgetown susceptible to more widespread disaster – drought, flood and fire. The most serious drought to date occurred during the 1997–1998 El Niño event (*Stabroek News*, 1999a). In the last quarter of 1997, surface water supply from the GS&WC was reduced from 10–12m gallons/day to 1–2m gallons/day. In response, the Civil Defence Commission (CDC) mounted Operation Mellon, which used water trucks to distribute an additional 20,000 gallons/day of water to affected parts of the city (CDC, 1998). Catastrophic fires are historical due to the judicious spacing of wooden buildings and an expansion of the city fire service. Contemporary fire hazard has tended to be restricted to individual or at most neighbouring buildings.

Flooding is the most important environmental hazard in Georgetown. The proximate causes of flooding are found in the everyday environmental stresses of inadequate solid waste management, drainage, drinking water provision and sanitation. Georgetown is potentially at risk from flooding from three sources: the intrusion of water from the Atlantic Ocean and Demerara River, which form the city's northern and western boundaries; the overflowing or breaching of water conservancies lying to the south of the city; and the accumulation of rainwater and overflowing of drains within the city. The first of these sources of risk has largely been mitigated through the construction of sea and river defences, which remain sturdy. This is not the case for water conservancy earth dams, which have suffered from 40 years of neglect. Neglect is also behind the low capacity of the city's drainage system to cope with storm rainfall, and this is exacerbated by a reliance on gravity drainage which can only operate at low tide.

Flooding related to inadequate city drainage has only been noted in the second half of the 20th century and can be explained by the badly managed urbanization process. Impervious areas in Georgetown increased by 50 per cent between 1963 and 1993, raising the volume of runoff channelled through Georgetown's drainage system. At the same time, drainage capacity was lost due to the infilling of drains, inadequate maintenance of existing drains, the use of drains for informal refuse disposal and the use of drainage reserves for informal housing and petty agriculture, which made drain cleaning more difficult. Since 1989, uncontrolled urban expansion into unserviced areas has similarly increased the risk of flooding from high rainfall. Sea-level rise will further reduce the efficiency of the city's gravity drainage system and may induce a rise in ground-water level. A sea-level rise of 1m will cause the permanent inundation of the entire developed coastline (Diaram, 1999). Climate change adds further uncertainty to hydraulic systems, with global warming being associated with increased precipitation (Fowler and Hennessy, 1995). In 1996, a national emergency was declared in response to flood rains due to La Niña, which produced more than double the mean monthly rainfall totals in May and June (Khan, 1998)

Flooding occurs several times a year in Georgetown. Between 1 January 1990 and 30 November 1999, the press reported on 29 floods in Georgetown. Halcrow (1994) ranked Albouystown as being at high flood risk.

URBAN DEVELOPMENT AND GOVERNANCE

Administration of drainage and irrigation, sea and river defences, roads and health services is a complex mix, with responsibilities being shared between line ministries of central government, the GCC, neighbouring regional administrations and semi-autonomous public sector agencies such as the

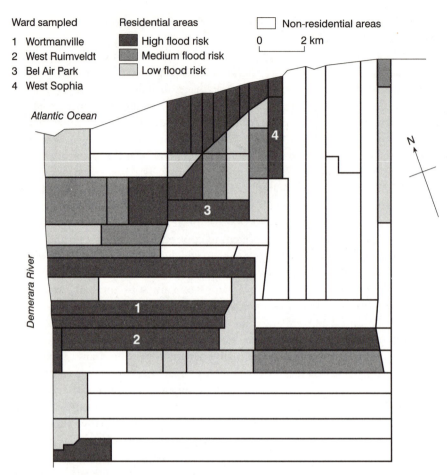

Ward sampled

1 Wortmanville
2 West Ruimveldt
3 Bel Air Park
4 West Sophia

Residential areas

High flood risk
Medium flood risk
Low flood risk

Non-residential areas

0   2 km

Atlantic Ocean

Demerara River

Source: Based on Halcrow (1994)

Figure 6.1 *Flood risk, Georgetown*

GS&WC. A small number of civil society actors also play a role in providing education, health care and charitable relief such as feeding school children, and more recently the Private Sector Commission has commented on city administration and policy.

Access to safely constructed housing and to land that is not at risk from natural hazard is becoming increasingly rare in urban Guyana. This is despite only 10 per cent of the national land area having been developed for agriculture or settlement. There is no shortage of adequate land, nor the materials with which to restore or build safe housing, but there is a shortage of entitlements, which means a growing number of people are denied access to these resources. The main reason for this is that the costs of legal shelter solutions are beyond the reach of lower-income households without substantial subsidies, which the government itself cannot afford (Payne, 1996).

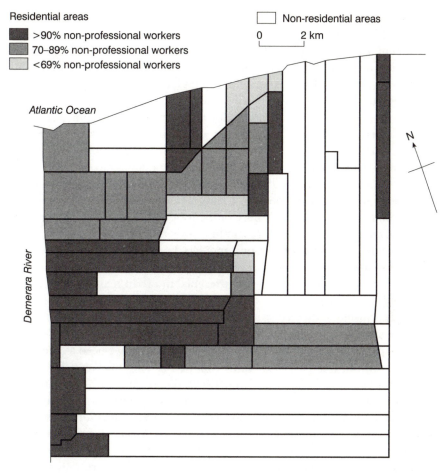

Residential areas

■ >90% non-professional workers
▨ 70–89% non-professional workers
□ <69% non-professional workers

□ Non-residential areas

0   2 km

Atlantic Ocean

Demerara River

N

Source: National Housing and Population Census, 1991

Figure 6.2 *Economic status, Georgetown*

Access to housing in the formal sector is difficult for those on a low income, with private rental accommodation being the dominant form of housing in Georgetown (46 per cent in the 1991 census). However, a combination of rent control and macro-economic problems since the 1970s have meant that a large proportion of rental stock has not been maintained for many years. The public provision of urban infrastructure and services in Georgetown has declined along with housing over the last 25 years. Two recent attempts at improving the delivery of services in Georgetown have been undermined by political competition between the city and national government. First, since 1993 the Inter-American Development Bank has funded an Urban Rehabilitation Programme to finance improvements to roads, drainage, solid waste management and sanitation in Georgetown. The programme requires consent between the city and national government before works can begin. It was not until 2002 that consensus was reached between the GCC and national government, largely for political reasons.

Tension between central government and the GCC is long-standing, with the GCC having been dissolved in 1994 and replaced by an interim government appointed by the president. There are claims from the GCC that central government has withheld subventions for infrastructure development projects and has even failed to pay rates for government buildings. There are counterclaims by the national government that the GCC is unable to manage funds transparently. No independently audited city budget has been presented since 1987 (*Stabroek News*, 1999b). Tensions between the city and national governments are again symptomatic of the greater problem of partisan politics, which is undermining Guyana's development opportunities. Instead of being the central coordinator of development in Georgetown, the GCC has become a partisan and ineffective institution, and has been marginalized by central government and the public, who increasingly fail to pay rates.

The beginnings of a civil society presence in urban management can be seen. The Private Sector Commission, an umbrella NGO for private business in Guyana, specifically addressed issues of poor city management in a press release on 13 October 1999: 'The current arrangements in place for the country's capital are clearly not working... It may well be, for instance, that we need a completely different form of city government, free of politics and managerial structure that seems to paralyze it' (*Stabroek News*, 1999c, p3). Community involvement in local management is, however, very limited. The exception to this is in high-income residential areas with access to economic and professional resources, where some infrastructure maintenance can be undertaken at private expense (Pelling, 1997). Outside the central urban areas, community groups are more common. Many have been formed since 1992, as a direct response to the availability of funding for community-sponsored development projects in peri-urban and rural areas (Pelling, 1998). National funding agencies (SIMAP and Basic Needs) that manage these programmes are prohibited from funding projects in Georgetown because of potential overlap with the planned Urban Rehabilitation Programme, which misses an opportunity for building local human and social capital. Some exceptions have been made by SIMAP for local infrastructure rehabilitation projects, but these are not commonly open to applications from community groups.

Lack of access to and the poor quality of housing in the formal sector has led to a rapid expansion in informal sector squatting (Table 6.1). But despite a policy of squatter settlement regularization being in place since the mid-1990s, not one plot had been regularized by 1999. As a result it is impossible for households in these settlements to obtain access to formal credit to improve the conditions of their housing or environments. This is partly because the Central Housing and Planning Authority (CHPA) has been unwilling to grant titles, and secondly because some residents have been unwilling to realign their existing plots or

Table 6.1 *Squatting in Greater Georgetown*

Year	Source	Squatter households per thousand households
1980	Population census (1991)	1/1000
1990	Pelling (1992)	35/1000
1995	Payne (1996)	70/1000
1999	Scott (1999)	9283 units in Region 4

buildings. Any attempt by the authorities to impose a solution would create more problems, whilst accession to intransigence only increases the difficulties and costs of regularization. No organizational channel, such as an NGO, presently exists through which the authorities can seek to achieve a compromise.

Despite a history of collective response to environmental risk in the early squatter settlements (Pelling, 1997), over time organization has become more fractured. It is important to understand why squatting groups have not been able to organize because, together with low-income private rental households such as those predominant in Albouystown, they are the most vulnerable to flood hazard. The Sophia squatting area to the east of Georgetown is the largest, and has been organized by the CHPA into a number of blocks, each with smaller sub-divisions or 'fields'. The CHPA has tried to encourage each field to have its own representative community group, but this has not happened. Some fields have very active community leaders, but most have inactive groups or are effectively groupless.

In addition to competing personal issues, such as leaders needing to invest time in organizing, visiting the CHPA etc, as well as earning a living and maintaining a family, the principal barrier to community organization has been a conflict between local and national political activists and community organizers. This problem was perhaps the major concern of community leaders from the squatter settlements interviewed as background for this chapter. Typical views are that 'They [political activists] try to bombard you in any possible way, we try to keep clean... Its a mixed community and we don't want racialism, we want people to understand unity' (Lewis, 1999a); or that 'in the early stages [of establishing the squatter settlement] there was much unity amongst the people', but before the 1992 election the devil got going and politics came into Sophia' (Blair, 1999).

Community leaders identified a number of strategies which they felt had been employed by political activists to undermine community organization and force people to rely upon political patronage. Tactics included:

* Breaking trust between the community and its leaders:

    'The politicians tried to come in and discredit the results [of the community group elections]. People support the group not the politicians' interference... they tried to set up their own body' (Robb, 1999).

- Infiltrating and breaking up community groups:

  'politicians intend to penetrate this area. The organization has people who are on the committee not working for the committee [which resulted in the formation of a splinter community group and]... disrupted relations with donors' (Thompson, 1999).

  'some leaders are so mixed up with the politicians that they end up tarnishing their image in the community and the politician has them' (Blair, 1999).

- Promising help before elections:

  'running up to election time organization becomes more difficult... campaigning technique is negative. The grassroots politicians will find out who has a problem' (Blair, 1999).

- Blocking relationships with potential funders by controlling information:

  'Funding agencies want to deal with people, not parties. Politicians get in-between so, for example, they make it difficult to know about opportunities for funding' (Cameron, 1999).

- In addition, the system itself is liable to discrediting community leaders. For example, politicians or government officials will promise something and then not deliver. This is felt to be just another part of the political culture that community organizers have to confront:

  'Putting people against one another. Discrediting leaders by saying yes, then another person says no about it' (Bynoe, 1999).

The work of political activists is rooted in the racial political culture of Guyana. Squatting communities are especially important to national and city politicians, not only because of their large electorate but also because of their evolving community structures, where political allegiance has yet to be constructed and where communities could vote against race lines. As an organizer of a women's group (Claudette, 1999) put it, 'Politicians are scared of the organization'.

A key tactic of community groups aiming to weaken the influence of political activists is to have mixed-race leadership (Robb, 1999). Some leaders have also attended a leadership training course run by the University of Guyana and funded by UNDP. This has had a great impact on the ability of leaders to identify and confront political influence, and recognize and separate their own private goals from public goals in the community or their groups.

The effects of self-help on physical vulnerability are very variable, with some fields having road access and piped drinking water, and others having only mud banks for access, drainage ditches for bathing and rainwater to drink. This is partly a function of the age of the settlements. The originally settled fields have passed through a period of intense community action including drain clearing, bridge building and road repairing (Pelling, 1992, 1997) as is common in self-help settlements. Promises made by the government since 1992 that land title will be available have still not been fulfilled, and this has made people reluctant to continue working until the government moves further (Sukul, 1999). Lack of government assistance in the face of rhetorical support for participatory development has also alienated residents, who felt the government owed them something: 'they want to work you, and use you, in spite of the fact' (Chan, 1999). Lack of plot ownership not only prevents householders from acquiring loans from banks, but is also seen as a reason not to apply to funding agencies (SIMAP, Basic Needs) (James, 1999).

In Georgetown, the self-help/participatory model of urban development and disaster mitigation does not seem to be functioning. Scope for manoeuvre in the current political climate is slight, with political competition between leaders at the national level and an aversion to local non-political organization at the grassroots level acting as a double barrier to political reform.

DISASTER MITIGATION AND RESPONSE CAPACITY

The lead disaster response agency is the Civil Defence Commission (CDC). The CDC was disbanded in 1995 as part of public sector restructuring, only to be reinstated in 1996 in response to a national emergency caused by flooding of coastal areas triggered by La Niña. The lack of preparedness for natural disasters in 1996 can be seen in the CDC's own critical conclusions:

> 'Mobilization of food relief was initially slow because of the lack of functional disaster response capacity and absence of stored food. Initially there was too much uncoordinated relief activity in the disaster areas... Mobilization of NGO participation was sub-optimal and inconsistent. Regional disaster relief responses were sub-optimal. Coordination of foreign donor aid to disaster response activities needed better organization and more realistic rules of procedure' (CDC, 1997, p18).

Guyana's second national emergency triggered by a natural disaster was called in response to drought and fires triggered by the 1997 El Niño event. The CDC was active in coordinating responses in rural and urban areas. Georgetown's drinking water supply was critically reduced during this period, and the CDC coordinated Operation Mellon to distribute additional water by truck within the city. The role of the CDC in the 1997 drought and 1996 flood was limited to a national-level response, with no public sector organization focusing on prevention or preparedness. This is symptomatic of a wider institutional orientation in the public sector, which is geared towards responding to emergency needs rather than maintaining or strengthening infrastructure to mitigate risk, and which displays a reluctance to support independent community initiatives. The absence of regional or community relief organizations during the 1997 drought was identified as being particularly problematic because it delayed the processing of claims for relief aid (CDC, 1999).

Four non-governmental actors have been involved in disaster response: the Guyana Relief Council (GRC), the Guyana Red Cross, Food for the Poor and the Beacon Foundation. Formal independence of some of these organizations from the state is comparatively recent, and they all share a tendency towards centralized management and a primary focus on disaster relief with little evidence of efforts to support vulnerability prevention and leadership at the local level. Food for the Poor and the Beacon Foundation are broadly concerned with poverty amelioration and have extensive networks to distribute food parcels and donate food to disaster relief missions.

The GRC specializes in providing relief to families following house fires in Georgetown. House fires are most common amongst low-income households who tend to reside in old wooden rental dwellings, and especially in single parent families where young children are left at home during the day. The GRC receives 20 per cent of its management costs from the government but is otherwise self-financing, drawing on fund-raising and donations from individuals, local businesses, diplomats etc. Until 1994 the GRC was run as a para-statal organization under the office of the prime minister, and problems of aid capture were recorded (GRC, 1999). In 1994 the GRC was registered under the Friendly Societies Act. It now operates independently of government although a close association remains, with the prime minister's wife being its president. There are however no claims from the press of impartiality. The GRC does not means-test its beneficiaries and hopes to avoid claims of partiality by helping everyone who asks. Financial transparency has become a key issue with funding being increasingly reliant upon private sector donations.

The Red Cross has been represented in Guyana since 1948, with varying degrees of independence. It contributes to national emergency relief projects as well as running training courses in first aid and sexual health. A major challenge has been to stimulate community-level interest. There are eight groups nationwide, with five in Georgetown. More training is needed for local groups and it was felt that difficulties in generating local support were symptoms of Guyana's developmental history: 'people are lacking in confidence, and the history of dependency stops people from coming forward and leading... there is a need for training in self-esteem for young people' (Guyana Red Cross, 1999). At the national level, NGOs lack skills and personnel. This has been addressed partly in the Red Cross by the building up of financial auditing skills as part of the CIDA-funded Building Community Capacity Programme.

ALBOUYSTOWN

Albouystown is located in the south of Georgetown and is one of the few racially mixed areas of the city (Dick, 1991, in Trotz, 1995). The 1981 census recorded 35 per cent of the population as Indo-Guyanese, a high proportion for a ward in the largely Afro-Guyanese Georgetown. Historically, Albouystown has been the destination of rural migrants. The opening up of squatting areas in eastern Georgetown has provided an alternative destination for migrants and also attracted some of Albouystown's longer-term residents. As a consequence, the population of Albouystown declined from 8000 in 1980 to 6000 in 1990 (1981, 1991 census data). Despite this, Albouystown remains one of the most densely populated wards in the city (Trotz, 1995).

Demand for affordable housing in Georgetown in the 20th century led to the unauthorized sub-division of dwellings. Tenement yards and range houses (consisting of a building divided into several one-room flats, which share common toilet and bath facilities – if they have any) and a large number of internally sub-divided rental properties are commonplace in Albouystown and other low-income inner-city wards (Pelling, 1992). Environmental services are woefully inadequate. Trotz noted that:

> *'garbage collection was non-existent, the drainage and sewerage systems have virtually broken down... Piped water in houses has been a rarity for over a decade, and residents often created their own supply by breaking water mains, which leads to contamination since most mains are located above stagnant drains'* (1995, p82).

Major obstacles to improving the condition of housing have been the large number of rental properties in Albouystown and the uneconomical proposition of housing improvement for owners (Kanneh, 1993). Vulnerability to everyday hazards, flooding, fire and drought are a result.

Vulnerability in Albouystown will firstly be discussed using indicators of household access to economic, social and physical resources; secondly, through a description of household losses and responses to past flood events; and finally, the adaptive potential of the Albouystown community is explored using indicators to assess social ties within the community, and engagement in the wider political process. Table 6.2 shows a summary of data.

Albouystown is highly vulnerable to environmental hazard (and other socio-economic shocks). A high proportion of households suffer economic poverty (53 per cent of households have at least twice as many dependants as workers, and 59 per cent of households have at least two people per room), and have household heads without education beyond primary schooling (48 per cent). There is a high proportion of households with children under the age of five years, the most vulnerable group to health impacts. Residential mobility can be seen in the low mean duration of residence (47 per cent of households have

Table 6.2 *Vulnerability and risk*

Variable	Indicator
Household asset profiles	
Economic resources	Workers/dependants ratio of 1/2 or more, 53%
	Rooms/residents ratio of 1/2 or more, 59%
Education of household head	Primary, 48%; secondary, 51%; university, 1%;
	adult or further education classes, 26%
Overseas remittances	72% have relatives living overseas, 38% receive
	remittances
Household structure	Common law, 47%; married, 18%; single, 20%; visiting,
	10%; widowed, 3%; divorced, 2%
Demographic profile	Generations in household: 1, 9%; 2, 69%; 3, 19%; 4, 2%
	Households with members aged less than five years,
	50%
	Households with members aged more than 65 years, 6%
Dwelling tenure	Private landlord, 79%; rent-free, 10%; own, 11%
Length of residence in Alb	Mean 17.5 years, 23% less than five years
Length of residence in house	Mean 10 years, 47% less than five years
Experience of flooding	
Yard flooded in last heavy rain	64%
Dwelling flooded in last heavy rain	15%
Impacts of last flood	
Physical losses	6%
Health impacts*	20%
Response to flooding	
Raised yard	18%
Adapted dwelling	Rebuild drains or build up house, 9%

Notes: Percentages are for positive responses unless indicated.
* See Table 6.3 for more detail.

been resident in their house for less than five years); the transience of community members is likely to restrict the building up of social networks. The majority of dwellings are privately rented (79 per cent) with the consequences for building maintenance and vulnerability to environmental risk discussed above. More positively, security is likely to come from the high number of community members with family resident in Albouystown (47 per cent of household heads are in a common-law union, 18 per cent are married and 10 per cent have visiting relationships), and from the possibility of accessing financial support from relatives living overseas (72 per cent): 38 per cent of households receive money at least once a year in this way.

Some 64 per cent of respondents had flooded yards following the 'last heavy rains', which most respondents identified as being about six weeks before the survey, although only a few households (15 per cent) had floodwaters within their houses on this occasion. Flood impacts were mostly felt in terms of health impacts (20 per cent of households), but some physical impacts were also

Table 6.3 *Health impacts of the most recent flood*

Age (years)	Cold	Fever	Diarrhoea	Skin rash	Arthritis
<5	13	21	19	11	0
6–16	6	5	6	3	0
17–65	2	2	0	3	1
>65	0	0	0	1	0

reported (6 per cent). In Table 6.3, the breakdown of health impacts as reported by the respondents shows the vulnerability of children under five years to fever, diarrhoea, cold and skin rashes immediately following the flood. Despite the low proportion of households owning their dwelling (11 per cent), almost 20 per cent had attempted to reduce exposure to floodwaters by raising their yard and 9 per cent had modified their dwelling in some way: most commonly by the construction of a barrier over the threshold or the raising of the dwelling's floorboards.

Table 6.4 *Adaptive potential*

Indicator	Values
Informal social support	
Spoke to a neighbour today	83%
Where does your closest friend live?	Same house, 48%; neighbour 29%; God is closest friend, 5%
Leave doors unlocked whilst going to the local shops	40%
Share food with neighbours	36%
Clean drains with neighbours	63%
Clear streets with neighbours	53%
Shop for neighbours	64%
Play sport with neighbours	21%
Local community group Membership:*	
Church	60%
Sports	6%
Community-based	5%
Political party	18%
Participation in elections	
Most recent national elections	yes, 76%; no, 14%; too young, 9%
Most recent city elections	yes, 74%; no, 16%; too young, 9%
Social distress	
Do you feel worried about crime in Albouystown?	75%
Have you attended a crime prevention meeting?	2%

Notes: Percentages are for positive responses unless indicated.
* See Table 6.5 for more detail.

Table 6.5 *Local group membership*

Group	Male (age in years)			Female (age in years)		
	<16	17–65	>66	<16	17–65	>66
Church	31 (40%)	31 (31%)	23 (37%)	21 (40%)	68 (49%)	55 (64%)
Sports	2 (3%)	17 (17%)	2 (3%)	1 (2%)	7 (5%)	0 (0%)
Community group	0 (0%)	0 (0%)	1 (2%)	1 (2%)	2 (2%)	3 (3%)
None	44 (57%)	52 (52%)	36 (58%)	29 (56%)	62 (45%)	28 (33%)
Total %	77 (100%)	100 (100%)	62 (100%)	52 (100%)	139 (100%)	86 (100%)

Given the observed exposure to flooding in Albouystown, and adaptations of individual households to flood risk, to what extent have households come together and organized to reduce vulnerability? Table 6.4 shows that participation in formal organizations was low, with the exception of church attendance (60 per cent) and membership of political parties (18 per cent).

In Table 6.5, the demographics of group membership show the key role played by women above the age of 16 as members of churches and also community groups. Two of the most prominent community groups were women's groups. About half the number of men attended church compared to women; young men were most commonly involved in sports groups.

Low participation in formal organizations does not mean that the community is fragmented, so much as indicating that social capital has not been invested into formal structures – it remains latent. This is perhaps best demonstrated in the low proportion of sports club members (6 per cent) compared to the higher number of respondents who played sport with neighbours (21 per cent). Indeed, the community appears to be full of positive and frequent social interaction: 83 per cent of respondents spoke to their neighbour on the day of the survey; for those people whose closest confidant or best friend was not a member of their household, almost two-thirds were neighbours. These social contacts were readily translated into positive informal actions to improve the local environment (63 per cent cleaned drains with neighbours and 53 per cent cleaned garbage from the street with neighbours). Such actions were focussed on the immediate living environment and tended to involve young and adolescent men.

The contradiction between high informal and low formal organization and action to mitigate vulnerability and risk has a number of possible explanations. Economic poverty is often used to explain why people have little time and energy to invest in non-immediate activities. In Albouystown, this is likely to have been compounded by a lack of trust in local leaders and their groups, which have a history of being short lived and of low financial accountability. Reinforcing cynicism is a history of political co-optation of grassroots organization in Albouystown, with party activists frequently also being involved in community organization. The political dynamic is especially important in

Albouystown, which has been a principal support base for the PNC and more recently the GGG (whose leader comes from Albouystown and is the current Mayor of Georgetown). The importance of politics in the community is reflected in party membership (18 per cent) and high voter turn-out (74 per cent in city elections). These pressures are therefore likely to have acted to reduce formal organization and the potentially high gains in terms of vulnerability reduction that they could deliver, whilst less risky and costly forms of informal organization are commonplace despite the more limited range of developmental outputs.

Community organization

The most established groups in the ward were service organizations, including a Seventh Day Adventist church, a mosque, a YMCA branch and a sports club (the Young Achievers Boxing Association). These organizations were not principally engaged in development work, although they did play a role in sustaining local social capital. There was a single community-based development group, True Vision, and a second organization engaged exclusively in environmental rehabilitation, the Albouystown Neighbourhood Development Committee. These two groups are the only cases of local organizations concerned with vulnerability reduction, and we turn our attention to them now.

True Vision was founded in 1995 and its stated aim is 'to organize community based initiatives to respond directly to the social and material needs of the most vulnerable members of the community' (UNDP, 1998c). Its leadership structure evolved from initial self-appointment to annual elections from 1997. However, this said, its leadership has not changed since 1995. At the time of the interview, there were three paid staff (treasurer, office assistant and handyman) and 15 members, and the major on-going activity of the group was a daily feeding programme for 50 school children and 150 elderly residents of Albouystown. Drain cleaning and garbage collection days had been organized using the labour of 30 local residents but it had proven difficult to maintain such levels of community involvement in environmental projects. The environmental programme was self-financed, with funds for the feeding programme raised from donations by national (Food for the Poor – a local branch of a US religious charity) and international (Guyana Christian Charities (Canada) Inc) supporters. Personal subscriptions from community supporters were not encouraged because it was felt that people would be unwilling to give. This was explained by Thorne, chairman of True Vision:

> '*A lot of organizations just spring up for their own personal gains. People think of this [True Vision] as another one where they hear it, so they are reluctant to help... Overseas donors are better 'cos there is less politics... But they need to know that what they fund reaches the people they want*' (Thorne, 1999).

One of the key managerial problems was a lack of human skills necessary for providing the financial transparency required by external donors. There was a tension between the desire to employ local people and the necessity of having basic skills within the organization. This has meant that the few skilled people in True Vision have had to spend time training any new members in basic secretarial skills. Management itself has not been able to access any training in organizational management, nor in the type of role that a community group can play. The organization relies heavily on the experiential skills of its chairman, who has worked voluntarily as a branch representative in the Transport and General Workers Union and as a local political organizer for the PNC. In 1993, the chairman left the PNC after 27 years of active membership, and in the same year moved to Albouystown, founding True Vision in 1995.

True Vision has also been constrained by the high cost of obtaining legal registration as an NGO (G$35,000 or UK£175). This makes it hard to access support from government and international agencies. There is also talk of restructuring the organization, as some members have recently moved to live in other areas of the city. The biggest problem in the enabling environment was the politicization of community organization, and the negative effect this has on membership and community relations. As Thorne said, 'All organization in Albouystown play a lot of politics. I want True Vision to be different, and so to grow' (Thorne, 1999). The reluctance of community members to concern themselves with groups was also felt to be because of a history of local leaders using community groups as platforms for their own political or socio-economic advancement.

In 1997, Thorne founded the Albouystown Neighbourhood Development Committee. This was to be a networking body for all civil society organizations working in Albouystown. The Committee gained funding and technical support from SIMAP and UNDP together with local self-help labour for the construction of two foot bridges in Albouystown. Despite these successes in risk reduction and community mobilization, the organization failed to overcome tensions between political factions and non-political organizers, and after one year the Committee was disbanded.

There has been one major effort by external development agencies to link together environmental improvements and the strengthening of community cohesion in Albouystown. This initiative was undertaken by the CHPA, which formed the Albouystown Neighbourhood Development Association (ANDA) in 1991. ANDA was formed as part of a participatory project funded by the UNDP for environmental and social development. ANDA's major success was the management of a garbage collection and disposal project over two years from 1991, which only ended when responsibility for funding was shifted to the GCC. Following long periods between payments from the council, the organization eventually collapsed (Kanneh, 1993). Despite this failure of sustainability, the experience demonstrated that a CBO could organize local solid waste management and that divestment of some of the GCC's responsibilities could produce positive results. However, the experiment has not been repeated. ANDA's history is indicative of problems for community organization in Albouystown. From inception, with the selection of a locally well-known supporter of the ruling party (PNC) as the group's organizer (unknown to the external project organizers), the group was politically oriented, which served to exclude non-party supporters, including the Indo-Guyanese residents of Albouystown. Barriers to community mobilization were also created by the (correct) perception of residents that they paid rates, and that garbage collection was thus the responsibility of the GCC.

SUMMARY

In Georgetown, flood hazard is principally a product of maldevelopment. There are certain physical phenomena and characteristics of settlement location that shape the geography of flooding, but flood hazard could be mitigated with available technology and management systems. That this has not occurred is a product of Guyana's political economy.

In the 1990s, Guyana moved from a centralized and undemocratic regime towards a more democratic model of government. Free national and local elections have been held and there is much mention of civil society participation in government and donor rhetoric. However, the political culture of Guyana has been slower to change. Amongst political activists and public servants, there remains an approach to development which sees grassroots actors as recipients rather than partners in development. Amongst grassroots actors, there is a reluctance to become involved in local organizations, reducing the chances of a community-led response to environmental hazard and vulnerability.

At a national level, disaster response has historically been undervalued. The reinstated Civil Defence Commission coordinates disaster response and has successfully entered into partnerships with civil society actors like the Guyana Red Cross and Guyana Relief Council. This is a good model: perhaps because of the youth of the organization and its leadership, it has been able to develop with financial transparency as a key goal, and appears to have distanced itself from political influence. However, there is a lack of engagement on the part of the CDC and disaster-oriented NGOs with community-level preparedness and vulnerability evaluation. Disaster management remains reactive, possibly reflecting the political dangers and resource expenditures that come with moving towards community involvement.

The resilience of the political culture (despite a change in ruling party), the slowness with which civil society actors are emerging, and the deepening and spreading of inequality and vulnerability to environmental hazard are linked. In city and national government there are many instances in which partisan political gain has been put before good management. In the absence of any strong critical civil society, private sector or grassroots voices, dissent is kept to a minimum – although there are important exceptions to this. The cost is a decaying urban infrastructure and the loss of skilled individuals, prolonging the status quo, as potential agents of change migrate to the Caribbean or North America.

What can be done to address these issues? Nationally, much is being done to address constitutional reform, reform of regional government, education of local government representatives and institutional strengthening in civil society. These all point in the right direction, but successful change is proving slow and painful. At a local level, community leaders might benefit greatly from training to show the difference between political and social development goals, and the benefits of an apolitical approach. National NGOs need to develop capacity to promote community-led action in preparedness and vulnerability reduction. A similar role should be considered by the CDC. More helpful than anything, perhaps, would be: a clear distancing of political parties and their leaders from racial identity politics and the cultures of patronage that undermine the long-term hopes for public sector reform; and the evolution of a civil society that is representative of and responsive to the needs of those who are most vulnerable in Guyanese society.

Chapter 7

Patrimonial Regimes and the Maintenance of a Constructive Civil Society: Santo Domingo, The Dominican Republic

---

'The municipality is a problem, it does not function well, they have no funds. They blame the central government and vice versa... Work is done if you have a good local CBO which can attract an NGO' (Schvenson, 1999).

'It's hard enough to get people involved in immediate environmental problems. To generate interest in natural disasters, which happen every 20 years is really a struggle' (Catafesta, 1999).

INTRODUCTION

These two quotes, the first from an officer in an international development organization, the second from a local academic and community activist, go to the heart of the opportunities and frustrations offered by public action to reduce disaster losses in Santo Domingo. From the perspective of an international organization, Schvenson argues that linking with grassroots actors is a preferred strategy for reducing vulnerability amongst those most at risk in the context of a centralized and partisan state. However, as the local academic and activist Caterina Catafesta reminds us, from a grassroots perspective things are not so simple. At the best of times, good community leadership and enthusiasm for local public action are rare and precious commodities. If grassroots actors are to play their full potential in reducing disaster vulnerability, an active local community and a willing international community and state are required.

Our goal in this chapter is to uncover the ways in which the dominant political system at work in Santo Domingo has shaped the adaptive potential of grassroots actors – and whether grassroots actors have been able to influence the dominant political system to open new spaces for adaptation. In the preceding chapters we have seen how grassroots actors have a range of skills and resources which can be used in reducing vulnerability to disaster. We have also seen the ways in which the potential offered by these resources can be suppressed or enhanced according to three types of social relationship: relations within the community (do people work together or individually to overcome common problems); relations between grassroots actors and the state (city or national government, the police etc); and relations between grassroots actors and other civil society actors (local NGOs, international NGOs, political parties). These three types of relationship and their impact on adaptive potential are explored at the city level and through the eyes of a case-study community, Los Manguitos. Beforehand, though, it is worth noting a few points by way of introduction and background. This we do below, providing a thumbnail sketch of contemporary urban politics in Santo Domingo, and in the following section, where the nature of environmental hazard in the city is discussed. The chapter serves as an exemplar of the struggles for public action in an authoritarian, patrimonial political system.

AUTHORITARIAN RULE IN THE DOMINICAN REPUBLIC

Change in systems of governance can provide opportunities to enhance the adaptive potential of a society. Recent trends in local academic and journalistic writing, as well as statements from government and donors, on citizen–state relations in Santo Domingo suggest a growing consensus for the need to decentralize the public sector, democratize government and build greater capacity within civil society (Collado, 1997; Pérez, 1996; Fernandez, 1996). However, the extent to which this new language of development reflects any real change in the structure and orientation of politics nationally, and in the city, is less clear. The tension between reformist and conservative elements within the urban polity form the backdrop for this chapter.

Governance in Santo Domingo has changed little in the last 30 years. Decision-making is largely centralized in the office of the president. The fragile nature of democracy in Santo Domingo is captured by its description as 'restricted' (Matias, 1997) and 'transitory' (Choup, 2000). Duarte, Brea and Holguín (1998) argue that a culture of paternalism pervades Dominican politics; they found that 81 per cent of Dominicans liken a good government to a father to whom one can go to resolve problems. This paternalistic culture provides popular legitimization for centralized government, and normalizes the culture of clientelism that is endemic (Matias, 1997). Despite this, pressure from international actors, civil society and some national politicians has contributed towards a period of slow reform at the turn of the millennium. The pace of change has been increasing since the fair election of the Dominican Liberation Party (PLD) to government in 1996 (the first uncontroversial fair election result) and the Dominican Revolutionary Party (PRD) in 2000. Although the old political elite still has much influence and there is resistance to change at both the municipal and national levels, the beginnings of a more decentralized and democratic institutional structure are emerging.

As part of this process of democratic transition, civil society actors have also undergone recent changes in their political orientation and in the kinds of work they undertake. Until the early 1990s, at the local level the aims of two groups of local activist – community organizers and grassroots, left-wing political workers – converged. The goals of local development were understood in terms of poverty alleviation, and this in turn was seen as being tied in with democratic reform of the state. Since the mid-1990s, however, the political goals of party activists and the developmental goals of community organizers have diverged, and the local NGO sector has matured (Pérez, 1992, 1997). This can be seen in the disappearance of many politically motivated groups working at the local level, and a resurgence of 'professional' NGOs. Tactically, community organizers and NGOs have moved away from a directly confrontational relationship with municipal and national government characterized by frequent street protests in the 1970s and 1980s, towards a critical but more cooperative relationship at the turn of the millennium. This is perhaps demonstrated best by NGOs and CBOs being as likely now to propose and enact alternative or complementary development projects to the state, where once their role was more limited protest and lobbying (Cela, 1999).

From the 1970s to the present day, women have formed the mainstay of local community organizations. In a study of community organization in an inner city *barrio*, Villa Julia, Catafesta (1999) found that women and youths were the most active participants in community development and local environmental improvements. She argues that women's activity is a result of their concern for their young children, that women are less politically motivated than men, and that women have a greater stake in local environmental improvements because of their role in household reproduction, which brings them into close daily contact with the local environment. This echoes many of the more general arguments put forward by Moser (1996) in Chapter 3. The intensity of community organization in low- and very-low-income *barrios* like Villa Julia has been maintained since the street protests of the 1970s, but in recent years the older generation of local leaders has begun to express concern that young activists are not coming through, raising doubts over the future vibrancy of local organizations in Santo Domingo.

ENVIRONMENTAL HAZARD

The most frequent type of catastrophic hazard affecting Santo Domingo comes from hurricanes. In the Dominican Republic, some 20 hurricanes made landfall between 1871 and 1998. The season lasts from June to November. The city is also prone to earthquakes, with the most recent shock in 1941 having caused widespread damage. There is little direct risk of flooding from sea-level rise in Santo Domingo, which is largely built on a raised coral platform. However, interior deforestation for agricultural land and settlement reduces forest by 0.6 per cent annually (SESPAS, 1996) and this has increased runoff rates and the risk of flash flooding amongst riverside settlements within Santo Domingo (Ramia, 1994).

Hurricane Georges hit the Dominican Republic on 22 September 1998; its eye passed to the north of Santo Domingo and moved in a westerly direction towards Haiti. Direct economic damages have been estimated at 2.2b Dominican dollars (DR$, equivalent to 14 per cent of national GDP). There were 300 officially recorded deaths nationwide (UNDP, 1999a). In Santo Domingo, 19,408 refugees were registered in 142 refuges (*Listin Diario*, 1998).

Degradation in the urban environment means that risk from chronic everyday hazards is also high. Only 30 per cent of the city has adequate provision of housing and basic services (Rumbo, in Choup, 2000). Despite this great need, management of the urban environment has low political priority in Santo Domingo. Service provision is unable to keep up with rapid population growth, and the urban environment continues to degrade (Morel, 1996). Reform of public sector provision has been led by privatization initiatives: for example, solid waste management was privatized in 1994. But contractual problems have reduced the effectiveness of private sector-based provision.

The sectors of the city most exposed to flooding lie adjacent to the rivers Isabela and Ozama. Figure 7.1 shows these rivers and also the distribution of poverty within the city. The congruence of poverty with riverine location is striking. The figure also shows high rates of poverty in peripheral settlements. Riverine and fringe settlements have the lowest levels of access to environmental services such as sanitation, garbage collection and drinking water, and the highest rates of poverty.

The close relationship between poverty and vulnerability to disaster is shown by comparing the data in Figure 7.1 with the distribution of *barrios* worst impacted by Hurricane Georges, shown in Figure 7.2. The marginal settlements identified in Figure 7.1 have experienced the greatest impacts, and are most at risk.

URBAN GOVERNANCE AND ADAPTIVE POTENTIAL

A culture of *'no planificacion'* in the public sector

The birth of the modern city of Santo Domingo can be traced back to 1930, when the city was destroyed by Hurricane Zerún. In the same year the dictator Trujillo gained the presidency and commenced a modernization project, which at its height consumed 62 per cent (Greenfield, 1994) of the national budget. Trujillo had a vision of the city as an engine for national economic growth and as a symbol of national (and personal) identity and pride: the city was re-named

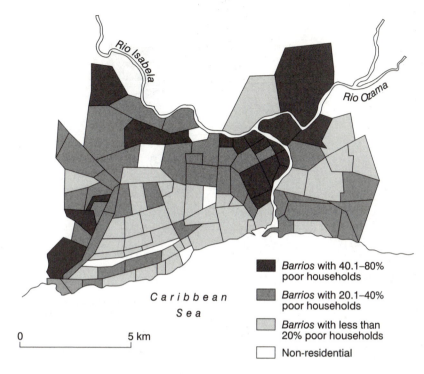

Source: Pelling (2002) using data from Oficina Nacional de Planification (ONAPLAN) (1997)

Figure 7.1 *Household poverty, Santo Domingo*

Ciudad Trujillo. Successive presidents have sought to put their own stamp on the city and have continued to fund prestige development projects rather than investing in basic services and infrastructure (Morel, 1996). The inequality produced by such development is best shown by President Balaguer's Faro de Colon monument, which displaced 30,000 low-income families from inner-city neighbourhoods (see Figure 7.2). In total, 180,000 people were evicted from all over Santo Domingo to allow prestige development and also to disrupt local political opposition movements (Azuela, Duhau and Ortiz, 1998). In 1990–1991, the UN Commission for Human Rights issued a public condemnation of the city's development strategy (Cela, 1999).

Fuelled by rural underdevelopment and encouraged by urban modernization, population has grown rapidly, from 1.8 million in 1981 to over 3 million in 1991, with estimates that the population exceeded 5 million in 2000. Growth has coincided with widening economic inequality. Growing numbers of people have been excluded from the formal urban land market. In 1981, 64 per cent of the city population lived on 20 per cent of the urban land area, and by 1990 the informal sector accounted for 71 per cent of all housing (Fernandez,

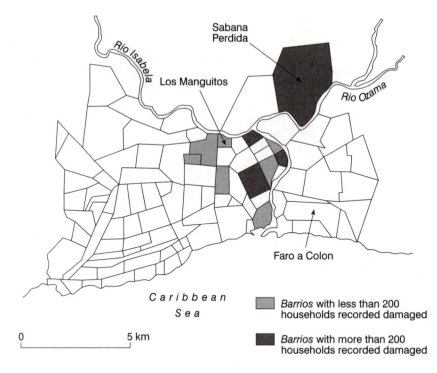

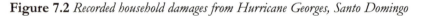

Reproduced from *International Development Planning Review* by permission of Liverpool
University Press
Source: Pelling (2002) using data from UNDP (1998b)

Figure 7.2 *Recorded household damages from Hurricane Georges, Santo Domingo*

1996). Exclusion from the formal housing market together with forced
displacement from inner-city *barrios* undergoing prestige redevelopment has
resulted in the rapid growth of informal settlement on the fringes of the city
and in hazardous places adjacent to the rivers Isabela and Ozama.

National and city politics are closely linked. Both have been shaped by
almost 60 years of patrimonial rule under presidents Trujillo (1930–1938 and
1942–1952) and Balaguer (1960–1962, 1966–1978 and 1986–1996). Over this
time an increasing array of municipal functions have been drawn under
centralized state control, and clientelism has become endemic. Central
government has captured most of the municipal government's responsibilities,
with the exception of garbage collection. Urban development is frequently
berated for its lack of transparency and culture of *no planificacion* (lack of
transparent planning). There is no urban development plan and planning
decisions appear to be directed by presidential whim (Cela, 1996).

However, nominally, municipal government for Santo Domingo is
undertaken by the Ayuntamiento Distrito Nacional (ADN), which has
jurisdiction over adjacent peri-urban and agricultural settlements as well as the

urban core. The inclusion of non-urban areas in the administrative definition of Santo Domingo has produced excluded rural zones of high vulnerability. Such areas have small electorates and tend to lose out in public sector spending. This is particularly the case with informal fringe settlements that lack legal tenure, and peri-urban agricultural communities or *bateys* that are home to Haitian labour migrants. Because neither Haitian migrants nor their children are eligible to vote, these communities are especially marginalized and suffer high vulnerability.

Decentralization is a key component of the democratization process. There have been many plans to decentralize planning within Santo Domingo (Pérez, 1996; Matias, 1997; CPRME, 1998) but these have never come to fruition. Struggles between conservatives and reformists for decentralization have often been enacted as conflict between the national government and the ADN. Article 55 of the constitution allows the state to take over any specific duty of the municipal government if it is deemed by the state to be incompetent. The power of the president has recently been extended over the ADN through the creation of special presidential committees. The Presidential Committee for the Support of Barrio Development (Comisión Presidencial de Apoyo al Desarollo Barrial), whilst providing new resources for *barrio* development, also has the effect of encouraging community actors to bypass the ADN and, in so-doing, reinforces centralized control. The tension between the ADN and the central government is heightened when an opposition party has control of the ADN, as has been the case for all but four years between 1986 and 2000. There are many claims and counterclaims of financial mismanagement and political interference between the national and city authorities, which creates a conflicting working relationship, undermining public sector potential for vulnerability reduction.

Despite the reluctance of central government to decentralize, some state agencies have been more progressive, with positive outcomes for adaptive potential. The Ministry of Health has been the most proactive with primary health care in Santo Domingo divided between five sub-districts. It is claimed that reforms had immediate benefits in service delivery with decreased maternal and infant mortality rates, and enhanced community involvement in disease prevention programmes following Hurricane Georges (*Hoy* in Choup, 2000).

Civil society

Contrasting with a corrupt and overly centralized public sector, Santo Domingo has a vibrant civil society with the number of CBOs exceeding 1000 and the number of NGOs running into the hundreds (Cela, 1999). However, both the legal regime which governs civil society activity, and the city's political history, have constrained this sector's contribution to adaptive potential (García and Mercedes, 1996; Matias, 1997). To receive support from the ADN, and consequently most international donors, grassroots organizations must be formally registered with the ADN as *junta de vecinos* (neighbourhood groups). *Junta de vecinos* work and draw popular support from within demarcated territories that sometimes cut across communities with shared economic status and housing conditions. This fragments organic community organization whilst, as Guzman (1999) argues, at the same time encouraging competition and conflict between groups for membership and resources. Such tension and instability make it easier for political activists to undermine and capture community organizations and prevent challenges to dominant vertical chains of partisan clientelism.

The requirement for *junta de vecinos* to have annual elections of management boards with 19 members is often beyond the administrative capacity of smaller groups. Such groups are therefore excluded from ADN support and must look to personal appeals to the president or to international NGOs for support (Choup, 2000). This undermines attempts to build political space for adaptive potential through decentralization. As Choup (2000, p17) argues:

> *'Despite efforts to make demands through decentralized appeals to government institutions, that is to play by democratic rules, a direct appeal to the president still yields the best results for the community'.*

As exemplars of this process, Choup (2000) points to land invasions in Sabana Perdida, where communities have been named after the colour of political parties in office (Villa Blanca and Villa Morada). These are cases where the immediate demands of coping took priority over (and set back) the longer-term goal of institutional modification.

Until free and fair elections were held in 1996, civil society groups were primarily concerned with a leftist agenda of protesting for working-class interests and lobbying for a democratic transition. There is a long history of conflict with the state (Pérez, 1997). The legacy of this politicized relationship continues to restrict vulnerability reduction and adaptation to hazard. First, a lack of trust undermines cooperation between state agencies and civil society groups. Second, the political orientation of community organization has made some people reluctant to participate in public action, and this undermines the representativeness of CBOs. Third, because many CBOs and NGOs are oriented towards pursuing national rather than local agendas, neighbourhood development concerns are often not prioritized by community leaders.

Networks

Networks are a great strength of civil society in Santo Domingo. They enable the vertical and horizontal spread of information and resources between communities, CBOs, NGOs and INGOs. Vargas (1994) found that 44 per cent of CBOs were members of confederations. The largest NGO network is the Red de Redes de ONGs (the Network of NGO Networks) (Cela, 1999). The city's networking capacity has been used by civil society actors to try and build

---

Box 7.1 *IDAC: integrating disaster response and social development*

Instituto de Acción Comunitaria (IDAC) was founded in 1983 and registered as an NGO in 1992. It works with local community groups from isolated Haitian communities in Santo Domingo's periphery to alleviate poverty. Core areas of activity are community development and leadership building, education, integrated local economic development and sanitation. Its orientation is towards long-term social development. IDAC is recognized as an established NGO with an extensive network of contacts with local community organizations.

    Following Hurricane Georges, in 1998, IDAC was one of a small number of NGOs that provided a link between international aid donors and local community groups. Taking on this new role was greatly facilitated by IDAC's prior involvement in a vulnerability reduction programme organized by another NGO, the Dominican Disaster Mitigation Committee (DDMC), in 1997. Importantly, as part of this programme IDAC had coordinated the training of 679 community disaster managers who worked successfully during the emergency period to administer first aid and coordinate local disaster response. With part funding from DDMC, IDAC also worked with two communities to reduce local vulnerability to flooding by the construction of foot bridges and drains for flood and residential water.

    IDAC's local partners felt that the disaster management training and infrastructure works had played important roles in containing losses to Hurricane Georges. Furthermore, it was recognized that during the relief period IDAC was the only outside institution to have provided aid. IDAC worked with the European Community Humanitarian Office to distribute relief aid and to rebuild a community centre following the hurricane.

---

links with the ADN. For example, the Citizens' Forum (Foro Cuidado), formed by 197 member groups in 1999, aims to pressurize central government towards decentralization through the transfer of resources and responsibilities to the ADN. This and other networks are sophisticated tools for institutional modification, using popular mobilization and an academic/professional critique of development policy to assert pressure for democratic change.

Networks of CBOs, especially those linked to development NGOs, have become the favoured vehicles for INGO support. This is true of development as well as emergency aid. For such networks to function well during catastrophes, their members need to exhibit a high degree of flexibility and willingness to adopt a wide range of practical measures to achieve their development objectives. Box 7.1 provides an example of an NGO, Instituto de Acción Comunitaria (IDAC), which has successfully integrated the immediate needs of disaster recovery with its longer-term social development objectives.

There is a danger that vertical links by NGOs into otherwise horizontal networks of local organizations can make CBOs dependent upon patronage from dominant NGOs with access to international funding. Similarly, there is pressure on NGOs to act simply as local service organizations and sub-contractors for INGOs, rather than representatives of grassroots actors with independent aims and strategies. The accountability of many NGOs towards funders, rather than community partners, can be seen in the business model of management adopted by many NGOs. Such NGOs, like IDAC, are headed by permanent directors accountable to boards of trustees. Such arrangements are efficient: they encourage stability and are attractive to INGOs, but they are in danger of reversing democratic gains in the wider polity. At the grassroots, the business model fits closely and does not challenge the model of patrimonial organization received from political party organizations. In both cases, decision-making authority is vested in a single leader who is not obliged to stand for election. CBOs using either model will not be effective in exposing members to democratic modes of decision-making, but instead reinforce entrenched norms of vertical dependence and *caudillismo* (dependence on a single leader).

DISASTER MANAGEMENT CAPACITY

An uncoordinated state sector

Preparation for and response to catastrophic disaster in Santo Domingo has historically suffered even greater neglect than vulnerability and the management of everyday environmental hazard. The biggest problem has been a lack of inter-agency cooperation. This is as true between actors within the state as it is between the state and civil society. The state sector is dominated by Civil Defence, but also includes the armed forces, the Meteorological Office, the emergency services and the Office of the President. A National Emergency Committee was established in 1992 with funding from the UNDP to strengthen state activity and to draw up a national disaster plan. Lack of commitment from government meant that little progress was made on this plan, which was abandoned during Hurricane Georges.

Centralized governance has failed to provide a focal point for disaster management. Instead, a number of public sector and civil society actors operate with no transparent coordination, and at times visible conflict. Where coordination has arisen this is arguably the result of political expediency and expanding central control. The history of the Dominican Red Cross (DRC) is a case in point, being greatly influenced by policy changes from central government. The DRC was controlled through the Office of the President from 1927 to 1998. The director and president of the Dominican Red Cross are appointed by, and accountable to, the Office of the President. The DRC was reformed in 1998 under Law 41:98. Box 7.2 describes the consequences of a new-found independence for the DRC: efficiency has increased, but relations with partner institutions in the public sector have become worse.

International support for civil society

Lack of commitment in the public sector has forced many donors to work directly with grassroots actors. This can also be read as a local manifestation of the New Policy agenda. In Santo Domingo this process was very evident. The

---

Box 7.2 *The Dominican Red Cross: state capture and release*

Law 41:98 returned control of the DRC to its members for the first time since 1927. A number of positive changes in the style and scope of work performed by the DRC have resulted from this:

- There is no longer the threat of staff changes when a new party comes into power. All staff are now institutionally appointed.
- There is no longer the need to employ large numbers of staff for political reasons. In 1999, 350 out of 500 paid staff were dismissed. This has reduced the partisan image of the DRC as well as making financial savings.
- The DRC is now recognized by international NGOs.
- INGOs are now enthusiastic to support the DRC (see Table 7.1).
- The IFRC/RC moved its Central America and Caribbean office to Santo Domingo in 1998. This has created an environment for skills transfer and strengthening in the DRC.

A short-term negative consequence of independence and the rising stature of the DRC is increasing tension with Civil Defence. These two organizations played a very similar role in disaster management within the state and have a history of competition over state resources. With the DRC's independence and access to international support, Civil Defence is in danger of being marginalized. This would reduce the overall capacity of the Dominican Republic to manage disaster.

UNDP provides an instructive example: after the failure of the National Emergency Committee during Hurricane Georges, the UNDP shifted from support of state agencies to direct aid for grassroots actors. Within Santo Domingo this took the form of technical support for a community-based rehabilitation project in Sabana Perdida (see Box 7.3).

Networks of vertical and horizontal organization were critical for CBOs to access information and support, and for INGOs and NGOs in reaching target beneficiaries or partners at the local level. During Hurricane Georges, the most effective and equitable distribution systems were those that used pre-existing networks, where participating organizations knew each other well and had high levels of trust. This is in contrast to state-managed aid that was distributed through Civil Defence chapters or political party branch offices. Both routes have been criticized for being open to political interference in allocation of aid. The scale of international aid distributed through local civil society groups following Hurricane Georges was such that a coordinating committee was established. The Comité de Emergencias Post-Huracán de Organizaciones de la Sociedad Civil had 40 members and oversaw the distribution of food, water, shelter and clothing. Table 7.1 provides some examples of the types of networks used and goods distributed. The DRC emerges as a key nodal institution.

As the examples above show, INGOs were highly active in supporting disaster response and rehabilitation. Indeed, one newspaper poll showed that 19 per cent of the general public considered INGOs to have been the most active

Box 7.3 *The UNDP and grassroots rehabilitation*

The UNDP acted swiftly following Hurricane Georges, holding meetings with government officials and national and international institutions to help structure a coordinated rehabilitation process. As an outcome of these discussions, the UNDP was able to modify two existing projects (Sustainable Human Development, and Housing and Human Settlements) and launch an Emergency and Rehabilitation Programme after Hurricane Georges. The project was conceived as a means of supporting the transition from emergency response towards integrated sustainable development, with target beneficiaries being the most vulnerable groups affected by the hurricane.

Recognition of rehabilitation as an opportunity to promote sustainable development can be seen in the programme's emphasis on skills training and income generation – particularly amongst women. The project site in Sabana Perdida lies on the northeastern periphery of Santo Domingo (Figure 7.2).

Sabana Perdida is a rapidly expanding and largely informal settlement of about 10,000 households. It is recognized as a marginal *barrio* with high levels of unemployment and low levels of service provision. Some 4000 residents were made homeless following Hurricane Georges, the majority having lived in exposed locations alongside the Rio Ozama. Despite its material poverty, Sabana Perdida has a wealth of local organizations (Choup, 2000). Following the hurricane, representatives from different community groups, political parties and institutions came together to form a local action plan, Integrated Action Padre Santiago Hirujo for the Reconstruction of Sabana Perdida. The plan combined short-term needs with long-term development objectives.

The UNDP was able to support the objectives of the local action plan through a number of local projects:

*   Emergency relief to 10 temporary shelters, 1800 beneficiaries.
*   Construction of 26 new houses, 26 families benefited.
*   Reconstruction of 530 homes, 530 families benefited.
*   Construction of a seamstress school, 50 women (and their families) benefited.
*   Construction of a sports court, 200 youngsters benefited.
*   Training in safe housing construction and disaster preparedness, entire community benefited.

In each of these projects, local community groups were responsible for democratically selecting the beneficiaries.

The experience of organizing and working with the UNDP has added strength to an already capable local community sector. The house construction and reconstruction projects were managed locally by an NGO formed specifically for this role, and which has since re-invented itself as the Comité Nacional de Desarrollo Integral Comunitario (CONDIC). CONDIC is led by two experienced community leaders who have successfully maintained community enthusiasm after the completion of the housing rehabilitation project. This has been done by organizing weekly community actions, such as drain cleaning, to keep a focus on community development beyond the disaster rehabilitation period. CONDIC became a registered NGO in 1999, and has subsequently become one of six NGOs involved with Office of National Planning (ONAPLAN) in a nationwide programme of community development, and has received support from this programme for further housing improvements.

Table 7.1 *INGO responses to Hurricane Georges*

INGO	Network and aid provided
European Community Humanitarian Office	Used local NGOs to distribute food to 13,000 families in shelters over three months (nationwide).
United Nations Development Programme (UNDP)	Funded CONDIC, a community group, to repair 530 houses and build 23 houses in Santo Domingo.
Organization of American States	Supported 17 CBOs in mitigation projects, value US$300,000.
United States Agency for International Development (USAID)	Used the DRC to distribute food to 26,000 families over six months (nationwide).
Spanish (Catalan) Red Cross	Provided hygienic first aid kits to hurricane shelters.
CARITAS International	Provided funding for the construction of 300 new houses to re-house flood victims, administered through Centro Juan Montalvo, a local NGO.

type of institution in disaster response, with an additional 34 per cent of respondents naming foreign nations. This compared to 19 per cent for the state, but only 6 per cent for CBOs and none for NGOs (*Hoy*, 1998).

INGOs tend to be less involved in support for projects targeting everyday vulnerability and community-level disaster preparedness, a major gap in provision. A notable exception to this was the Organization of American States, which financed a locally based NGO, the DDMC. The DDMC is involved in community-led infrastructure improvement projects and more widespread attempts to raise the profile of disaster and the need to reduce vulnerability across Dominican society. Because of the uniqueness of the DDMC, it is worth spending some time reviewing its activities.

The Dominican Disaster Mitigation Committee

The DDMC was legally constituted in 1995 and has five main areas of work: training of trainers, coordination and communication, information, community education and community initiatives. Within these broad areas of work, the DDMC has enhanced adaptive potential through two key projects. First, a community education programme: between 1995 and 1999, 578 meetings were held in high-risk communities to raise awareness of risk, vulnerability and options for mitigation. Second, a programme of community-based projects to build risk-reducing infrastructure: these projects were supported not only to reduce physical risk within vulnerable communities, but also as a tool for strengthening local leadership capacity. This was achieved in part by handing over financial management for the projects to community groups, who also had to raise at least 50 per cent of the costs for any infrastructure work. In addition, the community had to provide labour for the project and agree to a post-project maintenance programme. Since 1996, 17 projects have been completed worth US$300,000 and with 25,000 beneficiaries.

DDMC's mission to enhance awareness of vulnerability and disaster as development issues was approached through a number of complementary programmes. An effort was made to work with established actors in disaster management, such as the DRC, with whom the DDMC developed a disaster training programme for local Red Cross chapters. The DDMC was also successful in drawing support from the private sector. The media proved particularly willing to collaborate; 1400 minutes of TV time alone were donated to the DDMC. The insurance industry was also prepared to work with the DDMC to promote the use of disaster-resistant construction standards amongst architects.

Communities in Santo Domingo benefited from increased national awareness but, more directly, seven communities were included in the DDMC's community risk-reduction programme (Table 7.2).

The degree of community input in these projects was generally high. For example, in the construction of two bridges in La Galleria it was the community that decided on the bridge locations and two CBOs (Asociación de Mujeres and Junta de Vecinos La Galeria) that organized 100 families to contribute towards costs and provide labour. Maintenance of the bridges was supervised by the Junta de Vecinos La Galeria.

In Mata Mamon, disaster preparedness workshops given by the DDMC as a preliminary component of its involvement with the community proved invaluable during Hurricane Georges. The community was very badly hit by the hurricane: 75 per cent of houses were damaged or destroyed, and the neighbourhood was flooded and received no outside assistance for ten days. Because of its training, before the hurricane the community organized the evacuation of vulnerable people from areas of risk, and after the hurricane rescued people from the river and rebuilt houses. When, after ten days, the Red Cross provided food aid it was the community group that organized distribution.

Strong community leadership was doubly important in Mata Mamon as it was excluded from official state relief. It was felt locally that this was for political reasons. Other neighbouring communities had received aid but this had been distributed through local political party branches (Mata Mamon, 1999).

As noted above, politicization in the distribution of resources was a common observation of CBO leaders. This cross-cut with the interventions of the DDMC in shaping the types of support that community groups were able to access. In the quote below (APRODEMI, 1999) politicization is linked to a group's success in accessing funds for risk reduction projects, and its failure to receive relief aid following Hurricane Georges:

> '*The Junta de Vecinos Nazareno applied [for a mitigation project] and got help. This is very unusual. ProComunidad [government agency] works with*

Table 7.2 *Community initiatives facilitated by the DDMC in Santo Domingo*

Community	Works undertaken	Beneficiaries (direct and indirect)	Contribution towards costs
La Galeria	Sewer system	160 (direct) 670 (indirect)	DDMC: 47 per cent community: 45 per cent NGO: 8 per cent
La Mina Guaricano	Anti-landslide wall	200 (direct) 800 (indirect)	DDMC: 25 per cent community: 67 per cent NGO: 8 per cent
Barrio Norte Guaricano	Storm drains, 250m	100 (direct) 389 (indirect)	DDMC: 20 per cent community: 69 per cent NGO: 11 per cent
Los Guandules La Victoria	Storm drains, 240m	325 (direct) 163 (indirect)	DDMC: 45 per cent community: 30 per cent NGO: 25 per cent
La Union Los Alcarrizos	Storm drains, 315m	380 (direct) –	DDMC: 29 per cent community: 54 per cent NGO: 5 per cent municipality: 12 per cent
Mata Mamon San Luis	Flood dyke	520 (direct) –	DDMC: 31 per cent community: 34 per cent NGO: 19 per cent government: 16 per cent
La Union La Victoria	Storm drain, 260m	475 (direct) 90 (indirect)	DDMC: 42 per cent community: 33 per cent NGO: 25 per cent

communities directly. They were successful because of politics, maybe someone in the Junta de Vecinos has good links with the PRD [ruling party]... The Red Cross and Civil Defence were bad, they did not have much to offer in terms of material and food, etc. Distribution was disorganized – perhaps some people got too much, maybe if you are a friend of the distributor you will get more'.

In La Mina, institutional strengthening was an outcome of the DDMC programme. Before the DDMC's involvement, this community had only a weakly functioning CBO. Through community involvement in the DDMC project, local leadership was reinvigorated and a second disaster mitigation project has been planned (APRODEMI, 1999). The intermediary NGO that provided a link between the DDMC and community leaders (APRODEMI) felt it had also benefited from this experience. Its ability to manage projects had been demonstrated and it felt confident enough to approach other potential supporters. Indeed APRODEMI has since received a donation of drinking water filters from the World Food Programme.

LOS MANGUITOS

Los Manguitos is a marginal, densely populated *barrio* first settled in 1975 by 200 rural migrant families. In 1999 the population was 33,000. Risk comes from the *barrio*'s location on the flood plain and tributary ravines of the Rio Isabela (Figure 7.2). The vulnerability of the people who live here is indicated by their lack of access to economic, social and physical assets. The extent of economic poverty can be seen in the high dependency ratios of households (42 per cent of households had two or more dependants for every income contributor). Similarly, the demographic and human resource profiles of the *barrio* indicates human vulnerability: 43 per cent of households had at least one member under five years of age (vulnerable to health impacts of disaster), and there was a lack of access to education and informational resources (23 per cent of the adult population were illiterate).

Dwelling constructions ranged from scrap metal to reinforced concrete, and 53 per cent of households were overcrowded with more than two members for every room. The settlement was illegal but with the mean length of residence at 22 years there was established de facto ownership with an informal housing market. Rental housing can indicate risk, as landlords are unwilling or unable to maintain their buildings: 36 per cent of households were rented. Electricity was first obtained following organized protest in the 1980s, drinking water was supplied in 1994 and in 1998 the municipality extended a sanitation system into Los Manguitos. Despite this, Espillat and Ballenilla estimated in 1998 that 36 per cent of households had inadequate access to drinking water and sewerage.

Community social capital

Given the economic exclusion of Los Manguitos's residents, has any local organization evolved to ameliorate vulnerability? If so, how do local institutions interact with wider city processes and flows of power? Table 7.3 presents a summary of findings from the household survey (see Appendix 1 for methods used). At this time, social capital was clearly present in Los Manguitos as indicated by the high frequency of informal social contact (91 per cent of respondents had spoken to their neighbour on the day of the interview and 44 per cent had their closest friend living in Los Manguitos). Respondents also reported frequently being engaged in informal social activities with positive environmental outcomes (66 per cent had joined with neighbours to clear the street) or in acts that maintained social bonds and were fun (60 per cent had joined with neighbours to celebrate carnival or Christmas).

Informal cooperation tends to be reactive – for example, cleaning garbage from streets rather than organizing an educational programme to reduce littering and dumping in the first place – but it can be a strategically useful source of support when the unexpected occurs. Following Hurricane Georges, respondents recall the abundance of informal support. Neighbours were frequently called upon for help, particularly when respondents wanted to keep watch over their home and possessions and were wary of the conditions that they would encounter in government shelters (50 per cent of respondents with damaged homes stayed with neighbours and only 30 per cent with family).

From a theoretical perspective there are clear advantages for community members taking part in this kind of informal cooperation. Perhaps most importantly, informality allows the flexibility to respond to problems as they arise, and requires few assets for participation (ie, no formal group membership or financial outlay is demanded). But informal cooperation has its limits. Whilst no formal group membership is required, reciprocity with neighbours will be required to maintain informal networks over the long term. For any households or individuals excluded from informal community networks, social isolation is likely to exaggerate their relative vulnerability. The data collected from Los Manguitos suggests that in this *barrio* at least, marginalization of social groups within the wider community was not a hindrance to informal cooperation.

The data in Table 7.3 indicate that a transformation from social capital into developmental social organization had taken place within Los Manguitos, so that informal and formal systems of community cooperation had begun to operate together. This is demonstrated in the high proportion of households (77 per cent) that had at least one member belonging to some kind of local social organization (the most popular were two local churches). Importantly, 19 per cent of respondents were a member of a *junta de vecinos*, indicating a reasonably high participation rate in community development and coping initiatives. Political party affiliation was also high at 39 per cent, and there were high levels of participation in elections, indicating the importance of political identification in the barrio, which had been at the forefront of political protests during the 1980s.

These data suggest that in marginalized communities like Los Manguitos, where vulnerability to environmental hazard is high, a firm base of community cohesion, political engagement and civil society organization can be found. The question remains whether these social and political assets held at a communal level are sufficient for accessing externally or generating locally the resources needed to build coping responses and to push for positive institutional modification in the city.

Community organizing

The history of social organization in Los Manguitos is typical of the marginal *barrios* in Santo Domingo. Before the mid-1980s, community activity was limited to cultural and sporting activities, but with the creation of *junta de vecinos* and youth/women's groups in the 1990s development projects were possible. Los Manguitos hosted six community-based development organizations (three *junta de vecinos*: Los Manguitos, Grito de Capotillo and Ruben Diaro; two youth/women's groups: MOCUGRECA and AMDEM; and one developmental

Table 7.3 *Social organization, Los Manguitos*

Indicator	Response
Informal social support	
Spoke with a neighbour today	91%
Closest friend lives in Los Manguitos	44%
Have you ever cleaned the street with neighbours?	66%
Have you ever celebrated carnival or Christmas with neighbours?	60%
Have you ever shopped for a neighbour?	44%
Have you ever played sport with a neighbour?	39%
Have you ever joined in a neighbourhood tree-planting programme?	10%
Local community group membership	
Member of any local group	77%
Member of a local church	46%
Member of a *junta de vecinos*	19%
Member of a cultural or youth group	15%
Member of a sports group	2%
Member of a *san* (a saving circle)	28%
Member of a political party	39%
Participation in elections	
Voted in last national election (1996)	70%
Voted in last municipal election (1998)	63%
Plan to vote in the next national elections (2000)	75%
Responses to Hurricane Georges	
House was damaged by Hurricane Georges	64%
If your home was damaged where did you seek refuge…	
with a neighbour	50%
with your family	30%
in a church	11%
in a government refuge	7%
in a shop	2%
in a CBO building	1%

CBO which sought to represent all of Los Manguitos, Centro Desarrollo Capotillo), two churches and political party branch offices. There was also a community health care clinic and a community primary school, both partly staffed by local volunteers. The community has also worked with an external NGO, Instituto Dominicano de Desarrollo Integral (IDDI). This amounts to a good deal of potential for organizing to confront vulnerability, but was this potential realized? Table 7.4 presents a summary of the actions, advantages and constraints of organizations of three different kinds: informal social organizations (discussed above), CBOs and external NGOs.

The principal barrier to coordinated adaptation between CBOs was personal and political rivalry between the leaders of what had become competing community groups. This was a legacy of the politicization of local organization in the 1970s and 1980s. Some *junta de vecinos* were led by well-known local party

Table 7.4 *Summary of findings*

Organizational Level	Actions	Advantages	Constraints
Informal social organization	• Local environmental improvements. • Neighbourliness and reciprocity. • Disaster refuge. • Self-contained strategy.	• Risk-averse strategy. • High degree of flexibility. • Little social capital or economic resources required.	• Ad hoc. • Actions limited by the individual or family's resources.
CBO	• Local environmental improvements. • Disaster evacuation, repair and rehabilitation. • Builds social networks through sports and cultural activity. • Can respond rapidly to changing local demands.	• Can bring local knowledge and values into planned strategy. • Can give a voice to minority groups or socially isolated individuals.	• Politicization of leadership. • Youth ambivalence. • Unrepresentative leadership. • Lack of cooperation between CBOs.
External NGO	• Strategically addresses local poverty and environmental hazard. • Builds young leaders. • Strengthens ties between CBOs. • Increases local human capital through skills training. • Accesses external funds for projects.	• Can access external resources. • Can mediate local tensions. • Can facilitate exchange of ideas and information horizontally between CBOs or vertically from other external actors. • Can facilitate or enter into public–private partnerships.	• Short/medium-term commitment, any longer risks dependency. • Rivalry with CBOs for community support. • Agenda limited by funding priorities of donors.

Source: Pelling (2002)

activists, which alienated non-party supporters and made cooperation difficult between opposing party groups. One *junta de vecinos* was formed out of a local party group in an attempt to gain more local influence. For all the groups funding was scarce: to prevent allegations of corruption, money was collected from residents for specific projects rather than through any regular membership fees. *Junta de vecinos* are entitled to apply for support from the municipality, but as one leader put it: 'Going to the municipality, you have to make politics if you want help, but *junta de vecinos* … are apolitical, so no help – it's the same with the government' (Aroyo, 1999).

There appeared to be a crisis in local leadership on two counts. First, there was a disproportionately high number of middle-aged male leaders from skilled or professional backgrounds (teachers, lawyers) who clearly are not representative of the population of Los Manguitos. Only one group had a female leader. This gender bias contrasted with group membership, which for all groups was dominated by women and girls. This gendered division of labour within the CBOs was explained by women not wanting to lead but having spare time to contribute to local activities. Underlying this was a culture of machismo, which stressed values for men of self-reliance and individualism as well as support for traditional hierarchical forms of social organization (which reinforced their own power over women). This made it hard for men to join groups and for women to become leaders. Second, there was an anxiety amongst some leaders that there were few young people interested in taking on leadership roles. This was a concern for one leader:

> 'It is time for younger people to take leadership, but the youth are not interested. Young people are more individual and involved in drugs crime... because of a lack of education and jobs' (*Junta de Vecinos* Los Manguitos, 1999).

In Los Manguitos, CBOs had only a little involvement in projects to improve the physical environment or reduce poverty. However, they did respond to Hurricane Georges. Groups evacuated people from the most dangerous dwellings, Civil Defence arrived but too late, when many evacuations had already been completed. AMDEM and MOCUGRECA and a local church used their premises as temporary shelters for about 200 homeless residents. Los Manguitos received no disaster aid, and local groups organized the clearing of debris for one week following the hurricane and organized work parties to rebuild 67 houses that were badly damaged.

The capacity of local organizations to respond to Hurricane Georges was weakened by a lack of cohesion and cooperation between leaderships, which was born out of political and personal competition. This is well illustrated by the attempts of MOCUGRECA to form a local chapter of the DRC:

> 'A Red Cross group was formed as a satellite to the group in 1993. However, soon after another Red Cross group was formed in the Church San Juan Bautista. During Hurricane David, the church group wanted our group to come under their control. In 1995 this was agreed to by the [Dominican] Red Cross as the church has more resources [but we refused], and since then the [Dominican] Red Cross has stopped helping the MOCUGRECA Red Cross group' (MOCUGRECA, 1999).

In addition to households and CBOs, the third tier of organization in Los Manguitos was a developmental NGO, the IDDI, which had a city-wide remit. In 1992, IDDI was invited into the community by leaders who had seen its work in organizing a community refuse collection service for a neighbouring *barrio*. Since then, IDDI had generated funding for drainage, drinking water and sanitation systems as well as organizing the refuse service. Despite developing such a high number of 'coping strategies', IDDI's central concern was to enhance local institutional capacity, to facilitate cooperation amongst the CBOs and to train and motivate a younger cohort of leaders.

IDDI's institutional objectives had partly been achieved through running the refuse business (UCOREBAM) as a joint concern managed by all the local organizations and initially funded by USAID. There is no doubt that inter-group cooperation had increased since IDDI's intervention: 'groups became less passive, and activating these groups then encouraged two new groups [AMDEM and MOCUGRECA] to form' (IDDI, 1999). This view was supported by a leader of AMDEM: 'since IDDI the other organizations are stronger and we work more with them in health education and environmental projects' (AMDEM, 1999). A good indicator of the extent of institutional strengthening in Los Manguitos was shown during Hurricane Georges, when all CBOs worked together. In one week the *barrio* was clean with no outside assistance. The first government supplies arrived after two weeks. As a leader from AMDEM said, 'The community feels that the [CBOs] are the places to go in times of disaster – whatever the cause' (AMDEM, 1999).

There was a strong tension between IDDI's guiding presence and a local dependency upon IDDI as a mediator of local antagonisms. IDDI feared that if it pulled out then fighting between the CBOs would cause the refuse service to collapse. IDDI was criticized by some leaders for having taken good young people away from their organizations, and into IDDI's training and health promotion programme. One leader said: 'the promoters respect IDDI and look to IDDI more than UCOREBAM, for example if there is a meeting at UCOREBAM some don't attend, if there is a meeting at IDDI most do. This takes power away from UCOREBAM and the community groups' (UCOREBAM, 1999).

SUMMARY

The governance regime of Santo Domingo is in transition from authoritative/centralized to democratic/decentralized. But progress is slow. The state sector is in competition with itself, with central government having captured most of the expected responsibilities of municipal government. Civil society actors have begun to move from being principally interested in political protest to being developmental professionals. The high quality of NGO leadership and networked organization in Santo Domingo has been recognized by international funding agencies, and has been mobilized as a strategy for mitigating vulnerability.

Overall, this strategy is to be welcomed. It is likely to contribute to the democratization process and to strengthen the adaptive potential of Dominican society. It also restricts opportunities in the public sector for rent-seeking, and the maintenance of politically partisan and clientelistic relationships with citizens. But there are contradictions within this strategy and in civil society action in Santo Domingo more generally. By choosing to withdraw from supporting the public sector, efficiency gains have been made for vulnerability reduction projects – less money is lost to bureaucracy or rent-seeking, and this has allowed the support of many community-level coping mechanisms. However, it seems that the longer-term aims of institutional modification have not been so easily facilitated.

The study of Los Manguitos revealed existing stocks of social capital, and this was corroborated by the large numbers of developmental CBOs and NGOs in Santo Domingo. But building these stocks into cooperative organizations that operate to promote democracy has proven difficult. The examples of IDDI, DDMC, UNDP and IDAC have shown the variety of ways in which NGOs can work to foster local organization. They are examples of best practice in the simultaneous building of local leadership (institutional modification) and environmental/social improvement (coping mechanisms). It has been more difficult to build linkages with the public sector, and the municipality in particular. CBOs prefer to go directly to central government or NGOs for support, and this has two negative implications for long-term institutional modification. First, it weakens the position of the municipality and reinforces the centralized governance structure of the Dominican Republic. Second, it risks making CBOs dependent upon the patronage of NGOs, and INGOs in turn. The example of IDDI best showed this problem. Cooperation between previously competing CBOs had been built up through the community-based garbage collection business, but despite IDDI's wish to withdraw to prevent the build-up of dependency, it feared that without its strong neutral presence the CBOs would quickly revert to in-fighting. The CBO leaders also recognized this and similarly wanted IDDI to remain active in the community.

Section III

Towards Safer Cities

Chapter 8

Action for Safer Cities

THE SOCIAL ROOTS OF URBAN VULNERABILITY AND RESILIENCE

The aim of this book has been to present an examination of the influence of contrasting institutional/political relationships on the (re)production of human vulnerability to environmental hazard in cities. This was prompted by a gap in the theory and practice of vulnerability mitigation, which tends to engage principally with rural contexts, despite urbanization being increasingly linked to human losses caused by catastrophic and everyday environmental hazard. A clear theme within theoretical and practical work on environmental risk in rural areas is the inter-relatedness of livelihood assets with vulnerability. Livelihood instability can exacerbate vulnerability just as the hazard impacts experienced by vulnerable populations are likely to undermine livelihoods. A focus on livelihoods has broadened the scope of disaster mitigation policy to include questions of social structure and social agency. Social structures are important – the labour market, market access for locally produced goods, access to skills, training and credit and political organization all play a part in shaping livelihood opportunities. Other structures such as the application and monitoring of land-use planning and building codes and the organizational capacity of local government and emergency services to anticipate and respond to catastrophic disaster will contribute directly to shaping urban vulnerability to environmental risk.

But, as the opening example of local response to a landslide in Patayas showed, individual agency is also important. Experiences of exposure and risk and of direct disaster impacts are spatially bounded. This means that despite the deeper systemic and historical roots of vulnerability and hazard, vulnerability to disasters with a natural trigger and their direct impacts tend to manifest in clearly defined places and at specific times. There is a similarity here with economic or social stresses or shocks, which tend to be generated widely as systemic pressures acting across the urban political economy or certain of its sectors, but which also have local manifestations in time and place; the intensity of urban un(der)employment or political violence varies spatially and socially across the city. Being spatially bounded means that the vulnerability to environmental risk is amenable to policies and projects that raise local capacities of resilience in addition to wider structural reforms in urban social, political and economic life that tackle risk at the city level. A focus on the local brings social agency under the policy spotlight. How can local actors – individuals, households, families, community groups etc – be enabled to develop the skills and resources appropriate for building resilience to reduce vulnerability to environmental risk in the city? Answering this question is perhaps easier in theory than in practice. Whilst many tools exist for building local resilience, for good reason local actors are often unwilling to take on the extra burden of mitigating their own vulnerability.

Why should the vulnerable, many of whom have to expend their resources, time and energy just getting by, be expected to plan for future uncertainties and risk? For many individuals and households this is a non-question – they simply cannot. But work on rural environmental risk management and urban development has shown that where individuals or households may have a little spare capacity in their asset profiles to invest in vulnerability reduction, at the level of the community resources and willingness to act may be available (see the journal *Environment and Urbanization* for many case studies). For urban risk management, then, local agency lies with individuals but also with formal and informal groups of residents and neighbours who, based on regular social contact and the trust that this has engendered, have built up social support networks. Recent work on social capital is useful in identifying different types of social relationship. Two broad classifications are of relevance here. The first makes a broad distinction between 'latent' (Fukuyama, 2001) or 'cognitive' (Moser and McIlwaine, 2001) social capital and organizational social capital. Latent or cognitive social capital is found in social norms, the expressions of trust that individuals have for each other. Organizational social capital is found in social behaviour. The amount of formal social capital held by residents of a specified area is indicated by the number, orientation and activities of social groups and networks. Some networks are informal and at a casual glance may be invisible: neighbours getting together to repair a damaged house, for example. Others, such as community groups, are more formally constituted and have greater visibility to outside observers or policy-makers. Of course, social groups, networks and organizations need not contribute to building resiliency – some may have an ambiguous relationship, others may appear more counter-developmental or 'perverse', such as drugs gangs. A second categorization of social capital focuses on the links between social actors. It differentiates between bonding, bridging and linking capital. Bonding capital is held between individuals in a group – it is what holds the group together: a shared interest, experience or belief system, for example. Bridging capital is held horizontally between different social groups – say two community-based groups which join forces to clean a shared drain. Linking capital is held vertically between organizations: this could include a link between a community group and a partner organization outside of the community, such as a developmental NGO or local government agency.

Local social capital in all its categorized forms plays a key role in shaping a local area's adaptive potential. But social capital does not exist in isolation from other assets: it is cross-cut by the changing livelihood status of individuals, groups, their leaders, members and non-members. Economic poverty not only excludes people from market consumption and access to basic needs, but can also act as a barrier to involvement in social and communal activities outside the household. As a household's economic resources (savings etc) and income declines, it becomes harder to expend time and resources on community-level work or obligations. Even simple neighbourly ties based on reciprocity can become difficult to sustain as households come close to Swift's point of collapse. When money is short, loans and gifts cannot be extended and even common hospitality may be too great a burden, leading to increased social isolation for the poorest and reducing the representativeness of local social organization (McIlwaine, 1998; Moser, 1998). This can be a particularly acute problem for single-headed households, many of which may be female-headed. In a similar fashion, community-level organization – especially of a formal kind – is often riven by religious, ethnic or political differences (Desai, 1995; Pelling, 1998). In some communities, local organization may be predominantly counter-developmental, as in the case of drug- or crime-related gangs.

Attempts by actors from within and outside local communities to enhance or realize adaptive potential by building or activating stocks of local social capital will always be difficult. There are two particularly tough barriers to overcome, especially for external actors who will initially lack a clear insight into local personalities and party politics. First, there is the heterogeneity of interests within the community, which at times can undermine community cohesiveness, fracturing social capital and preventing the building and maintenance of local social organizations with which to strategically confront local developmental concerns, including the many aspects of vulnerability. Second, in those neighbourhoods where CBOs are present, they are as likely to be antagonistic as they are to support one another. As the case studies have shown, these barriers are deeply connected to the development path of the wider society in which the community is placed, as well as to the personalities found in that community. But the case studies have also shown successful contributions being made at the local level to reduce vulnerability. Three key generalizations from this empirical work are:

1   that informal social organization exists and could be used as a target for reaching groups excluded from more formal organizations;
2   that external organizations can act as a stabilizing force to extend inclusiveness and reduce negative forms of competition between existing formal community organizations; and
3   that community-level action to enhance coping needs to be supported by wider engagement with the political/institutional structures of the city, which can in turn open up more political space for community-level adaptation.

In this final chapter, the core findings of the theoretical discussion and case studies are brought together to identify the limits of community-level action for vulnerability reduction. What can or should local actors be asked to do to reduce their own vulnerability, and how can external actors best work with local actors to build local resilience? Differences in the political orientation and institutional structures of the case studies allow some comment to be made on the relative impact of past and contemporary development strategies on experiences of environmental hazard and potential for resilience. This discussion starts with an overview of the ways in which urbanization, environmental change and hazard are linked; the role of institutional frameworks or city governance regimes on shaping risk is then reviewed; possibilities for political actors in the city to resist, work with or change these structures as a means of opening scope for adaptive potential is then compared between the case studies, and general principles for building adaptive potential are outlined. These findings are then linked back to the literature reviewed in Chapters 1 to 4, before closing with suggestions for further research.

URBANIZATION, ENVIRONMENTAL CHANGE AND HAZARD

Within all the case studies, regardless of local political and economic characteristics, weak environmental legislation and a lack of adequate capacity or willingness amongst government and non-governmental actors to enforce legislation or foster cultural norms meant there were few barriers to environmental change and consequent hazard production in and around the city. Decisions not to intervene in the rapid expansion of urban areas and the consumption or modification of environmental assets, or to become directly involved in this process of environmental change, were of course encouraged by the imperatives of economic growth on the one hand and survival on the other, and in this way were themselves set within the broader pressures of national and global economic, political and environmental change. A number of relationships between urbanization and environmental change were identified and these are brought together below into two main areas of interaction: external environmental change and environmental change within the city.

External environmental change

Institutional responses to global climate change and sea-level rise are in their infancy. Across the case studies, dedicated state funding for structural mitigation – for example, the construction of sea walls in direct response to global climate change – was notable for its absence. In Georgetown, the city most directly at risk from sea-level rise, the Guyanese Environmental Protection Agency had commenced a study to identify coastal vulnerability to sea-level rise, but this was in its earliest stages of scoping. Environmental degradation in rural areas also increased hazard in the city, especially when hydrological regimes or coastal systems were affected. In each case there was an inability or unwillingness to enforce existing legislation to control rural resource extraction. In Guyana, much of the loss of coastal mangroves and sand cheniers (ridges), which had acted as natural sea defences, was accounted for by small business or individual household extraction. Ironically, householders have for many years extracted chenier sand to build up their own house yards as a coping response to flooding. The result is a short-term reduction in individual exposure to flood risk but an increase over the long term in collective exposure and vulnerability as natural sea defences are degraded.

Watershed management plans and coastal zone management plans had been prepared in each case study, but implementation was slow because of broad institutional inertia (some individuals in environment agencies were exceptionally dynamic but constrained by inertia in government overall), financial constraints, a lack of human resources and possibly the influence of powerful vested interests. The latter was especially apparent in Bridgetown and Santo Domingo, both of which had a more pronounced contemporary experience of large-scale capitalist investment in activities based on natural resource exploitation in the cities' peripheries and hinterlands than had Georgetown. Examples included deforestation of hill-slopes for intensive agriculture around Santo Domingo, and land-use change from sugar cane plantations to golf courses around Bridgetown. Both land-use changes led to increased rates of runoff and urban flooding. In Barbados, the island's tourist economy had contributed to this through beach-based tourism developments whose physical presence and lack of waste management facilities had led to the degradation of inshore coral reefs and the interruption of coastal sedimentary cycles, leading to increased risk from coastal flooding and erosion.

Environmental change in the city

Planned and unplanned developments were seen to have contributed to increasing city-wide environmental risk. In all cities though, but especially in the poorer cities of Santo Domingo and Georgetown, urban growth took place primarily through the informal housing sector outside of formal planning control. Squatting on peripheral land or marginal land in the city created growing populations without access to basic services, infrastructure or formal political representation. In itself this increased risk exposure, but in a double whammy of risk production many urban squatter settlements were also sited close to key components of urban environmental infrastructure, for example sources of drinking water, drainage canals or rivers. Settlement in these sites made the maintenance of basic services more difficult and introduced new pathways in the production of environmental risk, for example through potential for the contamination of drinking water or reduced storm drainage capacity. It is important to note that squatters living in these sites were merely the vehicles of risk production in the city; the real motor was a lack of affordable and appropriately located urban housing.

Squatting in Santo Domingo was an outcome of state land clearance and the redevelopment of low-income, inner-city neighbourhoods in the 1980s. In Georgetown, most squatters were escaping from the unhealthy environment of inner-city rental accommodation, and taking a chance on the possibility for improved environmental and economic conditions that squatting could offer. In Barbados, squatting was less widespread, a reflection of higher incomes and government housing policy. However, some squatting sites had been established during the 1990s, many residents having been labour migrants from neighbouring islands. A large proportion of squatters originated from St Lucia and St Vincent. In Bridgetown the largest squatter settlement consists of 100 squatter households that have colonized the Bell Water Reserve. This is the source of one-third of Bridgetown's drinking water. Hence, household wastes from the squatters threaten to produce a city-wide hazard. Planners face a dilemma of providing drainage and sanitation services for the squatters to alleviate local and city-wide environmental risk, or clearing the squatter settlement by force if necessary. The problem with the former proposal is that it would send out a message to other potential squatters that targeting well reserve lands is a quick route to gaining services, whilst the latter policy option goes against the instincts and training of the Barbadian planners. At the time of writing, no final decision has been made. This planning dilemma serves to highlight the complexity of urban risk management, where different scales of risk – local housing quality/city-wide drinking water – can operate in the same location simultaneously, and where the solution to an identified risk may unleash further and possibly more dangerous risks for the future.

A STRUCTURAL VIEW: INSTITUTIONAL FRAMEWORKS AND ADAPTIVE POTENTIAL

In this section, urban risk and vulnerability production are viewed from a structural-historical perspective. This helps in revealing the extent to which present-day vulnerabilities and capacities for building adaptive potential are the outcome of historical development paths, as opposed to contemporary development policy. This is important, since we need to know reasonably the degree to which contemporary policy interventions can hope to build resilience and security. To what extent might successful policy outcomes be made more elusive when the root causes for urban risk and vulnerability are deeply historical and structural?

Historicizing vulnerability

The evidence presented below reinforces the existing theoretical consensus that contemporary vulnerability and adaptive potential are rooted in history – in this case, in the historical coevolution of the city within national and global political economies and environmental change. Human vulnerability and hazard are at the same time outcomes of and pressures shaping the historical progression of these relationships. The bullet points below outline a chronology of the coevolutionary production of vulnerability, from the colonial period to contemporary experiences of participatory development, based on the case study material presented in Chapters 5, 6 and 7.

- The colonial period laid the foundations for much contemporary vulnerability through settlement patterns (coastal and low-lying settlements), social composition (Georgetown's mixed racial composition being a source of competition and community fracture in contrast to Bridgetown's relative racial homogeneity) and government form (Barbados is still run on a Westminster-style system with local members of parliament (MPs) being accountable to their electorate, thereby increasing community access to decision-making but also generating dependency upon long-serving MPs).
- The post-colonial period was one of nation building and political consolidation. This led to the radicalization of politics in the Dominican Republic and Guyana, which persists today and deeply shapes both political agendas, and on a more fundamental level access to political power and the distribution of resources with which to confront local vulnerability in the city. Barbados enjoyed relative political and economic stability in the transition to independence, and this has continued into the post-colonial period with relative economic prosperity indicating low levels of vulnerability.
- The Cold War period acted to normalize political polarization that had emerged out of power struggles during the post-colonial period. In Guyana, international isolation led to economic crisis, the rapid decay of urban infrastructure and widespread environmental hazard. In Santo Domingo, where a series of right-wing governments have been in conflict with left-wing grassroots and workers' organizations since this period, political parties have co-opted local organizations, which tend to focus on national political issues and overlook local issues of poverty and vulnerability reduction.
- The hegemony of the USA and market liberalism from the late 1980s onwards, exemplified best by SAPs, re-shaped urban political economies and stimulated a growth in urban poverty. In Georgetown, large-scale redundancies in the, predominantly urban, Afro-Guyanese public sector workforce effectively created a new vulnerable sector in Guyanese society. Barbados, with the most stable economy and already operating a liberal democracy, also underwent structural adjustment with some increases in unemployment amongst unskilled public sector workers. However, the new unemployed in Bridgetown have received attention from the state and developmental civil society organizations, ameliorating the negative social impact of structural adjustment in this case.
- The participatory agenda of the 1990s was used alternatively to cut labour costs and add sustainability in donor-financed projects, and/or as a means

of empowering local actors in predominantly NGO-funded projects. The result has been an increased flow of resources into civil society. In Georgetown and Bridgetown, the small size of civil society frustrated donors. In Georgetown, large amounts of money were spent in the early and mid-1990s on locally sponsored development initiatives in attempts to stimulate the growth of local community capacity in this post-socialist society. Whilst some useful projects were completed that did genuinely reduce vulnerability – school refurbishments, road upgrading, drain and drinking water infrastructure rehabilitation etc – large sums of money were captured by local political/business elite groups, and an opportunity for building positive social capital through the implementation of participatory development projects was lost. In Bridgetown, the small number of developmentally oriented groups is linked to a decline in communal activities in general in this prosperous and liberal society. Existing groups are in danger of being swamped by new roles and responsibilities as the participatory agenda washes over Barbados. In Santo Domingo, civil society is large but partisan, and competition between differently aligned groups has resulted in the government blocking civil society projects (eg, at the time of writing, a contract to re-house 300 families made homeless by Hurricane Georges, awarded by a Spanish NGO to the Dominican NGO Juan Montalvo, had yet to receive approval from the Ministry of Housing after ten months).

Contemporary institutional structures and adaptive potential

Table 8.1 maps out the main elements of each city's institutional framework. These are composed of the public sector, private sector and civil society organizations that contribute to shaping the political environment in which local adaptive potential either grows or is suppressed. They also contribute to disaster mitigation in their own right at the city level. The capacity of each city to respond to vulnerability is discussed below.

• In Santo Domingo, public sector agencies were involved in emergency warning, response and relief, but with many gaps in provision. A key weakness was a lack of internal coordination, which led for example to the failure to issue and act upon a 36-hour evacuation warning preceding Hurricane Georges. Actors from within civil society provided a wide range of support, including basic needs, community-level training in disaster prevention strategies and primary health care, facilitation of local structural mitigation works and providing emergency response and relief. A large international NGO community used local NGOs as a network to reach communities in the disbursement of aid following Hurricane Georges. International donors engaged in institutional modification through the

Table 8.1 *City-wide adaptive potential*

	Georgetown	Santo Domingo	Bridgetown
Institutional framework			
Government structure	Local, regional and national government	Local and national government	National government
Approximate size of urban developmental civil society	20 CBOs 10 NGOs	1000s of CBOs 100s of NGOs	10 CBOs 10 NGOs
NGO network groups	Very limited, not inclusive membership	Many networks with political influence	None
Disaster mitigation			
The state	Civil Defence reinstated in 1996, relief only	Civil Defence active in prevention and relief	CERO/DERO active in prevention and relief
Civil society	A few NGOs active in relief only	Many NGOs/CBOs active in all aspects of disaster mitigation	Few organizations, very limited involvement in relief
Private sector	None	Institute of Architects building codes, TV/radio time	Radio time and paper space
International network membership	PAHO, CDERA since 1996, IFRC/RC	PAHO, ECHO regional office, IFRC/RC regional office	PAHO, CDERA headquarters, IFRC/RC
Urban environmental services			
Public sector	Long-term lack of investment, crisis management across the city in all sectors	Great inequality in service provision with the poor majority being excluded	Good coverage of basic needs
Civil society	Isolated projects stimulated by outside actors. The sector is blighted by politicization. Some limited success in squatter settlements	Vibrant CBO/NGO sector but within state partnership	Isolated projects. Community action lacks popular support and there is dependency on the state
Private sector	Limited resources and experience, hostile relationship with city council	Experienced, linked to corruption in city government	Experienced, close relationship with national government

preferential funding of civil society actors, the restructuring of the city government and efforts to create a constructive dialogue between civil society and the public sector through the funding of a City Forum event, where civil society groups and the municipality came together to discuss future development plans.

- In Georgetown, a reforming state-centred regime, the central government (through the Civil Defence and the Hydrometeorological Service) provided flood warning and relief management services. Civil Defence was revived in 1996 following nationwide flooding and has been successful in coordinating relief efforts involving both the state and civil society in response to floods and drought in the city and nationally. The suppression of civil society and its slow recovery rate meant that only a small number of CBOs were active in the provision of basic infrastructure, with four NGOs engaged in disaster relief work. Only the Guyana Red Cross was involved in disaster preparedness, and this on a modest scale. A lack of human resources, opportunism and politicization within civil society constrained the effectiveness of civil society groups despite increasingly available financial resources. It is difficult to judge whether most vulnerable groups have been able to access relief provided by civil society groups or the public sector. Institutional modification requires a long-term investment by local and international actors to reorient the public and private sector as well as civil society following 25 years of state control. It did not seem likely that the present regime or international actors were prepared to undertake such a commitment.

- In Bridgetown, a liberal democracy, perhaps surprisingly the state was the principal provider of services. The CERO coordinated disaster relief through local DEROs. The system was only partly functional, as 16 out of 28 groups were inactive. CBOs were rare and covered only small areas of Bridgetown. However, they were successful in improving access to services amongst low-income communities, and some groups had also undertaken community risk and vulnerability mapping. Overall, a lack of popular participation constrained both the state-led and NGO/CBO-sector vulnerability amelioration programmes. This is likely to also constrain local responsiveness in the event of a catastrophic disaster where the state's ability to function will be compromised. In contrast to the other case studies, here it was the state that led the way in institutional modification, which continued to weaken civil society by the co-option of its leaders. There was little resistance from civil society. International donors had attempted to increase funding to civil society, but there are few appropriate applicants and funding was in danger of having the perverse effect of overstretching and overburdening civil society groups. A case in point is UNDP's Global Environment Facility small grant scheme, which had supported two projects in Barbados.

A number of generic observations can be made from the case studies, and they are set out below:

Challenges to developing adaptive potential

International donors emerged as political actors with great potential for shaping supportive institutional frameworks. A number of challenges to donor interventions were identified:

- Entrenched cultures of opposition and mistrust between the public sector and civil society reduce the likelihood of partnerships forming to confront vulnerability. Donors need to work to build norms of behaviour and that can encourage cooperation between the sectors.
- The participatory agenda produces a tendency amongst donors to ignore the public sector. Though there are good reasons for this, if taken too far opportunities for collaborative public action and even democratic principles are undermined as the elected city council is pushed further away from local development actions, with its relevance being popularly questioned and its responsibilities taken over by non-elected leaders in civil society.
- International agendas are often applied by donors without a deep understanding of local political contexts. This creates inefficiencies, especially when donors seek to make changes in the institutional environment of the city by funding community-sponsored development projects that in some cases only reinforce clientelism and strengthen local elites.
- A longer time frame is needed for projects that seek institutional modification in the city. Contemporary project management and assessment time frames are inappropriate and create a barrier to the adoption of innovative strategies to enhance adaptive potential.
- Re-applying local examples of good practice, when these exist, is better than developing new programmes. Formal networks between CBOs and NGOs and informal networks between local leaders increase the possibility that local actors will identify and re-apply good practice without turning to external actors for strategic input. This reduces dependency on donors and encourages local innovation, and should be supported. In small cities and states, where human and social capital might be limited, regional networks offer an alternative orientation for networking and sharing information.

Findings suggest that in cities where vulnerability is high, even when manifest adaptations are inadequate to the scale of risk, underlying adaptive potential is likely to be strong. Structural constraints on the unleashing of adaptive potential varied across the case studies according to political regime form and historical development trajectories. Politically partisan non-state organization and an overly centralized state sector constrained action in Santo Domingo; the historical suppression of local organization under a so-called socialist regime continued to act as a barrier to citizen participation in Georgetown; successful private sector-led economic development and a strong and stable state constrained the capacity of organized civil society activity in Bridgetown. In each case, state and private sector or government and individual-oriented adaptations to environmental risk predominated over civil society-directed or communal efforts to reduce vulnerability amongst a range of related social and environmental ills suffered by the economically, socially and politically marginalized. But despite heavy structural constraints on civil society action, social capital was identified within communities at risk, and at times blossomed successfully in collective action to counteract those pressures producing local risk and vulnerability. It is to the power of local actors that we now turn.

CITIZEN AGENCY AND ADAPTIVE POTENTIAL

Whilst a historical-structural perspective is useful in identifying the broad and deep lines of power that shape risk and vulnerability, it underplays the ability of individual actors to resist or re-shape these forces at the local level. In this section we look at local capacity from across the case studies – can grassroots actors build local organizational capacity with which to advance collective adaptive potential in the face of historical-structural constraints? If so, what might the role be of external and international development agencies in this process of building local organizations and orienting their work to make a positive contribution towards building collective resilience?

Table 8.2 summarizes findings from the household questionnaire surveys conducted in each city. In every case social capital was present, as indicated by observed ties of informal social support. Differences in social capital and organization are partly influenced by cultural and historical context, but also by those institutional arrangements outlined in the previous section, and here we see the interaction of historical-structural forces with local agency in the production of adaptive potential.

• The most comprehensive range of local social organization and action was found where informal social support had been built up into local community group membership in Los Manguitos. At the time of the study there were six active CBOs and one active NGO in this neighbourhood. The NGO, IDDI, had been invited into the community by local community groups and had worked with them to form a jointly managed community business to collect garbage, called UCOREBAM. UCOREBAM represented a coping strategy and, through the building of cooperation between previously antagonistic CBOs, a means of institutional modification. On the other hand, the long-term sustainability of this short-term pact was doubtful because of deeply rooted political conflict between the CBOs. Hence IDDI was resigned to staying within the community longer than planned, to maintain group solidarity.

Table 8.2 *Social capital and social organization*

Variable	Albouystown, Georgetown (%)	Los Manguitos, Santo Domingo (%)	The Pine, Bridgetown (%)
Informal social support			
Spoke to neighbour today	83	91	65
Where does your closest friend live?	same house, 48; neighbour, 29	same house, 36 neighbour, 60	same house, 32; neighbour, 34
Leave doors unlocked whilst going to the shops	40	33	61
Share food with neighbours	36	44	35
Clean drains with neighbours	63	n/a	29
Clean streets with neighbours	53	66	24
Shop for neighbours	64	44	33
Play sports with neighbours	21	39	23
Local group membership			
Religious group	60	46	48
Sports group	6	29	7
Community group	5	24	11
Political party	18	39	29
Participation in elections			
Most recent national elections	81	70	80
Most recent city elections	79	63	n/a
Knowledge of disaster prevention			
Have you ever attended a disaster prevention meeting?	n/a	12	6
Do you know where your nearest hurricane shelter is?	n/a	43	61

Notes: All data are percentage values for positive responses.
n/a = question was not applicable.

- Elsewhere, high levels of informal social interaction remained undeveloped or latent. This was the case in Albouystown (with the exception of high levels of religious group membership). Efforts by UNDP, the CHPA and local leaders to build up organizations in Albouystown had all failed. In Georgetown's political history, community organizations have been repressed or co-opted, and in Albouystown active community members have been used as foot soldiers for competing political parties. The continued influence of political parties was shown in high rates of political party membership and in high voter turn-outs at national and city elections. Residents were wary of local organizations because of their perceived lack of financial transparency, as well as their political orientation. Only two developmental CBOs were identified: both had little popular support and meagre resources.

- Informal social ties in the Pine had been built upon by a long history of successful community organization. This was centred upon the CBO PCW, which had been active in welfare and social development since the 1980s. The ability of PCW to continue engaging the community may be due to its on-going innovation and ability to reorient its programmes in response to changing tastes and demands from the community and external actors. The most recent example was an emphasis on sports as a way of encouraging youth involvement with community action and self-improvement. The breadth of this CBO's engagement with the community is registered by 96 per cent of respondents having heard of the PCW and just under a quarter having been, at some time, its client. Potential barriers to citizen agency in this case came from two quarters. First, ties between the CBO and community were loosening with the co-option of senior leaders from PCW to government appointments, including that of Minister for Social Mobilization in 1999. Second, the scarcity of human capital from within the community had made it difficult to recruit middle-management staff, with existing staff facing increasing workloads.

Across the case studies, women were over-represented in membership and under-represented in leadership roles in CBOs. Gender division was weakest in the Pine. The reasons given by respondents for high group membership included women having more spare time, being more interested in neighbourhood issues because of spending time locally, and being more interested in health and environmental issues because of their caring roles within the household. The reasons for low leadership levels included less access to secondary education, the advantage men have in negotiating with outsiders (also largely men), and women not wanting to be leaders. Underlying such reasoning were cultures of machismo, which stress the value for men of self-reliance, self-sufficiency, individualism and traditional lines of authority (which reinforced their own power over women). Machismo made it hard for men to join community organizations and difficult for women to hold leadership positions.

Constraints on social organization for vulnerability reduction

A number of constraints on social organization were observed, and whilst it is difficult to generalize beyond the specific contexts of the case studies it seems likely that the constraints identified here will be found elsewhere, to varying extents, in the cities of Africa, Asia and Latin America and the Caribbean.

- The priorities of donors and NGOs/CBOs seldom converge, creating insecurity, opportunism and long-term difficulties for local actors. One response has been for NGOs/CBOs to generate their own income. Community businesses and business-like organizational management structures were observed that offered stability, but at the cost of abandoned democratic structures. Efficiency was in danger of over-ruling equity.

- Modernization has a contradictory effect on community organization. The privatization of leisure time, increased social and physical mobility and a shift in individual identification from place of residence to lifestyle and professional group meant that socio-economic development was associated with the underdevelopment of community organization and negative consequences for local adaptive potential.

- There are key moments in the life history of communities, with peaks in support for the transformation of social capital into social organization. Examples of these moments include the colonization of squatter settlements, the response and early reconstruction phases of a disaster event, and following consciousness-raising exercises by external activists. These moments are opportunities for local organization building and the setting of local goals that meld together vulnerability reduction and human development. The constraint here is in the fleeting nature of such opportunities. For external actors, taking advantage of such openings for community organization requires the ability to respond quickly to changing local circumstances and the maintenance of an information network.

- Communities are characterized by heterogeneity and internal competition as well as cooperation. Similarly, CBOs are often organized to compete with each other for external support and group membership and local influence, whether they draw membership and legitimacy from defined social groups or spatial territories. Whilst a degree of competition amongst local actors can be healthy for organizational fitness, international agencies seeking to enhance local adaptive potential should have regard to the need to overcome competitive norms and build community consensus without excluding marginal groups.

- Community organizers were often in competition with local party activists. Party activists needed to prevent apolitical organization and were able to undermine self-help activities by claiming resources from party networks or influence with politicians. It was common for party activists to have co-opted or prevented local organization and so to have maintained community ties of dependency and clientelism. Community leaders had developed strategies in response. These tended to focus on a symbolic and actual distancing of the organization and its structure from political groups – mixed membership and leadership was a common tool.

- The contested legitimacy of leadership. Where organizations do not have structures of internal democracy, they tend to reinforce dominant norms of autocracy, paternalism and dependency found within the wider society. However, democratic models are perceived as reducing organizational efficiency, with delays in decision-making and leadership changes interrupting programme cycles. There is likely to be a preference among leaders for efficiency and continuum in leadership and for the abandonment or subversion of democratic models of organization. The human and financial resource constraints of community groups at times make it impractical to open leadership positions up to elections, and where this had taken place organizations were open to capture by political activists. The personalities of individual leaders made a big difference: if they were generally perceived to be open to new ideas and to be unprejudiced in their views and actions, the group gained more widespread support. Where community groups were in competition with political activists, such openness and inclusivity was worn as a distinct badge of difference by community organizers.

OPPORTUNITIES AND BARRIERS TO BUILDING ADAPTIVE POTENTIAL

Building social organization for vulnerability reduction

Knowledge of local social organization is key for interventions from external actors, both governmental and non-governmental. Vulnerability reduction initiatives tend to be most successful when piggybacked onto the activities of established CBOs or NGOs. This is a common observation for local development work, but in the case of vulnerability reduction has particular salience. Mobilizing new local groups around the theme of vulnerability reduction is made difficult by the non-immediate nature of many threats. More than this, forming new groups creates additional transaction costs and real costs for the community and external agents, and raises the question of group sustainability, with groups liable to failure once external support is removed. However, when existing communities and community leadership are known to exclude social groups (women, youths, ethnic or religious minorities or supporters of political parties) the additional costs of new group formation are likely to be less than the inefficiencies and inequities that would lie in working with pre-existing organization.

Being gender-conscious

Women are often the most active community members in informal and formal community organizations. However, most community organizations are led by men and few organizations explicitly seek to target women's issues. Women have been targeted in interventions because of their gendered roles in household (and by extension) community maintenance. Women's participation has, therefore, been seen as a means to achieve community involvement rather than as a mechanism for women's empowerment. Women are often identified as having a high vulnerability to environmental hazard, and vulnerability reduction programmes need to consider women as a target as well as a tool for vulnerability reduction action.

The relationship between vulnerability and adaptive potential

Adaptive potential is composed of coping strategies, which alleviate the immediate causes of vulnerability and are set within an enabling environment, and institutional modifications, which seek to change the enabling environment itself to enhance coping. Grassroots organization to reduce vulnerability is most likely to occur where vulnerability is high and visible and where there are no institutional constraints on building social capital up into social organization. External interventions seeking to reduce vulnerability need to act on two levels: first, fostering positive local social organization to confront vulnerability; and second, supporting institutional frameworks in the city that will not constrain local social organization.

Scope for building partnerships with the private sector

The private sector is often limited to the role of a state-contracted provider of basic services or infrastructures. However, the scope for greater integration in vulnerability reduction through partnerships with civil society was observed, for example, through the generation and self-regulation of building codes and architectural quality standards and in setting aside TV, radio and printed press space for education on local vulnerability reduction initiatives. Civil society organizations offered technical input and oversight to guarantee good practice and private sector organizations contributed access to professional networks and media space.

Challenges for donors seeking to foster local adaptive potential

International donors emerged as political actors with great potential for stimulating institutional modification in the city. Two key challenges to donor interventions were identified. First, contemporary project management forms and assessment time frames are inappropriate. Time frames for project completions were too short and became a barrier to local innovation to enhance adaptive potential. Projects with the explicit goal of enhancing local leadership or community-level capacity for organization to build adaptive potential were still trapped within time frames designed for physical infrastructure projects. Social development is a long-term commitment: short-term interventions tended to be counter-productive, raising expectations without delivering the social or physical goods. Project formats that succeeded best brought together extended periods of social development work (leadership training, citizenship rights education, community mapping etc) with opportunities to apply for (and generally win) support for a physical infrastructure project. The tying together of the social and physical infrastructure components made for a complicated project pro forma and increased management costs, but the benefits in terms of project impact appeared well worthwhile.

A second and related challenge was the difficulty in measuring project impact where the goal is vulnerability reduction or ultimately reduced exposure to disaster loss – how can one measure the extent to which something does not happen? The need for vulnerability indicators is well recognized by local and international agencies. Proxies in use were inclusivity of community leadership, the success rate of grant applications from community groups, the ability of communities to self-organize and accounts from community members following disaster events. These were all qualitative, rapid assessment measures. Alternatives, including the change through time of local distributional inequalities in household asset profiles, would require considerable resource investment, and for many agencies the costs were prohibitive.

URBAN ENVIRONMENTAL RISK: A NEW RESEARCH AGENDA FOR POLICY REFORM

Even in the most marginalized urban neighbourhood, local actors do have some capacity to respond to environmental hazard. For particular actors, circumstances may give individual actions preference over communal responses to hazard and vulnerability. This may be because of risk-aversion reasons, for fear of communal rent-seeking, because the individual places value on individualism and self-sufficiency, or because of the need to attend to other competing demands on an individual's time and resources. The case studies suggest that this is not because of a lack of social capital, which was shown to be present. This said, the extent to which latent social capital can cross over into building up social organizations to make a positive contribution towards vulnerability reduction will vary in different political contexts. This is a central concern for building adaptive capacity. The case of Los Manguitos demonstrated the difficulty such a project faces: in this case, community heterogeneity, competition between leaders and the politicization of local development goals all conspired to reduce the willingness of neighbours to join together in formal organizations. A substantial literature exists on urban micro-politics and social development in the city, but areas for further research remain. Importantly, much of the existing literature focuses on Latin America and Asia. African cities, which are the fastest growing today, have received less attention despite their high levels of risk, particularly to flooding but also to social disasters such as civil war, medical disasters such as the AIDS pandemic and the complex disasters that result from two or more of these kinds of disaster overlapping. Whilst African cities have similarities in terms of administrative models with their Latin American and Asian counterparts, and the principles of vulnerability reduction (including adaptive potential as outlined in this monograph) have application, the characteristics of urban African societies in particular call out for additional case-study work to refine more specific policy guidance.

The importance of access to political decision-makers in the city or at a more local level in shaping peoples' vulnerability and capacity for resilience needs to be conceptualized within a broader bundle of household assets. A household's livelihood asset profile determines individual and household status and the proximity of a household to Swift's (1989) theoretical point of collapse, where the household as a unit of economic production and social reproduction is no longer viable. The focus of this monograph and the bulk of research upon which it is based has been on political and social assets. There is a need for greater understanding of the ways in which urban livelihoods are formed by individuals and households, and how they function and contribute towards individual, household and collective vulnerability and resilience. There are a number of basic research questions about urban livelihoods that would inform questions of vulnerability. For example, the literature on urban labour markets tends to draw up a dichotomy between the formal and informal sector. At a local level, such a division may be less important as people undertake employment in both sectors simultaneously. Recent changes in the structure of urban economies brought about by structural adjustment or the presence/absence of foreign investment have been linked to the formation of new groups of the poor. How these groups have responded to poverty, identifying the tactics and assets employed to cope with or move out of poverty, and subsequently applying policy to assist those able to move on and support those who have not yet been able to move out of economic poverty, are key areas of research for the future. At an individual level, the role of psychological status in determining whether an individual is able to muster sufficient agency to cope with poverty, or feels unable to respond to the structures of the urban (and local/global) political economy, could also be usefully examined. There is some movement in this direction (see, for example, Narayan, 2000), but a great deal of scope exists both for basic research into urban livelihoods, and in a more applied agenda to investigate how livelihoods are linked with the social and political aspects of adaptive potential and vulnerability/resilience to external shocks, including those of the environment.

The case studies indicated that the best chance for building local adaptive potential came from partnership, primarily involving NGOs, many of which had links with the municipality and/or international donors. In Bridgetown, beneficial linkages with government community development workers from CERO provided a focus for building community-level adaptive potential, showing the potential offered by state actors as partners in vulnerability reduction. The role of the private sector was more ambiguous, with donations of air time from media companies contributing towards preparedness and post-disaster charity assisting in recovery, but no examples emerged of direct business

support for local coping mechanisms or lobbying for positive structural/
institutional changes in the city that could open up new space for coping
mechanisms to evolve. Perhaps the single exception to this was the Dominican
Architects Association which, in partnership with the NGO DDMC, had
undertaken to promote the monitoring of building construction to oversee the
implementation of building codes. There is clearly much scope for the private
sector to play a more active role in fighting social vulnerability. There is very
little research into the private sector's contribution to reducing vulnerability, and
this is an area for further research. Large companies often train workers in on-
site safety procedure, but is or could this be extended to training in external risk
management? Has the corporate social responsibility agenda included
vulnerability or risk-reduction efforts? Are companies linked to foreign
investment more or less likely to support workers by investing in measures to
reduce vulnerability where they live as well as where they work – both being an
outcome of their employment?

Clearly, challenging local vulnerability requires institutional change in the
city and beyond as well as in the community. Vulnerability can be indicated in
the city by exposure to risk, economic poverty/inequality and political
marginality. Using these indicators, all the case studies shared a high level of
vulnerability. Bridgetown, as the most economically developed, had the least
poverty and indicated lower absolute levels of exposure to risk, but inequality
and political marginalization were present. Santo Domingo, with a history of
right-wing, authoritarian rule, and Georgetown, a post-socialist city, both had
high levels of inequality and vulnerability. But a low per capita GNP and the
depth of political marginalization experienced by residents of Georgetown
suggest that comparative absolute vulnerability was highest there. The central
point to emerge from these comparative studies is that past and contemporary
development strategies, systems of political organization and the distribution of
power within the city do make a difference in the scale and depth of
vulnerability to environmental risk.

The vision of a city as a symbol of political power and national identity was
most acute in Santo Domingo. The largest of the city case studies (with a
population approaching 5 million), it approached mega-city status. Santo
Domingo's position as an urban centre with regional significance, coupled with
the autocratic style of national/city leaders, was linked to a preference for
prestige developments and reduced investment in health and education. In this
case, the pressure on decision-makers hoping to compete at a global level is
even more intense, with the symbolic value of prestige developments being
seen as a strategy for attracting foreign investment (Short and Yeong-Hyun,
1999). The links between global competitiveness and the place of poverty
amelioration and vulnerability reduction in strategies for attracting foreign
investment is an area ripe for further investigation on two levels. First, is urban
disaster a factor in foreign investment decision-making, and if it is could this
mean that investment in social as well as more traditional physical infrastructure

systems to build up adaptive potential will become more cost effective in global cities at risk? Second, to what extent can risk management and vulnerability reduction policies act to build security into urban labour forces, so that even after large-scale physical events such as earthquakes and hurricanes, production will not be suspended because of workforce losses or the inability of workers to travel to the workplace? Linked with this are wider questions of poverty, civil unrest, violence and global terrorism.

Across the case studies, a responsive and representative municipal government with sufficient power to carry out its mandate of delivering basic services and infrastructure to all the city's residents could have been pivotal in shaping resilience and vulnerability. In Georgetown and Santo Domingo, authoritarian and socialist development paths had resulted in the centralized state control of many municipal functions, and there was a reluctance to decentralize authority. International donors played a key role in working with the public sector, as well as civil society and the private sector, to prepare the way for a more decentralized model of urban governance. In Santo Domingo, the European Union funded and provided technical assistance for a reorganization of central and municipal government. Whilst decentralization with appropriate funding offers the opportunity for local actors to build closer links with urban decision-makers, little research work has been undertaken on the influence of urban decentralization on the capacity of cities to prevent and respond to environmental risk. A body of work on the influence of decentralization and privatization on environmental service provision – drinking water and garbage collection in particular – is available, but this should be extended by research into the consequences of such policies for disaster mitigation. Disaster risk reduction involves actors whose efficiency is maximized at various scales of organization from the city to the neighbourhood. How have decentralization and associated privatization policies affected individual sectors such as emergency services, civil defence, Red Cross networks, first aid provision, and the capacity of the city to provide emergency cover for services such as electricity and drinking water etc, and the coordination of these sectors in urban disaster planning?

As Töpfer (1999), in his role as the Director of HABITAT, argues, the precepts of good governance have much to offer in the fight to reduce the growing losses from environmental hazard in urban areas. However, notwithstanding the central role of municipal government, good governance requires local institutions at the community level that can represent and respond to the needs of citizens, and a supportive array of non-state actors. Social development is an important component of good governance. Without meaningful social development, requiring long-term support between development partners, physical development projects will not achieve their fullest potential for vulnerability reduction either in terms of equity or efficiency. However, building an awareness of the social roots of vulnerability into city disaster management strategy should not be allowed to replace a physical science approach: the two are complementary. Research and development of clear policy guidance and practical tools, including vulnerability indicators and methods for identifying adaptive potential and vulnerability reduction following project interventions, is needed to convince policy-makers and politicians of the utility of a social development approach to urban vulnerability reduction.

The Standard Methodology

In each case study, adaptive potential was studied first at the city level to identify general processes, and secondly through a community case study, which allowed more detailed analysis of organizational capacity and institutional inter-relationships. Qualitative and quantitative data were collected using a standard methodological approach (Table A.1), but it was important that this was flexible enough to respond to the research priorities of each case study. So, for example, when cases of good practice in supporting adaptive potential were identified, additional interviews were undertaken. This was the case in Bridgetown, with CERO and the NGO PCW, and in Santo Domingo with the NGO the Asociación Dominicana de Mitigación de Desastres.

Published academic and consultancy work, internal documentation from government and civil society organizations and the press from 1995–1999 were initially reviewed. Semi-structured interviews with key informants and household questionnaire surveys were then conducted. Questionnaires were conducted by teams of four local women, who received training in survey techniques and were involved in the piloting and final draft of the questionnaire. The questionnaires used closed questions and were formatted with sections on membership of formal community associations, perceived environmental and social problems, participation in informal social activities and social indicators. Qualitative data were analysed using textual analysis, and quantitative data were analysed using the Statistical Package for Social Scientists (SPSS). Copies of the original datasets can be obtained from the UK's Economic and Social Research Council (ESRC) research archive.

Two types of semi-structured interviews were conducted in each city. Up to five interviews were used to supplement background data on urban governance and vulnerability. Interviews were held with local academics and international NGO officers identified from background reading and a snowball sample. These interviews were planned to obtain information on aspects of the national political regime, the perceived capacity of state, civil society and private sector actors to adapt to hazard and vulnerability, and on the performance of the overall system of urban governance in combating poverty, inequality and vulnerability. A larger group of interviews was conducted with the directors of organizations in civil society, the private sector and public sector that were

Table A.1 *The standard methodology*

Research aim	Data source(s)	Method(s)	Data analysis
Describe historical coevolution of environmental risk and human development Delineate institutional framework for urban governance Identify key actors from public sector, private sector and civil society with stakes in environmental risk management or the amelioration of vulnerability	Published and grey literature. Review of the press, 1995–1999. Key informants	Literature review in UK and in the field. Semi-structured interviews with local academics/ commentators	Iterative review of data. Allowing new findings to direct ongoing data searches
Assess adaptive potential of city-wide institutional framework	Key informants	Semi-structured interviews and agency documentation from a sample of organizations	Discourse and text analysis
Assess adaptive potential of case-study community	Households and community leaders	Questionnaire survey of approximately 200 households plus semi-structured interviews with community leaders	Quantitative analysis by SPSS, qualitative analysis using discourse and text analysis

involved in vulnerability reduction. 40 interviews were conducted in Georgetown, 54 in Santo Domingo and 35 in Bridgetown. The interviews solicited information on the organization's history, management structure, aims, major works, projects completed and underway, sources of finance, mechanisms of transparency and relationships with other organizations from civil society, the public or private sector or 'the community' of local households. Two directed snowball samples were used to identify respondents. First, a bottom–up sample, starting with CBOs in the community case study and then contacting partners with which they had vertical links. Secondly, a top–down sample, starting with international donor agencies and then contacting NGOs with whom they had links and finally CBOs with whom the NGOs had links.

For the majority of organizations, it was only possible to hold a single interview with limited formal public material being accessible. Where possible, an 'action research' strategy was employed to generate trust, in each case with an NGO (True Vision in Georgetown, IDDI in Santo Domingo and PCW in Bridgetown). This involved the researcher working with the organization being studied. This also allowed the researcher and key informants to discuss findings quickly, which resulted in changes in policy and practice amongst participating organizations (see impacts).

References

Abbott, J (1996) *Sharing the City: Community Participation in Urban Management*, Earthscan, London

Adams, W M (1990) *Green Development: Environment and Sustainability in the Third World*, Routledge, London

Adger, N (1996) *Approaches to Vulnerability to Climate Change*, CSERGE working paper #GEC 96-05, University of East Anglia, Norwich

Adger, W N (1999) Social vulnerability to climate change and extremes in coastal Vietnam, *World Development* 27 (2), 249–269

Adger, W N (2000) Institutional adaptation to environmental risk under the transition in Vietnam, *Annuls of the Association of American Geographers* 90, 738–758

Advocate Newspaper (1989) 'Relocated homes will be ready soon', 12 January, p3

Advocate Newspaper (1995a) 'Ripped apart', 4 August, p52

Advocate Newspaper (1995b) 'Dengue threat worries Lashley', 9 October, p5

Advocate Newspaper (1997) 'On sandy or sani soil?' 11 July, p12

Albala-Bertrand, J M (1993) *Political Economy of Large Natural Disasters: With Special Reference to Developing Countries*, Clarendon Press, Oxford

Alexander, D (1989) Urban landslides, *Progress in Physical Geography* 13, 157–191

Alexander, D (2000) *Confronting Catastrophe*, Terra, Harpenden

Alfonso, H D (1997) Political decentralisation and popular alternatives: a view from the South, in Kaufman, M and Alfonso, H D (eds) *Community Power and Grassroots Democracy*, Zed Books, London

Allen, J, Massey, D and Pryke, M (eds) (1999) *Unsettling Cities*, Routledge, New York

Allison, M, Harris, P J C, Hofny-Collins, A H and Stevens, W (1998) *A Review of the Use of Urban Waste in Peri-urban Interface Production Systems*, Department for International Development, London

AMDEM (1999) interview with director, 18 June

Amis, P (1997) India urban poverty: where are the levers for its effective alleviation? *IDS Bulletin* 28 (2), 94–105

Anderson, M (1990) *Analyzing the Costs and Benefits of Natural Disaster Responses in the Context of Development*, Environment working paper #29, World Bank, Washington DC

Anderson, M (1992) Metropolitan areas and disaster vulnerability: a consideration for developing countries, in Kreimer, A and Munasinghe, M (eds) *Environmental Management and Urban Vulnerability*, World Bank discussion paper #18, World Bank, Washington DC

Anon (1993) *Disaster Reduction*, Environment and Development Brief, UNESCO, Paris

Anton, D J (1993) *Thirsty Cities: Urban Environments and Water Supply in Latin America*, International Development Research Centre, Ottowa

APRODEMI (1999) community leader, personal communication

Aroyo (1999) leader of community group Junta de Vecinos Grito de Capitollo, personal communication

Azuela, A, Duhau, E and Ortiz, E (eds) (1998) *Evictions and the Right to Housing: Experience from Canada, the Dominican Republic, South Africa, and South Korea*, International Development Research Centre, Ottowa

Barnett, J (2001) Adapting to climate change in Pacific island countries: the problem of uncertainty, *World Development* 29 (6), 977–993

Bebbington, A and Riddell, R (1995) The direct funding of southern NGOs by donors: new agendas and old problems, *Journal of International Development* 7 (6), 879–893

Beck, U (1992) *Risk Society: Towards a New Modernity*, Sage, London

Becker, C (1999) Guyana Field Director, USAID, personal communication

Bennett, J (2000) Interagency co-ordination in emergencies, in Robinson, D, Hewitt, T and Harriss, J (eds) *Managing Development: Understanding Inter-Organisational Relationships*, Sage, London

Benson, C (1997) *The Economic Impact of Natural Disasters in the Philippines*, Working paper 99, Overseas Development Institute, London

Berke, P R and Beatley, T (1992) *Planning for Earthquakes: Risk, Politics, and Policy*, Johns Hopkins University Press, Baltimore

Berke, P R, Kartez, J and Wenger, D (1993) Recovery after disaster: achieving sustainable development, mitigation and equity, *Disasters* 17 (2), 93–109

Blaikie, P, Cannon, T, Davis, I and Wisner, B (1994) *At Risk: Natural Hazards, People's Vulnerability, and Disasters*, Routledge, London

Blair (1999) community leader, personal communication

Bolt, B A (1993) *Earthquakes*, Freeman, New York

Braun, B and Castree, N (eds) (1998) *Remaking Reality: Nature at the Millennium*, Routledge, London

Brennan-Galvin, E (2001) The future of the world's megacities, *Global Outlook*, Woodrow Wilson Center for Scholars, Washington DC, pp18–24

Brewster, L (1992) *A Report on an Inventory of Domestic, Industrial and Agricultural Sources of Pollution in Barbados*, Coastal Conservation Unit, Bridgetown

Briggs, J and Yeboah, I E A (2001) Structural adjustment and the contemporary sub-Saharan African city, *Area* 33 (1), 18–26

Brown, H A (1994) *Economics of Disaster with Special Reference to the Jamaican Experience*, Working paper #2, Centre for Environment and Development, University of the West Indies, Mona Campus, Jamaica

Bryant, R L and Bailey, S (1997) *Third World Political Ecology*, London, Routledge

Bryant, N (2001) *Floods Highlight Washington's Weakness*, BBC News, http://news.bbc.co.uk/hi/english/world/from_our_own_correspondent, accessed 18 August

Burton, I, Kates, R W and White, G F (1993) *The Environment as Hazard*, Guildford Press, London

Bynoe (1999) community leader, Sophia squatters' settlement, personal communication

Callaway, B and Creevey, L (1989) Women and the state in Islamic West Africa, in Charlton, S E M, Everett, J and Staudt, K (eds) *Women, the State and Development*, State University of New York, New York

Cambers, G (1987) *Report Showing Photographic Evidence of Severe Beach Erosion in Barbados*, Inter-American Development Bank, Bridgetown

Cameron, J (1999) community leader, Sophia squatters' settlement, personal communication

Castells, M (1972) *The Urban Question*, Edward Arnold, London

Castells, M (1983) *The City and the Grassroots*, Edward Arnold, London

Castells, M (1996) *The Rise of Network Society*, Blackwell, Oxford

Castree, N and Braun, B (2001) *Social Nature: Theory, Practice and Politics*, Blackwell, Oxford

Catafesta, C (1999) personal communication

CDC (Civil Defence Commission) (1997) *National Emergency Flood Relief*, CDC, Georgetown

CDC (Civil Defence Commission) (1998) Director, personal communication

CDC (Civil Defence Commission) (1999) *El Niño Crisis in Guyana 1997–1998*, CDC, Georgetown

Cela, J (1996) La ciudad del futuro o el futuro de la ciudad, *Antología Urbana de la Ciudad Alternativa*, Ciudad Alternativa, Santo Domingo, pp115–122

Cela, J (1999) personal communication

CERO (Central Emergency Relief Organization) (1998) personal communication, 30 July

Chambers, R (1989) Editorial introduction: vulnerability, coping and policy, *IDS Bulletin* 20 (2), 1–7

Chambers, R (1995) Poverty and livelihoods: whose reality counts? *Environment and Urbanization* 7 (1), 173–204

Chan (1999) community leader, Sophia squatters' settlement, personal communication

Charles, C L, McNulty, S and Pennell, J A (1998) *Partnering for Results: A Users' Guide to Intersectoral Partnering*, USAID, Washington DC

Charvériat, C (2000) *Natural Disasters in Latin America and the Caribbean: An Overview of Risk*, Working paper 434, Inter-American Development Bank, Washington DC

Chester, D K (2002) Overview: hazard and risk, in Allison, R J (ed) *Applied Geomorphology: Theory and Practice*, John Wiley and Sons, Chichester

Chester, D K, Degg, M, Duncan, A M and Guest, J E (2001) The increasing exposure of cities to the effects of volcanic eruptions: a global survey, *Environmental Hazards* 2 (3), 89–103

Choguill, C L and Choguill, M B G (1996) Toward sustainable infrastructure for low-income communities, in Pugh, C (ed) *Sustainability, the Environment and Urbanization*, Earthscan, London

Choup, A (2000) Municipal government, decentralization and civil society organizations: the case of Santo Domingo's grassroots organizations, paper presented at the Latin American Studies Association, Hyatt Regency Hotel, Miami, 18 March

CIDA (Canadian International Development Agency) (1999) personal communication with country representative

Clark, D (2000) World urban development: processes and patterns at the end of the twentieth century, *Geography* 85 (1), 15–23

Claudette (1999) community leader, Sophia squatters' settlement, personal communication

Clement, D (1990) *An Analysis of Disaster: Life after Gilbert*, Working paper 37, Institute of Social and Economic Research, University of the West Indies, Barbados

Coburn, A, Pomonis, A and Sakia, S (1989) Assessing strategies to reduce casualties in earthquakes, in *International Workshop on Earthquake Injury Epidemiology for Mitigation and Response*, Johns Hopkins University Press, Baltimore

Coleman, D and Schofield, R (eds) (1986) *The State of Population Theory: Forward From Malthus*, Blackwell, Oxford

Collado, F (1997) *Ventajas de la Descentralización Para el Desarrollo*, Editora Travárez, Santo Domingo

Colletta, N J and Cullen, M L (2000) *Violent Conflict and Transformation of Social Capital: Lessons from Cambodia, Rwanda, Guatemala and Somalia*, World Bank, Washington DC

Community Development Division (1998) *Groups and Organisations in Barbados*, Community Development Division, Bridgetown

Connolly, P (1999) Mexico City: our common future? *Environment and Urbanization* 11 (1), 53–78

Coppin, A (1995) Women, men and work in a Caribbean economy: Barbados, *Social and Economic Studies* 44 (2 & 3), 103–124

CPRME (Comisión Presidencial para la Reforma y Modernización del Estado) (1998) *Reforma del Estado y Descentralización*, Impresel, Santo Domingo

Cross, J A (2001) Megacities and small towns: different perspectives on hazard vulnerability, *Environmental Hazards* 3 (2), 63–80

Daily Nation (1998a) 'No one to support residents', 31 August

Daily Nation (1998b) 'Wash-out', 21 October

Degg, M (1986) Earthquake hazard assessment after Mexico (1985), *Disasters* 13 (3), 237–246

Degg, M (1992) Natural disasters: recent trends and future prospects, *Geography* 77, 198–209

Degg, M (1998) Natural hazards in the urban environment: the need for a more sustainable approach to mitigation, in Maund, J G and Eddleston, M (eds) *Geohazards in Engineering Geology*, Engineering Geology Special Publication, 15, Geological Society, London,329–337

Desai, V (1995) *Community Participation and Slum Housing: A Study of Bombay*, Sage, London

Desai, V (1996) Access to power and participation, *Third World Planning Review* 18 (2), 217–242

de Soto, H (1989) *The Other Path: The Invisible Revolution in the Third World*, I B Taurus, London

DFID (Department for International Development) (2000) *Partnerships with the Private Sector*, www.dfid.gov.uk/public/working/buspart/ (February 2002)

Diaram, R (1999) Guyana's experience with CPACC's screening assessment of coastal vulnerability, paper presented at a Vulnerability and Adaptation Workshop, University of the West Indies, Port of Spain, Trinidad, 20–22 July

Dierwechter, Y (2002) Six cities of the informal sector – and beyond, *International Development Planning Review* 24 (1), 21–41

Dillinger, W (1994) *Decentralisation and its Implications for Urban Service Delivery*, Urban Management Programme, UNDP/UNCHS/World Bank, Nairobi

Disaster Emergency Committee (2002) *Report on the Response to the Gujarat Earthquake, 2001*, Disaster Emergency Committee, London

Division of Housing (1998) personal communication, 7 September

Drakakis-Smith, D (1996) Sustainability, urbanisation and development, *Third World Planning Review* 18 (4), iii–x

Drèze, J and Sen, A (1989) *Hunger and Public Action*, Oxford University Press, Oxford

Duarte, I, Brea, R and Holguín, R (1998) *La Cultura Política Dominicana: Entre el Paternalismo y la Participacion*, Impresos Camilo, Santo Domingo

Duncan, N (1994) Barbados: democracy at the crossroads, in Carlene, E J (ed) *Democracy in the Caribbean: Myths and Realities*, Praeger, London

Edwards, S and Hulme, M (1996) Too close for comfort? The impact of official aid on nongovernmental organisations, *World Development* 24 (6), 961–973

Enarson, E and Morrow, B H (1998) *The Gendered Terrain of Disaster: Through Women's Eyes*, International Hurricane Center, Florida International University, Florida

Espillat, M and Ballenilla, C (1998) *Sistema Comunitario de Manejo y Control de Desechos Solidos Domésticos del Sector Los Manguitos del Barrio Capotillo*, Centro de Estudios Sociales P Juan Montalvo S J, Santo Domingo

Evans, P (1996) Development strategies across the public–private divide, *Development and Change* 24 (6), 1–9

Everett, J (1989) Incorporation versus conflict: lower class women, collective action, and the state in India, in Charlton, S E M, Everett, J and Staudt, K (eds) *Women, the State and Development*, State University of New York Press, New York

Ferguson, T (1995) *Structural Adjustment and Good Governance: The Case of Guyana*, Public Affairs Consulting Enterprise, Georgetown

Fernandez, A S (1996) Movimientos de pobladores: una alternativa para la participación popular, in Ciudad Alternativa, *Antología Urbana de la Ciudad Alternativa*, Ciudad Alternativa, Santo Domingo

Fiske, J (1989) *Reading the Popular*, Unwin Hyman, Boston

Fiszbein, A and Lowden, P (1999) *Working Together For a Change: Government, Civic and Business Partnerships for Poverty Reduction in Latin America and the Caribbean*, Economic Development Institute of the World Bank, World Bank, Washington DC

Flentge, J (2001) *A Radio Soap Opera Promoting the Culture of Prevention!* ISDR informe, www.eird.org/ing/revista/No3_2001/Pagina18.htm, accessed 13 September

Fowler, A (1997) *Striking a Balance: A Guide to Enhancing the Effectiveness of Nongovernmental Organisations in International Development*, Earthscan, London

Fowler, A (2000) Beyond partnership: getting real about NGO relationships in the aid system, *IDS Bulletin* 31 (3), 1–13

Fowler, A M and Hennessy, K J (1995) Potential impacts of global warming on the frequency and magnitude of heavy precipitation, *Natural Hazards* 11, 283–303

Freire, P (1985) *The Politics of Education: Culture, Power and Liberation*, Macmillan, Basingstoke

Friedmann, J (1992) *Empowerment: The Politics of Alternative Development*, Belhavan, Oxford

Friedmann, J (1996) Rethinking poverty: empowerment and citizens rights, *International Social Science Journal* 148, 161–172

Fukuyama, F (2001) Social capital, civil society and development, *Third World Quarterly* 22 (1), 7–20

García, A and Mercedes, A (1996) Organizaciones barriales, mejoramiento urbano y desarrollo de la ciudad, in Ciudad Alternativa, *Antología Urbana*, Ciudad Alternativa, Santo Domingo

Garza, G (1999) Global economy, metropolitan dynamics and urban policies in Mexico, *Cities* 16 (3), 149–170

Gazzoli, R (1996) The political and institutional context of popular organisations in urban Argentina, *Environment and Urbanization* 8 (1), 159–166

George, S (1992) *The Debt Boomerang*, Pluto, London

Germain, R D (2000) *Globalization and its Critics: Perspectives from Political Economy*, Macmillan, Basingstoke

Giddens, A (1984) *The Construction of Society: Outline of the Theory of Structuration*, University of California Press, Berkeley

Giddens, A (1993) *New Rules of Sociological Method*, Polity, Oxford

Gilbert, A, (1995) Debt, poverty and the Latin American city, *Geography* 80 (4), 323–333

Gilbert, A and Ward, P (1984a) Community action by the urban poor: democratic involvement, community self-help or a means of social control? *World Development* 12 (8), 769–782

Gilbert, A and Ward, P (1984b) Community participation in upgrading irregular settlements: the community response, *World Development* 12 (9), 913–922

Gilbert, R, Stevenson, D, Girardet, H and Stren, R (1996) *Making Cities Work: The Role of Local Authorities in the Urban Environment*, Earthscan, London

Gilbert, R and Kreimer, A (1999) *Learning from the World Bank's Experience of Natural Disaster Related Assistance*, Urban Development Division working paper series #2, World Bank, Washington DC

Giles, H and Brown, B (1997) And not a drop to drink: water and sanitation services to the urban poor in the developing world, *Geography* 82 (2), 97–109

Girardet, H (1999) *Creating Sustainable Cities*, Schumacher Briefings #2, The Schumacher Society, Bristol

Goodhand, J, Hulme, D and Lewer, N (2000) Social capital and the political economy of violence: a case study of Sri Lanka, *Disasters* 24 (4), 390–406

Government of Barbados (1996) *Habitat II: The Barbados National Report and Plan of Action*, Government of Barbados, Bridgetown

Government of Barbados (1998) *The Urban Renewal Programme (Greater Bridgetown Area)*, Government of Barbados, Bridgetown

GRC (Guyana Relief Council) (1999) Director, personal communication

Grant, R (1998) Director of Pinelands Creative Workshop, personal communication

Green, A and Matthias, A (1995) NGOs – a policy panacea for the next millennium? *Journal of International Development* 7 (3), 565–573

Greenfield, G (1994) *Latin American Urbanisation*, Greenwood Press, London

Gulkan, P (2001) *What Emerged From the Rubble*, ProVention Consortium Conceptual Articles, www.proventionconsortium.org/articles/innovations.htm, accessed 13 September

Guyana Red Cross (1999) Director, personal communication

Guzman, R (1999) interview at CONDIC, 5 May

Haggard, S and Kaufman, R (eds) (1992) *The Politics of Economic Adjustment*, Princeton University Press, Princeton

Halcrow plc (1994) *Primary Drainage System*, Georgetown Water and Sewerage Master Plan, Tn/GMP/09, Burdrop Park, Swindon

Haraway, D (1997) *Modest Witness@Second Millennium*, Routledge, London

Hardoy, J E and Satterthwaite, D (1989) *Squatter Citizen: Life in the Third World*, Earthscan, London

Hardoy, J E, Cairncross, S and Satterthwaite, D (1990) *The Poor Die Young: Housing and Health in Third World Cities*, Earthscan, London

Hardoy, J E, Mitlin, D and Satterthwaite, D (1992) *Environmental Problems in Third World Cities*, Earthscan, London

Hardoy, J E, Mitlin, D and Satterthwaite, D (2001) *Environmental Problems in an Urbanizing World*, Earthscan, London

Harris, N (1995) Bombay in a global economy, structural adjustment and the role of cities, *Cities* 12, 175–184

Harriss, J, Hunter, J and Lewis, C M (eds) (1995) *The New Institutional Economics and Third World Development*, Routledge, London

Hartnady, C (2002) *Earthquake Hazard in the Developing World*, submission to the International Strategy for Disaster Reduction consultation exercise in preparation for the Earth Summit 2002 conference, http://earthsummit2002.dyndns.org/pages/discussion.cfm?ID=1&week=1, accessed 28 April

Harvey, D (1973) *Social Justice and the City*, Blackwell, Oxford

Harvey, D (1993) The nature of the environment: the dialectics of social and environmental change, in Milliband, R and Panitch, L (eds) *Real Problems, False Solutions: Socialist Register 1993*, Merlin Press, London

Haughton, G (1999) Environmental justice and the sustainable city, *Journal of Planning Education and Research* 18 (3), 233–243

Hecht, S and Cockburn, A (1989) *The Fate of the Forest: Developers, Destroyers and Defenders of the Amazon*, Penguin, London

Heijmans and Victoria (no date) *Citizenry-Based and Development-Oriented Disaster Response*, Center for Disaster Preparedness, Quezon City, the Philippines (www.adpc.ait.ac.th/pdr-sea/cbdo-dr/cover.html)

Hewitt, K (ed) (1983) *Interpretations of Calamity: From the Viewpoint of Human Ecology*, Allen and Unwin, Boston

Hewitt, K (1995) Sustainable disasters? perspectives and powers in the discourse of calamity, in Crush, J (ed) *Power of Development*, Routledge, London

Hewitt, K (1997) *Regions of Risk: A Geographical Introduction to Disasters*, Longman, Essex

Hildebrand, M (2001) The cities alliance: a new global challenge to urban poverty, *Global Outlook*, Woodrow Wilson Center for Scholars, Washington DC, 16–17

Hobsbawm, E J (1996) The future of the state, *Development and Change* 27, 267–278

Hoy (1998) 'Hamilton and Son', 25 October

Hoy (1999a) 'Salud', 2 March

Hoy (1999b) editorial, 21 March

Huq, S (1999) Environmental hazards in Dhaka, in Mitchell, J K (ed) *Crucibles of Hazard: Mega-cities and Disasters in Transition*, United Nations Press, Tokyo

Hurrell, A (1994) A crisis of ecological viability? global environmental change and the nation state, *Political Studies* 42, 146–165

Hyden, G (1997) Civil society, social capital and development: dissection of a complex discourse, *Studies in Comparative Development* 32 (1), 3–30

IDDI (Instituto Dominicano Desarrollo Integral) (1999) Los Manguitos project manager, personal communication

IFRC/RC (International Federation of the Red Cross and Red Crescent) (1998) *World Disasters Report 1998*, Oxford University Press, Oxford

IFRC/RC (International Federation of the Red Cross and Red Crescent) (1999) *World Disasters Report 1999*, Edigroup, Switzerland

IPCC (Intergovernmental Panel on Climate Change) (1990) *Climate Change: The IPCC Scientific Assessment*, Cambridge University Press, Cambridge

IPCC (Intergovernmental Panel on Climate Change) (2001) *Climate Change 2001: Impacts, Adaptation and Vulnerability*, www.ipcc.ch

Jacobi, P (1997) Environmental problems in Sao Paulo: the challenge for co-responsibility and innovative crisis management, *Journal of Contingencies and Crisis Management* 5 (3), 131–139

James (1999) community leader, Sophia squatters' settlement, personal communication

Jordan, A and O'Riordan, T (1995) *Institutional Adaptation to Global Environmental Change (1): Social Institutions, Policy Change and Social Learning*, GEC 95-20, CSERGE, University of East Anglia

Junta de Vecinos Los Manguitos (1999) Director, personal communication

Kanneh, M S (1993) *Albouystown Upgrading Project: Terminal Report*, Central Housing and Planning Authority, Guyana

Kasperson, J X, Kasperson, R E and Turner, B L (1996) *Regions at Risk: Comparisons of Threatened Environments*, United Nations University Press, Washington DC

Kerr, D and Kwele, N (2000) Capital accumulation and the political reproduction of the urban housing problem in Botswana, *Urban Studies* 37 (8), 1313–1344

Khan, S M (1998) *Flood Rains in Guyana*, Hydrometerological Service, Guyana

Kreimer, A and Munasinghe, M (eds) (1992) *Environmental Management and Urban Vulnerability*, World Bank Discussion Paper 168, World Bank, Washington DC

LaPlante, J M (1988) Recovery following disaster: policy issues and recommendations, in Comfort, L K (ed) *Managing Disaster: Strategies and Policy Perspectives*, Duke University Press, Durham, USA

Leach, M, Mearns, R and Scoones, I (1997) *Environmental Entitlements: A Framework for Understanding the Institutional Dynamics of Environmental Change*, Discussion paper #359, Institute of Development Studies, University of Sussex, Brighton

Leitmann, J (1991) Environmental profile of São Paulo, in Munasinghe, M (ed) *Managing Natural Disasters and the Environment*, World Bank, Washington DC

Lewis, O (1966) The culture of poverty, *Scientific American* 214, 19–25

Lewis (1999a) community leader, Sophia squatters' settlement, personal communication, 31 October

Lewis, J (1999b) *Development in Disaster-prone Places*, Intermediate Technology Publications, London

Lipton, M and Maxwell, S (1992) *The New Poverty Agenda: An Overview*, Discussion paper #306, Institute of Development Studies, University of Sussex, Brighton

Lister, S (2000) Power in partnership? analysis of an NGO's relationships with its partners, *Journal of International Development* 12, 227–239

Listin Diario (1998) Seis milliones de personas vivieron en las zonas afectadas por el huracán, 9 October

Lomnitz, L (1977) *Networks and Marginality: Life in a Mexican Shanty Town*, Academic Press, New York

Losada, H, Bennett, R, Soriano, R, Vieyra, J and Cortés, J (2000) Urban agriculture in Mexico city: functions provided by the use of space for dairy based livelihoods, *Cities* 17 (6), 419–432

McCarney, P L (ed) (1996) *Cities and Governance: New Direction in Latin America, Asia and Africa*, University of Toronto, Toronto

McGranahan, G, Songsore, J and Kjellén, M (1996) Sustainability, poverty and urban environmental transitions, in Pugh, C (ed) *Sustainability, the Environment and Urbanization*, Earthscan, London

McGranahan, G, Jacobi, P, Songsore, J, Surjadi, C and Kjellén, M (2001) *The Citizens at Risk: From Urban Sanitation to Sustainable Cities*, Earthscan, London

McIlwaine, C (1998) Civil society and development geography, *Progress in Human Geography* 22 (3), 414–424

McIlwaine, C and Moser, C (2001) Violence and social capital in urban poor communities: perspectives from Colombia and Guatemala, *Journal of International Development* 13, 1–20

Main, H and Williams, S W (eds) (1994) *Environment and Housing in Third World Cities*, Wiley, Chichester

Mata Mamon (1999) community leader, personal communication

Matias, D (1997) *Partidos, Sociedad Civil y Reforma Municipal*, Union de Vecinos Activos, Santo Domingo

Matsukawa, T (2001) *Innovations in Disaster Management: Mobilizing Private Financing*, ProVention Consortium conceptual articles, www.proventionconsortium.org/articles/innovations.htm, accessed 13 September

May, P J, Burby, R J, Erikson, N J, Dixon, J E, Michaels, S and Smith, D I (1996) *Environmental Management and Governance: Intergovernmental Approaches to Hazards and Sustainability*, Routledge, London

Mearns, R (1995) Institutions and natural resource management: access to and control over woodfuel in East Africa, in Binns, T (ed) *People and Environment in Africa*, John Wiley and Sons, Chichester

Mercer, C (2002) NGOs, civil society and democratisation: a critical review of the literature, *Progress in Development Studies* 2 (1), 5–22

Minh-ha, T (1989) *Women, Nature, Other*, Indiana University Press, Indiana

Mitchell, J K (1996) Improving community responses, in Mitchell, J K (ed) *The Long Road to Recovery: Community Responses to Industrial Disaster*, United Nations University Press, Tokyo, pp1–41

Mitchell, J K (1999) *Crucibles of Hazard: Mega-Cities and Disasters in Transition*, UNU Press, Tokyo

Mitchell, J K (2001) What's in a name? issues of terminology and language in hazards research, *Environmental Hazards* 2 (3), 87–88

Mitchell, J K, Devine, N and Jagger, K (1989) A contextual model of natural hazard, *Geographical Review* 89 (4), 391–409

Mitlin, D (2001) Civil society and urban poverty: examining complexity, *Environment and Urbanization* 13 (2), 151–174

Mitlin, D and Thompson, S (1995) Participatory approaches in urban areas: strengthening civil society or reinforcing the status quo, *Environment and Urbanization* 7 (1), 231–250

Mitlin, D and Satterthwaite, D (1996) Sustainable development and cities, in Pugh, C (ed) *Sustainability, the Environment and Urbanization*, Earthscan, London

MOCUGRECA (1999) Director, personal communication

Mohan, G (2002) Participatory development, in Potter, R B and Desai, V (eds) *The Companion to Development Studies*, Arnold, London

Morel, E (1996) Cuenca hidrográfica y urbanización, in Ciudad Alternativa, *Antología Urbana*, Ciudad Alternativa, Santo Domingo

Moser, C (1996) *Confronting Crisis: A Comparative Study of Household Responses to Poverty and Vulnerability in Four Poor Urban Communities*, Environmental and Sustainable Studies and Monograph Series #8, World Bank, Washington DC

Moser, C (1998) The asset vulnerability framework: reassessing urban poverty reduction strategies, *World Development* 26 (1), 1–19

Moser, C, Herbert, A and Makonnen, R (1993) *Urban Poverty in the Context of Structural Adjustment: Recent Evidence and Policy Responses*, Urban Development Division, World Bank, Washington DC

Moser, C, Gauhurts, M and Gonhan, H (1994) *Urban Poverty Research Sourcebook: Sub-city Level Research*, World Bank, Washington DC

Moser, C and Holland, J (1997) *Household Responses to Poverty and Vulnerability, Volume 4: Confronting Crisis in Chawama, Lusaka, Zambia*, Urban Management Programme Policy Paper #24, Urban Management Programme, Nairobi

Moser, C and McIlwaine, C (2001) *Violence in a Post-conflict Context: Urban Poor Perceptions from Guatemala*, World Bank, Washington DC

Mosse, D (1994) Authority, gender and knowledge: theoretical reflections on the practice of participatory rural appraisal, *Development and Change* 25 (3), 497–526

Mossler, M (1996) Environmental hazard analysis and small island states: rethinking academic approaches, *Geographische Zeitschrift* 84 (2), 86–93

Mulwanda, M (1993) The need for new approaches to disaster management: the floods in Lusaka, Zambia, *Environment and Urbanization* 5 (2), 67–77

Munasinghe, M, Menzes, B and Preece, M (1991) Rio reconstruction and flood prevention in Brazil, *Land Use Policy* 8 (4), October

Munich Re (1998) *World Map of Natural Hazards* (2nd Edition), Munich Reinsurance Company, Munich

Narayan, D (2000) *Voices of the Poor: Can Anyone Hear Us?* Oxford University Press, Oxford

National Labor Committee, El Salvador (2001) Salvador earthquake: from poverty to misery, www.nlcnet.org, accessed 21 February

Nicholls, R J (1995) Coastal megacities and climate change, *GeoJournal* 37 (3), 369–379

Norgaard, R B (1994) *Development Betrayed: The End of Progress and a Coevolutionary Revisioning of the Future*, Routledge, London

North, D C (1995) The new institutional economics and third world development, in Harriss, J, Hunter, J and Lewis, C M (eds) *The New Institutional Economics and Third World Development*, Routledge, London

Nurse, L A (1989) *The Effects of Hurricane Gabrielle on the Barbados East Coast*, Coastal Conservation Project Unit, Bridgetown

Nurse, L A (1997) *Report on Baseline Study – Scotland District: 27*, Community Development Division, Bridgetown

ODA (Overseas Development Administration) (1995) *Megacities: Reducing Vulnerability to Natural Hazards*, ODA and the Institute of Civil Engineers, Thomas Telford Press, London

Ojeda, A C (2001) *Strategic Community Management for Reducing Vulnerability to Disasters*, ISDR informe, www.eird.org/ing/revista/No3_2001/Pagina13.htm, accessed 13 September

O'Keefe, P, Wisner, R and Baird, A (1977) Kenyan underdevelopment: a case study of proletarianisation, in O'Keefe, P and Wisner, R W (eds) *Landuse and Development*, International African Institute, London

ONAPLAN (Oficina Nacional de Planificación) (1997) *Informe Población*, Government of the Dominican Republic, Santo Domingo, 11 December

Ostrom, E, Schroeder, L and Wynne, S (1993) *Institutional Incentives and Sustainable Development: Infrastructure in Perspective*, Westview Press, Oxford

Özerdem, A and Barakat, S (2000) After the Marmara earthquake: lessons for avoiding short cuts to disasters, *Third World Quarterly* 21 (93), 425–439

PAHO (Pan American Health Organization) (1994) *A World Safe from Natural Disasters, the Journey from Latin America and the Caribbean*, PAHO, Washinton, DC

PAHO (Pan American Health Organization) (1998) Barbados, in *Health Conditions in the Americas*, Volume I, Scientific Publications, Washington DC

PAHO (Pan American Health Organization) (2001) *Strengthening Local Capacity For Disaster Reduction: The Experience of PAHO*, ISDR Informe, www.eird.org/ing/revista/No3_2001/Pagina12.htm, accessed 13 September

Payne, G (1996) *Shelter Sector Diagnostic Guyana*, Department of Civic Design, Inter-American Development Bank, Washington DC

Peak, L and Trotz, D A (1999) *Gender, Ethnicity and Place: Women and Identities in Guyana*, Routledge, London

Peet, R and Watts, M (1996) *Liberation Ecologies: Environment, Development, Social Movements*, Routledge, London

Pelling, M (1992) *Housing Strategies Employed by Lower-Income Groups in Greater Georgetown, Guyana*, occasional paper, Department of Geography, University of Guyana, Guyana

Pelling, M (1997) What determines vulnerability to floods: a case study in Georgetown, Guyana, *Environment and Urbanization* 9 (1), 203–226

Pelling, M (1998) Participation, social capital and vulnerability to urban flooding in Guyana, *Journal of International Development* 10, 469–486

Pelling, M (1999) The political ecology of flood hazard in urban Guyana, *Geoforum* 30, 249–261

Pelling, M (2001a) Sustainable cities, in Willis, K and McIlwaine, C (eds) *Middle America*, Addison Wesley Longman, London

Pelling, M (2001b) Natural disasters? in Castree, N and Braun, B (eds) *Social Nature: Theory, Practice and Politics*, Blackwell, Oxford

Pelling, M (2002) Assessing urban vulnerability and social adaptation to risk, *International Development Planning Review* 24 (1), 59–76

Pelling, M and Uitto, J (2001) Small island developing states: natural disaster vulnerability and global change, *Environmental Hazards* 3 (2), 49–62

Pelling, M, Özerdem, A and Barakat, S (2002) The macro-economic impact of disasters, *Progress in Development Studies* 2 (4), 283–305

Pérez, C (1992) *Movimientos Sociales Dominicanos: Identidad y Dilemas*, INTEC, Santo Domingo

Pérez, C (1996) *Urbanización y Municipio en Santo Domingo*, INTEC, Santo Domingo

Pérez, C (1997) Popular organisations in the Dominican Republic: the search for space and identity, in Kaufman, M and Alfonson, H (eds) *Community Power and Grassroots Democracy: The Transformation of Social Life*, Zed Books, London

Pérez, C (1999) interview at INTEC, 21 April

Pezzoli, K (1993) Sustainable livelihoods in the urban milieu: a case study from Mexico City, in Friedmann, J and Haripriya, R (eds) *In Defence of Livelihood: Comparative Studies on Environmental Action*, Kumarian Press and UNRISD, West Hartford

Pitt, M (2001) *Using Microfinance for Disaster Mitigation*, The World Bank Group, Disaster Mitigation Facility, www.worldbank.org/html/fpd/dmf/microfinance, accessed 31 August

Potter, R B (1995) Urbanisation and development in the Caribbean, *Geography* 80, 334–341

Potter, R B (2002) Global convergence, divergence and development, in Potter, R B and Desai, V (eds) *The Companion to Development Studies*, Arnold, London

Potter, R B and Lloyd-Evans, S (1998) *The City in the Developing World*, Longman, Harlow

Pred, A and Watts, M (1992) *Reworking Modernity: Capitalism and Symbolic Discontent*, Rutgers University Press, New Jersey

Puente, S (1999) Social vulnerability to disasters in Mexico City: an assessment method, in Mitchell, J K (ed) *Crucibles of Hazard: Mega-cities and Disasters in Transition*, UN University Press, Tokyo

Pugh, C (ed) (1996) *Sustainability, the Environment and Urbanization*, Earthscan, London

Putnam, R (2000) *Bowling Alone: The Collapse and Revival of American Community*, Simon and Schuster, New York

Putnam, R, Leonardi, R and Nanetti, R (1993) *Making Democracy Work: Civic Traditions in Modern Italy*, Princeton University Press, Princeton

Ramia, J (ed) (1994) *Humanidad y Naturaleza*, Fundación Ciencia y Arte, Santo Domingo

Rashid, S F (2000) The urban poor in Dhaka City: their struggles and coping strategies during the floods of 1998, *Disasters* 24 (3), 240–253

Riddell, B (1997) Structural adjustment programmes and the city in tropical Africa, *Urban Studies* 34 (8), 1297–1307

Robb, J (1999) community leader, Sophia squatters' settlement, personal communication

Rodriguez, A and Winchester, L (1996) The challenges for urban governance in Latin America: reinventing the government of cities, in McCarney, P L (ed) *Cities and Governance: New Directions in Latin America, Asia and Africa*, University of Toronto Press, Toronto

Rosenau, J (1997) *Along the Domestic–foreign Frontier*, Cambridge University Press, Cambridge

Sahr, W (1997) Semiotic-cultural changes in the Caribbean: a symbolic and functional approach, in Sahr, W and Ratter, B M W (eds) *Land, Sea and Human Effort*, University of Hamburg Press, Germany

Samoff, J (1990) Decentralisation and the politics of interventionism, *Development and Change* 21, 513–530

Sanderson, D (2000) Cities, disasters and livelihoods, *Environment and Urbanization* 12 (2), 93–102

Sanderson, D (2001) *Livelihoods, Disaster Risk Reduction, Urban Poverty*, CARE International UK, London

Satterthwaite, D (1997) Sustainable cities or cities that contribute to sustainable development? *Urban Studies* 34 (10), 1167–1691

Satterthwaite, D (1998) Meeting the challenge of urban disasters IFRC/RC, *World Disasters Report 1998*, Oxford University Press, Oxford

Satterthwaite, D (ed) (1999) *The Earthscan Reader in Sustainable Cities*, Earthscan, London

Scholte, J A (2000) *Globalization: A Critical Introduction*, Macmillan, Basingstoke

Schübeler, P (1996) *Participation and Partnership in Infrastructure Management*, Urban Management Programme, UNDP/UNCHS/World Bank, Nairobi

Schvenson, C (1999) interview at UNDP, 28 April

Scott, J C (1985) *Weapons of the Weak: Everyday Forms of Peasant Resistance*, Yale University Press, London

Scott, J C (1990) *Domination and the Arts of Resistance: Hidden Transcripts*, Yale University Press, London

Scott, N (1999) *Profiles of Squatting Areas in Guyana*, paper presented at the National Symposium on Informal Human Settlement, University of Guyana, Georgetown, April 15

Sen, A (1981) *Poverty and Famines*, Oxford University Press, Oxford

SESPAS (Secretaria de Estado de Salud Pública y Asistencia Social) (1996) *La Situación de Salud de Republica Dominicana*, SESPAS, Santo Domingo

Sharma, S (2001) Director of the Energy Environment Group, New Delhi, a note to the Mountain Forum – Asia elist mf-asia@lyris.bellanet.org

Short, J R and Yeong-Hyun, K (1999) *Globalization and the City*, Longman, Harlow

Shrivastava, P (1996) Long-term recovery from the Bhopal crisis, in Mitchall, J K (ed) *The Long Road to Recovery: Community Response to Industrial Disaster*, United Nations University Press, Tokyo

Smith, K (1992) *Environmental Hazards*, Routledge, London

Smith, M G (1984) *Uneven Development*, Basil Blackwell, Oxford

Smith, N (1997) *Community Participation in the Implementation Process: Barbados - A Case Study in the Management of Coastal Areas*, Award Report, Canadian International Development Agency, Bridgetown

Solway, L (1994) Urban developments and megacities: vulnerability to natural disasters, *Disaster Management* 6 (3), 160–169

Stabroek News (1999a) 'Some 11.5M gallons of water wasted each day in city', 25 September, p15

Stabroek News (1999b) 'City Budget' 6 October, p2

Stabroek News (1999c) 'Depoliticise management to turn city's fortunes around', 13 October, p3

Statistical Service (1993) *Population and Housing Census, 1990* Government of Barbados, Bridgetown

Steedman, S (1995) Megacities: the unacceptable risk natural disaster, *Built Environment* 21 (2/3), 89–94

Stren, R (1989) The administration of urban services, in Stren, R and White, R R (eds) *African Cities in Crisis: Managing Rapid Urban Growth*, Westview, Oxford

Sukul (1999) community leader, Sophia squatters' settlement, personal communication

Swift, J (1989) Why are rural people vulnerable to famine? *IDS Bulletin* 20 (2), 815

Swyngedouw, E A (1997) Power, nature and the city: the conquest of water and the political ecology of urbanisation in Guayaquil, Ecuador, *Environment and Planning* 29, 311–332

Sylves, R T and Waugh, W L (eds) (1990) *Cities and Disaster: North American Studies in Emergency Management*, Charles C Thomas, Springfield

Thomas, C Y (1982) Guyana: the IMF-World Bank Group and the general crisis, *Social and Economic Studies* 31 (4), 16–70

Thomas, C Y (1995) *Social Development and the Social Summit: A Look at Guyana, Jamaica and Trinidad and Tobago*, Institute of Development Studies, University of Guyana, Georgetown

Thompson (1999) community leader, Sophia squatters' settlement, personal communication

Thorne (1999) Director, True Vision, personal communication

Thouret, J C (1999) Urban hazards and risks: consequences of earthquakes and volcanic eruptions, an introduction, *GeoJournal* 49 (2), 131–135

Timmerman, P and White, R (1997) Megahydropolis: coastal cities in the context of global environmental change, *Global Environmental Change* 7 (3), 205–234

Tobin, G A and Montz, B E (1997) *Natural Hazards: Explanation and Integration*, Guildford Press, London

Töpfer, K (1999) *The Earthquake in Turkey*, United Nations Human Settlements Programme press release, 26 August

Trotz, A (1995) *Gender, Ethnicity and Familial Ideology: Household Structure and Female Labour Force Participation in Guyana*, unpublished PhD thesis, University of Cambridge, Cambridge

Trujillo, M, Ordóñez, A and Hernández, C (2000) *Risk-mapping and Local Capacities*, Oxfam working papers, Oxfam, Oxford

Tucker, B E, Erdik, M and Hwang, C N (eds) (1994) *Issues in Urban Earthquake Risk*, NATO ASI Series, Series E: Applied Sciences, 271, Kluwer, London

Turner, R K, Kelly, P M and Kay, R C (1990) *Cities at Risk*, University of East Anglia, Norwich

Twigg, J (2001) *Corporate Social Responsibility and Disaster Reduction: A Global Overview*, Benfied Greig Hazard Research Centre, CPRME (Comisión Presidencial para la Reforma y Modernización del Estado), University College London, London

UCOREBAM (1999) Director, personal communication

Uitto, J I (1998) The geography of disaster vulnerability in megacities, *Applied Geography* 18 (1), 7–16

UNCRD (United Nations Centre for Regional Development) (1995) *A Call to Arms: Report of the 17 January Great Hanshin Earthquake*, UNCRD discussion paper 95-2, Nagoya, Japan

UNCSD (United Nations Commission on Sustainable Development) (1997) *Barbados: Country Profile*, UNCSD, New York

UNDP (United Nations Development Programme) (1990) *Hazard Mitigation and Emergency Management Project: Barbados*, UNDP, Bridgetown

UNDP (United Nations Development Programme) (1996) *Guyana: Human Development Report*, UNDP, Georgetown

UNDP (United Nations Development Programme) (1997) *Consolidated Report on the Elaboration of a Poverty Eradication Plan for Barbados*, Government of Barbados/UNDP, Bridgetown

UNDP (United Nations Development Programme) (1998a) *Culture as a Tool for Sustainable Development: Case Study of the Pinelands Creative Workshop*, UNDP, Bridgetown

UNDP (United Nations Development Programme) (1998b) *Report on the Impacts of Hurricane Georges in the Dominican Republic*, UNDP, Santo Domingo

UNDP (United Nations Development Programme) (1998c) *Guyana Directory of Non-governmental Organisations, 1998*, UNDP, Georgetown

UNDP (United Nations Development Programme) (1999a) *Emergency/Rehabilitation Program: After Hurricane Georges in the Dominican Republic*, Programme Report (DOM 98/013), UNDP, Santo Domingo

UNDP (United Nations Development Programme) (1999b) *Guyana: Report of the 1999 Living Conditions Survey*, UNDP, Georgetown

UNDP (United Nations Development Programme) (2000) *Human Development Report 2000*, Oxford University Press, Oxford

UNDP (United Nations Development Programme) (2001) *Human Development Report 2001*, Oxford University Press, Oxford

UNDRCO (United Nations Disaster Relief Co-ordinator) (1991) *Mitigating Natural Disaster Phenomena, Effects and Options: A Manual for Policy Makers and Planners*, United Nations, New York

UN Habitat (1999) *Human Settlement Statistics*, www.unchs.org/guo/hssq/index.asp, accessed 15 January 2002

United Nations (1989) *Prospects for World Urbanization*, United Nations, New York

United Nations (1995) *World Urbanisation Prospects*, United Nations Population Division, New York

UNPD (United Nations Population Division) (1999) *World Population Prospects: The 1999 Revision*, UNDP, Washington DC

Vance, J E (1970) *The Merchant's World: The Geography of Wholesaling*, Prentice-Hall, Englewood Cliffs

Van den Bersselaar (2001) *Rural–urban Social Ties in Nigeria*, paper presented in the African studies series, University of Liverpool, Liverpool

Van der Linden, J (1997) On popular participation in a culture of patronage: patrons and grassroots organisations in a sites and services project in Hyderbad, *Environment and Urbanization* 9 (1), 81–90

Vargas, T (1994) *Las Organizaciones de Base en Santo Domingo*, Centro de Estudios P Juan Montalvo S J, Santo Domingo

Vasta (1999) *Community Participation in Postdisaster Reconstruction: Lessons Learned from the Maharashtra Emergency Earthquake Rehabilitation Program*, The World Bank Group, Disaster Management Facility, www.worldbank.org/html/fpd/dmf/best_practices2.htm, accessed 31 August 2001

Velásquez, D (2001) *Progress in the IMSS Solidarity Program in South Veracruz, Mexico*, ISDR Informe, www.eird.org/ing/revista/No3_2001/Pagina17.htm, accessed 13 September

Verba, S (1978) *Participation and Political Equality*, Cambridge University Press, Cambridge

Walker, K J (1989) The state in environmental management: the ecological dimension, *Political Studies* 37, 25–38

Walton, J and Seddon, D (1994) *Free Markets and Food Riots: The Politics of Global Adjustment*, Blackwell, Oxford

Watts, M (1983) *Silent Voice: Food Famine and Peasantry in Northern Nigeria*, University of California Press, Berkeley

Weinberger, K and Jütting, J P (2001) Women's participation in local organizations: conditions and constraints, *World Development* 29 (8), 1391–1404

White, G F, Kates, R W and Burton, I (2002) Knowing better and losing even more: the use of knowledge in hazards management, *Environmental Hazards* 3 (3–4), 81–92

WHO (World Health Organization) (1999) Health: creating healthy cities in the 21st century, in Satterthwaite, D (ed) *The Earthscan Reader in Sustainable Cities*, Earthscan, London

Wildavsky, A (1988) *Searching for Safety*, Transaction Books, London

Wisner, B (1996) The geography of vulnerability, in Uitto, J I and Schneider, J (eds) *Preparing for the Big One in Tokyo: Urban Earthquake Risk Management*, United Nations University, Tokyo

Wisner, B (1998) Marginality and vulnerability: why the homeless of Tokyo don't 'count' in disaster preparations, *Applied Geography* 18 (1), 25–33

Wisner, B (2001) Why post-Mitch lessons didn't reduce El Salvador's earthquake losses, *Disasters* 25 (3), 251–268

World Bank (1992) *Guyana: From Economic Recovery to Sustained Growth*, World Bank, Washington DC

World Bank (1997) *World Development Report 1997*, Oxford University Press, Oxford

World Bank (2000) *World Development Report 2000*, Oxford University Press, Oxford

Wratten, E (1995) Conceptualising urban poverty, *Environment and Urbanization* 7 (1), 11–36

Yacoob, M and Kelly, M (1999) *Secondary Cities in West Africa: The Challenge for Environmental Health and Prevention*, Woodrow Wilson International Center for Scholars, Comparative Urban Studies Occasional Paper Series # 21, Washington DC

Yodmani, S (no date) *Disaster Risk Management and Vulnerability Reduction: Protecting the Poor*, paper presented at the Asian and Pacific Forum on Poverty, organised by the Asian Development Bank

Young, L and Barrett, H (2001) Adapting visual methods: action research with Kampala street children, *Area* 33 (2), 141–152

Zapata-Marti, R (1997) Methodological approaches: the ECLAC methodology, in *Assessment of the Economic Impact of Natural and Man-made Disasters*, proceedings of the expert consultation on methodologies, Brussels, 29–30 September, Universite Catholique de Louvain, Belgium, pp10–12

Index

Page numbers in *italics* refer to figures, tables and boxes

actor-oriented approach 68
Adger, W N 10, 53–4, 63
ADN *see* Ayuntamiento Distrito Nacional
Africa 21, 22, 30
African Development Bank 70
Albouystown Neighbourhood Development Association 136, 136, 137
Albouystown Neighbourhood Development Committee 135, 136
Alexander, D 46
AMDEM *see* Asociación de Mejoramiento y Desarrollo de Los Manguitos
ANDA *see* Albouystown Neighbourhood Development Association
Anton, D J 14
Arup 76, 76
Asia 22, 30
Asian Disaster Preparedness Centre 56
Asian Urban Disaster Management Program 83
Asian Urban Disaster Mitigation Program 84
Asociación de Mejoramiento y Desarrollo de Los Manguitos 158, 159
asset 67
  social-political 61–2
  vulnerability 50, 52, 58
AUDP *see* Asian Urban Disaster Mitigation Program
authoritarian state regime 93, 140, 159
  paternalism 140
  Republic 93, 94, 95
  Santo Domingo, Dominican Republic 140–1
Ayuntamiento Distrito Nacional 144–7

Ballanilla, C 154
Bangladesh 21
Barbados 18, 97–117, 169–70
  Bridgetown 169–70, 171, 172, 173–4, 175, 182

gross domestic product 102
household insurance cover 104
infant mortality 102
Pine, the 109–115
population 101–2
unemployment 101
urban settlements 100
see also democracy, liberal
Barbados Labour Party 98
see also democracy, liberal
Barnett, J 7
Basic Needs Trust Fund 120
Beacon Foundation 130
Berke, P R 65
Blaikie, P 47, 54, 56, 58, 68
BLP *see* Barbados Labour Party
Bombay 23, 29
bonding capital 164
bounded rationality 70
Brazil 69
Brea, R 140
bridging capital 164
Bryant, N 53
building codes 36–7
  Himalayas 36
  National Building Code, of Jamaica 39
Building Community Capacity Programme 121
Burton, I 38, 47, 52–4
business-as-usual approach 10–1
  weaknesses 11
  see also ecological city

Cairncross, S 22
Cairo 23
California 21–2
Canadian International Development Agency 121
Cannon, T 47, 54, 56, 58, 68
CARE *see* Cooperative for Assistance and Relief Everywhere

Caribbean 22, 23
Caribbean Development Bank 120
Caribbean Disaster Emergency Response
    Agency 107, 171
Caribbean Red Cross societies *see* Red
    Cross
Castells, M 20
Catafesta, C 139, 141
CBOs *see* community-based organizations
CDB *see* Caribbean Development Bank
CDC *see* Civil Defence Commission
CDERA *see* Caribbean Disaster
    Emergency Response Agency
Central America 23, 28
Central Emergency Relief Organization
    105–7, 113–14, *171,* 172, 181
Central Housing and Planning Authority
    126, 127, 136, 175
CERO *see* Central Emergency Relief
    Organization
Chambers, R 16, 54–55
Chester, D K 22
China 20
Choup, A 146
CHPA *see* Central Housing Planning
    Authority
CIDA *see* Canadian International
    Development Agency
cities 14, 36, 96
    ecological 11
    largest 22
    mega 19, 23–4, 29, 37
    structural difference 41
    weaknesses 11
    see also business-as-usual; structural
        adjustment
Citizens' Disaster Response Network 85
Civil Defence 148–9, *149,* 158, 172
Civil Defence Commission 129, 137, 138
civil society 63, 97, 107, 126, 141, 146–7,
    157, 170, 172, 179
    Abyssinian Youth Group 107, 108
    Cornerstone Project 107, 108
    Future Centre Trust 107, 108
    see also Rastafarian
climate change 28
coastal flooding 10
    Manila 28
coastal zone management 167
    Santo Domingo 167
Coburn, A 20

coevolution 9–10
Cold War 169
Comité Nacional de Desarrollo Integral
    Comunitario *150*
Community Development Division 99
community-based organizations 17, 34,
    38, 42, 44, 61, 64, 83, 85, 99–100,
    119, 120, 136, 139, 141, 145–7, 149,
    152, 156, *157,* 158, 159, 160, 165,
    171, 172, 173, 174, 175, 176–7, 178,
    185
community-based self-help 4
CONDIC *see* Comité Nacional de
    Desarrollo Integral Comunitario
Cooperative for Assistance and Relief
    Everywhere 58, 78–9, *79,* 90
co-optation 87
coping strategies 52–4, 62, *63*
    loss absorption 52–3
    loss acceptance 53
    see also institutional modification
Cross, J A 84
cyclones
    Kolkata (Calcutta) 28

Daily Nation newspaper 99
Davis, I 47, 54, 56, 58, 68
DDMC *see* Dominican Disaster
    Mitigation Committee
De Soto, H 32
debt crisis 30
decentralization 63, 69, 145, 146
deforestation 27
democracy 177–8
    Bridgetown, Barbados 93, *94,* 94–5,
        97–103
    liberal 94, 95
democratic transition 140–1
democratization 69, 118
Department for International
    Development 55, 74
    Sustainable Rural Livelihoods Advisory
        Committee 55
dependency theory 47
DEROs *see* District Emergency Relief
    Organizations
Desai, V 80
DFID *see* Department for International
    Development
disaster *5,* 5, 11, 14, 42, 45, 67, 77, 148
    analysis 47

catastrophic 15–7
chronic 15
cycle 13
definition 6
indicator 6
management 8, 16, 44, *57,* 105, 137,
    148
mitigation 8–9, 34, 38, *75,* 75–6, *79,* 81,
    129–30, *171,* 183
natural 6, 7, 39, 47
preparedness 152
reduction 73, 183
resiliency 7
response 9
risk 7, 105
urban 6–7, 14, 18, 20, *26, 27,* 30, 35, 75
see also resilience
disaster impacts 32
direct 39, 40
economic 38, 41
systematic 39
see also systematic loss
Disaster Management Facility *72,* 72
District Emergency Relief Organizations
    105–6, 113–14, 115, *171,* 172
Dominican Architects Association 182
Dominican Disaster Mitigation
    Committee 151–3, *153,* 160, 182
Dominican Liberation Party 140
Dominican Red Cross *see* Red Cross
Dominican Republic 18, 39, 139–60,
    169–70
    barrio 141, 142, 144–5, 154, 155, 159
    households 154
    political system 139–40
    population 143
    poverty 142, *143,* 154
    Santo Domingo 139–60, 169–71, *171,*
        172, 173–4, *175,* 182–3
    social organization *156*
    Trujillo 142–3, 144
    see also authoritarian state regime; civil
        defence
Dominican Revolutionary Party 140
DRC *see* Dominican Red Cross
drought
    Afghanistan 23
    Bangladesh 23
    Barbados 103
    Chennai 28
    Delhi 28

Guyana 122
Hyderbad 28
India 23
Turkey 23
urban 28
see also sub-Saharan Africa 23
Duarte, I 140
Duncan, N 98, 101

earthquake
    Afghanistan 23
    Armenian 36
    Bangladesh 23
    Gujarat 60
    Himalayas 36
    India 23, 36, 73
    Japan 23, 40
    Loma Preta 7, 21
    Maharashtra Emergency Earthquake
        Rehabilitation Programme 73
    Metro Manila 7
    Mexico 41
    Philippines, the 23
    Salvador 74
    Santo Domingo 141–2
    Southeast and East Asia 23
    Taiwan 23, 36
    Tangshan 20
    Turkey 21, 22, 23, 28, 36, 40–1, *76,* 76
    World Earthquake Risk Management
        77
    see also Mexico City
ecology
    cultural 52
    human 47
    ecological city 11–2
Ecuadorian Red Cross *see* Red Cross
El Nino 129
empowerment 4
engineering responses 49
    flood defences 49
    India 49
entitlements perspective 50–1
environmental
    change 166
    degradation 35, 142, 166–7
    hazard 13, 14, 21, 46, 47, 131, 137, 180
    justice 12
    mitigation 10
    organizations 7
    physical 14

problems 11
quality 12
risk 4, 6, 9, 11, 15, 46, 47, *48*, 56, 70,
    163–4
urban services *171*
see also coping strategies; institutional
    modification
environmental determinism 47
Espillat, M 154
exposure 47, *48,* 48–9

famine
    China 34
fire
    Cape Town 32
    Guyana 122–3
    Japan 23
    Philippines, the 23
    Southeast and East Asia 23
    sub-Saharan Africa 23
    Taiwan 23
flood 14, 28, 56–6, 102, 109–10, 132–3
    132, 167
    Albouystown 132–134, 137
    Bangkok 28–9
    Bangladesh 14, 23, 28
    Barbados 103, 167
    Dhaka 14
    Georgetown 65
    Guyana 64, 122–3
    health impacts *133,* 133
    India 23, 68
    Japan 23
    Kolkata (Calcutta) 28
    Lusaka 64
    Philippines, the 23
    Republic of Korea 14
    Rio de Janeiro 29, 34, *35*
    risk zones 104–5, *124*
    Santo Domingo 142
    São Paulo 27, 29, 35, 64
    Seoul 14
    Southeast and East Asia 23
    sub-Saharan Africa 23
    Taiwan 23
    Turkey 23
    Vietnam 63
    see also coastal flooding
Flood Prevention Act 104
Food for the Poor 130
Freire, P 69

Freudenheim 42
Friedmann, J 64

Garza, G 33
Gauhurts, M 56
GCC *see* Georgetown City Council
gendered
    division 176
    division of labour 158
    women 141, 178–9
Georgetown City Council 120, 126, 136–7
Georgetown Sewerage and Water
        Commissioners 122
GGG *see* Good and Green Guyana
Giddens, A 88
Gilbert, A 31–2, 87
globalization 68–9
Gonhan, H 56
Good and Green Guyana 120, 135
governance 17
governance agenda 69
government
    central 73
    local 81, 85
    municipal 12–3, 81
    national 73
grassroots 64, 84–5, 88, 134, 139–40, 145,
        148
    actors 72, 83, 85, 87, 88, 139, 174
    junta de vecinos 146, 155, 156–7
    organizations 86–7, 179
    see also Asian Urban Disaster
        Management Program; community-
        based organizations
GRC *see* Guyana Relief Council
Green, A 14
GS&WC *see* Georgetown Sewerage and
        Water Commissioners
Guayaquil 80
Gulkan, P 75
Guyana 15, *16*, 18, 118–138, 169–70
    Albouystown 131–137, *175,* 175
    drainage 123
    economic status *125*
    Georgetown 169–70, *171,* 172, 173–4,
        182, 183
    housing 121–22, 125
    population 121
    sewerage 122
    squatting *127,* 127, 128
    see also flood risk; membership, political

party
Guyana Red Cross *see* Red Cross
Guyana Relief Council 130, 137
Guyana Water Authority 122
Guyanese Environmental Protection
     Agency 166
Guzman, R 146

Halcrow plc 123
Hardoy, J E 22, 85
Hartnaday, C 19
Harvey, D 4, 20
hazard *5*, 5, 51, 52, 53, 141–2, 169
   everyday 15
   geological 22
   mitigation 47
   natural 22, 23
   risk 14
   technological 39
   zones *25*
   see also loss absorption
Healthy Cities Programme 16
Hewitt, K 10, 20, 22, 47
Holguin, R 140
Holland, J 64
household density 32
   Bogota 32
   Santiago 32
   see also poverty, household
households 52, 54, 55, 59, 65–6, 131, *132*,
     181
housing 59
Human Development Index Rank 101
human organization 7
hurricane 141–2
   Barbados 104
   damage 16–7
   Dominican Republic 141
   economic damage 142
   Gabrielle 104
   Georges 142, 149, *150, 151,* 152–3,
     154–5, *156,* 158, 170–1
   Gilbert 39
   Jamaica 36, 39
   Mitch 27–8, 88

IDAC *see* Instituto de Acción Comunitaria
IDDI *see* Instituto Dominicano de
     Desarrollo Integral
IFIs *see* international financial institutions
IFRC/RC *see* International Federation of

the Red Cross; International
     Federation of the Red Crescent
indirect loss 40
   Kobe, Japan 40
   Philippines 40
informal sector 32
   Peru 32
informal social organization *157*
INGOs *see* international non-
     governmental organization
institutional modification 62, *63*
Instituto de Acción Comunitaria 147–8,
     160
Instituto Dominicano de Desarrollo
     Integral 156, 158–9, 160, 174
Inter-American Development Bank 70,
     125
international agencies 13
International Decade for Natural Disaster
     Reduction 73, 77
International Federation of the Red Cross
     see Red Cross
International Federation of the Red
     Crescent 79, 90, *171*
international financial institutions 17,
     70–2, 73, 80, 84
International Monetary Fund 30, 71
international non-governmental organiz-
     ations 13, 85, 146, 147–9, *151*, 151
International Secretariat for Disaster
     Reduction 77
international structures 68
interviews
   semi-structured 185–6

just-in-time 40
   Kawasaki Heavy Industries 40
   Toyota Motor Corporation 40

Kartez, J 65
Kates, R W 38, 47, 52–4
Kjellén, M 12

La Nino 123
La RED 78, *79*
land reclamation
   Latin America 61
landslide 3, 5, 163
   Bogota 28
   Kolkata (Calcutta) 28
   Manila 3–4

Rio de Janeriro 27
São Paulo 27, 29, 35
LaPlante, J M 13
Latin America 22, 30, 31, 32, 35
Leach, M 51
leadership 87–8, 107–8, 176, 177–8, 179
    community 87, 127–128, 177–8
LETS *see* local economic trading scheme
livelihoods 56
livelihoods approach *see* entitlements
        perspective
local economic trading scheme 108
localization 68–9
Los Angeles 23

macro-structural issues 34, 47
Manila 3–4
Marxism 47
McGranahan, G 12
Mearns, R 51
members of parliament 98–9
membership
    local group *134*
    political party 134
methodology *186*
Mexico City 23, 28, 31, 33, 36
    water catchment 11
    see also earthquakes
micro finance 81
migration 21, 54
    reverse 21
    see also Africa; Bangladesh
Minh-ha, T 88
Ministry of Housing 170
Mitchell, J K 13–4, 37–8
MOCUGRECA *see* Movimiento Cultural
        Gregorio Castillo
modernization 177, 178
Moser, C 56, 58, 59, 64, 141
Movimiento Cultural Gregorio Castillo 158
MPs *see* members of parliament
mud-flow 41

National Housing Corporation 109, 114
National Land-use Plan 104
networks 146–7
New Agenda, urban management 71, 90
NGOs *see* non-governmental
        organizations
Nicaragua 89
non-governmental organizations 17, 38,

42, 44, 55, 60, 62, 64, 65, 73, 77–8,
    79, 79–80, 81, 83, 100–1, 107, 113,
    119, 120, 126, 130, 136, 138, 139,
    141, 145–8, 149, *150, 157,* 159–60,
    170, *171,* 172, 173, 174, 176–7, 178,
    181–2, 185
    Mumbai (Bombay) 80
    National Labor Committee 55, 74
Norgaard, R B 7

Office of Foreign Disaster Assistance 83
opportunistic behaviour 70

PAHO *see* Pan American Health
        Organization
Pan American Health Organization 75,
        88–9, *171*
participatory development 10
partnerships 89, *89*
patronage 87
PCW *see* Pinelands Creative Workshop
PDC *see* Pinelands Development Council
People's National Congress 119, 135, 136
People's Progressive Party 119, 120
Philippines, the 81
Pinelands Creative Workshop 109,
        111–13, 114, 115, 176
Pinelands Development Council 111–12,
        115
PLD *see* Dominican Liberation Party
PNC *see* People's National Congress
political actions 42
political organization 10
Pomonis, A 29
population
    growth 28, 29, 45
    São Paulo 29
    see also population census
population census 29
poverty 29–30, 52, 55, 59, 181
    alleviation 58, 182
    economic 32, 33, 67, 134, 165
    household 64
    line 29–30, 121
    women 59
    see also urban poverty
power 4, 89
    material 4
    non-material 4
PPP *see* People's Progressive Party
PRD *see* Dominican Revolutionary Party

Presidential Committee for the Support
  of Barrio Development 145
Prevention of Floods Act 102
private sector 63, 73–4, *75*
privatization 63, 74
productive assets 32

questionnaires 185
  household 174, *175*

RADIUS *see* Risk Assessment Tools for
  Diagnosis of Urban Areas Against
  Seismic Disasters Programme 77, *78*
Rastafarianism 108
ratchet effect 52, 55
Red Cross
  Caribbean 107
  Dominican 148, *149,* 158
  Ecuadorian 80
  Guyana 121, 130, 137, 172
  International Federation of the Red
    Cross 79, 90, *171*
Red de Redes de ONGs 146
Relief and Disasters Programme, Guayas
  80
resilience *5,* 9, 47, *48,* 48–9, 51
  systems 7, *8*
resistance 47, *48,* 48–9, 64
risk *5,* 10, 111, *132,* 167, 182
  management 46, 183
  urban 37, 168
  see also urban risk maps
rural life 56

Sakia, S 20
Sanderson, D 49, 56, 58, 82–3
Sanitation Service Authority 114
SAPs *see* structural adjustment
  programmes
Satterthwaite, D 22, 85
Schvenson, C 139
Scoones, I 51
Scott, J C 51
sea-level rise 123, 166
secondary effects 40–1
semantic resistance 69
Sen, A 50
SIMAP *see* Social Impact Amelioration
  Project
Smith, K 101

social
  capital 59–60, 64–5, *112,* 164–5, 174, 177
  cognitive 164
  development 179
  exclusion 29
  fragmentation 56, 57
  institutions 51
  latent 164
  networks 60, 164
  structures 163
  see also bonding capital; bridging capital
Social Impact Amelioration Project 120,
  136
socialist regime 93
  cooperative socialism 119
  Georgetown, Guyana 93, *94,* 95,
    118–138
social-political change *43,* 44
  Chile 43
  Guatemala City 43
  Managua 44
  Mexico City 43
  Miami 43, 44
Solidarity Programme of the Mexican
  Social Security Institute 83
  Veracruz 83
Solway, L 36–7
Songsore, J 12
squatter settlements 32, 103, *127,* 127,
  167–8, 177
  Bridgetown 168
  Georgetown 168
  Mumbai (Bombay) 61
  Santo Domingo 166
structural
  adjustment 30–2, *31,* 33, 56, 66, 71, 74,
    119
  change 64
  policies 39
  Zambia 64
structural adjustment programmes 81–2
structural-historical perspective 168, 174
sustainable development 10
  sustainability approach 10
  see also participatory development;
    urban governance
sustainable urbanization 11–2, 16, 18
Swift, J 50, 52–3, 55, 58, 165, 181
systematic loss 40, 41
  see also indirect loss; secondary effects

Timmerman, P 9
Töpfer, K 183
Town and Country Planning Act 98
Town and Country Planning Advisory
    Committee 98
toxic gas leak 33
    Bhopal 33
Transport and General Workers Union
    136
Trotz, A 131
True Vision 135–6
Twigg, J 75–6

UCOREBAM *see* Unión Comunitaria para
    la Recogida de Basura del Barrio Los
    Manguitos
UK Drug Control Programme 114
UNDP *see* United Nations Development
    Programme
UNEP *see* United Nations Environment
    Programme
Unión Comunitaria para la Recogida de
    Basura del Barrio Los Manguitos
    159, 174
United Nations Commission for Human
    Rights 143
United Nations Conference for
    Sustainable Development in Small
    Island States 108, 109
United Nations Development
    Programme 108, 113, 121, 128, 136,
    148–9, *150,* 160, 172, 175
    Global Environment Facility 172
United Nations Environment Programme
    108
United States Agency for International
    Development 74, 83, 159
urban 19
    development 14
    governance 10
    growth 21, 44
    life 56
    management 164
    planning 34
    political economy 21
    population 22, *23*
    poverty 31, 32, 34
    scale 95
    society 14
    systems 13
    see also population growth

Urban Planning Commission 98
Urban Rehabilitation Programme 125–6
Urban Renewal Programme 103
urban risk maps 46
urbanization 10, 53, 95
USAID *see* United States Agency for
    International Development

volcanoes
    Amero, Columbia 41
    Goma 34
    Pinatubo, Mt 28
    Nyiragongo, Mt 49
vulnerability 46, 47, 49, 50–1, 52, 54–5,
    56, 59–60, 61, 65, 67, 111, 131–2,
    132, 154, 163, 168, 173, 179, 181
    analysis 68
    environment 10
    exposure 47
    household 58
    human *5,* 5, 10, 29, 44, 47, 49, 154, 164,
        169, 178–9
    indicators 180
    individual 61
    intermediate pressures 68
    mitigation 163
    physical *5,* 128
    production 169–70
    reduction 8, 166, 181, 182–3, 183–4
    resilience 47, 181
    resistance 47
    social *5,* 9, 182
    urban 29
    see also exposure; resilience; reduction;
        ratchet effect; environment hazard

Ward, P 87
Washington, DC 53
water
    inadequate 15–6, 168
watershed management 167
Webber, M M 7
Wenger, D 65
White, G F 38, 52–4
White, R 9
Wildavsky, A 7, 9
Wisner, B 46, 47, 54, 56, 58, 65, 68
World Bank 30, 70–2, *72,* 73, 74–5

Zambia 34
    see also disaster risk